DOVER · THRIFT · EDITIONS

Nicomachean Ethics

ARISTOTLE

DOVER PUBLICATIONS, INC.
Mineola, New York

DOVER THRIFT EDITIONS

GENERAL EDITOR: PAUL NEGRI
EDITOR OF THIS VOLUME: WILLIAM KAUFMAN

Bibliographical Note

This Dover edition, first published in 1998, is an unabridged republication of the work first published by J. M. Dent & Sons Ltd. in London in 1911 under the title *Aristotle's Ethics*.

Library of Congress Cataloging-in-Publication Data

Aristotle.
   [Nicomachean ethics. English]
   The Nicomachean ethics / Aristotle.
      p.   cm. — (Dover thrift editions)
   Translated by D. P. Chase.
   Originally published: London : J. M. Dent, 1911.
   Includes bibliographical references.
   ISBN 0-486-40096-4 (pbk.)
   1. Ethics—Early works to 1800. I. Chase, D. P. (Drummond Percy), 1820–1902. II. Title. III. Series.
B430.A5C5   1998
171'.3—dc21   97-39242
                                                            CIP

Manufactured in the United States of America
Dover Publications, Inc., 31 East 2nd Street, Mineola, N.Y. 11501

INTRODUCTION

THE *Ethics* of Aristotle is one half of a single treatise of which his
Politics is the other half. Both deal with one and the same subject. This
subject is what Aristotle calls in one place the "philosophy of human
affairs;" but more frequently Political or Social Science. In the two
works taken together we have their author's whole theory of human
conduct or practical activity, that is, of all human activity which is not
directed merely to knowledge or truth. The two parts of this treatise are
mutually complementary, but in a literary sense each is independent
and self-contained. The proem to the *Ethics* is an introduction to the
whole subject, not merely to the first part; the last chapter of the *Ethics*
points forward to the *Politics*, and sketches for that part of the treatise
the order of enquiry to be pursued (an order which in the actual treatise is not adhered to).

The principle of distribution of the subject-matter between the two
works is far from obvious, and has been much debated. Not much can
be gathered from their titles, which in any case were not given to them
by their author. Nor do these titles suggest any very compact unity in
the works to which they are applied: the plural forms, which survive so
oddly in English (Ethics, Politics), were intended to indicate the treatment within a single work of a *group* of connected questions. The unity
of the first group arises from their centring round the topic of character, that of the second from their connection with the existence and life
of the city or state. We have thus to regard the *Ethics* as dealing with
one group of problems and the *Politics* with a second, both falling
within the wide compass of Political Science. Each of these groups falls
into sub-groups which roughly correspond to the several books in each
work. The tendency to take up one by one the various problems which
had suggested themselves in the wide field obscures both the unity of
the subject-matter and its proper articulation. But it is to be remem-

bered that what is offered us is avowedly rather an enquiry than an exposition of hard and fast doctrine.

Nevertheless each work aims at a relative completeness, and it is important to observe the relation of each to the other. The distinction is
not that the one treats of Moral and the other of Political Philosophy,
nor again that the one deals with the moral activity of the individual
and the other with that of the State, nor once more that the one gives
us the theory of human conduct, while the other discusses its application in practice, though not all of these misinterpretations are equally
erroneous. The clue to the right interpretation is given by Aristotle himself, where in the last chapter of the *Ethics* he is paving the way for the
Politics. In the *Ethics* he has not confined himself to the abstract or isolated individual, but has always thought of him, or we might say, in his
social and political context, with a given nature due to race and hered-
ity and in certain surroundings. So viewing him he has studied the nature and formation of his character—all that he can make himself or
be made by others to be. Especially he has investigated the various admirable forms of human character and the mode of their production.
But all this, though it brings more clearly before us what goodness or
virtue is, and how it is to be reached, remains mere theory or talk. By
itself it does not enable us to become, or to help others to become,
good. For this it is necessary to bring into play the great force of the
Political Community or State, of which the main instrument is Law.
Hence arises the demand for the necessary complement to the *Ethics*,
i.e., a treatise devoted to the questions which centre round the enquiry;
by what organisation of social or political forces, by what laws or institutions can we best secure the greatest amount of good character?

We must, however, remember that the production of good character
is not the end of either individual or state action: that is the aim of the
one and the other because good character is the indispensable condition and chief determinant of happiness, itself the goal of all human
doing. The end of all action, individual or collective, is the greatest
happiness of the greatest number. There is, Aristotle insists, no difference of kind between the good of one and the good of many or all. The
sole difference is one of amount or scale. This does not mean simply
that the State exists to secure in larger measure the objects of degree
which the isolated individual attempts, but is too feeble, to secure
without it. On the contrary, it rather insists that whatever goods society
alone enables a man to secure have always had to the individual—
whether he realised it or not—the value which, when so secured, he
recognises them to possess. The best and happiest life for the individ-

ual is that which the State renders possible, and this it does mainly by revealing to him the value of new objects of desire and educating him to appreciate them. To Aristotle or to Plato the State is, above all, a large and powerful educative agency which gives the individual increased opportunities of self-development and greater capacities for the enjoyment of life.

Looking forward, then, to the life of the State as that which aids support, and combines the efforts of the individual to obtain happiness, Aristotle draws no hard and fast distinction between the spheres of action of Man as individual and Man as citizen. Nor does the division of his discussion into the *Ethics* and the *Politics* rest upon any such distinction. The distinction implied is rather between two stages in the life of the civilised man—the stage of preparation for the full life of the adult citizen, and the stage of the actual exercise or enjoyment of citizenship. Hence the *Ethics*, where his attention is directed upon the formation of character, is largely and centrally a treatise on Moral Education. It discusses especially those admirable human qualities which fit a man for life in an organised civic community, which makes him "a good citizen," and considers how they can be fostered or created and their opposites prevented.

This is the kernel of the *Ethics*, and all the rest is subordinate to this main interest and purpose. Yet "the rest" is not irrelevant; the whole situation in which character grows and operates is concretely conceived. There is a basis of what we should call Psychology, sketched in firm outlines, the deeper presuppositions and the wider issues of human character and conduct are not ignored, and there is no little of what we should call Metaphysics. But neither the Psychology nor the Metaphysics is elaborated, and only so much is brought forward as appears necessary to put the main facts in their proper perspective and setting. It is this combination of width of outlook with close observation of the concrete facts of conduct which gives its abiding value to the work, and justifies the view of it as containing Aristotle's Moral Philosophy. Nor is it important merely as summing up the moral judgments and speculations of an age now long past. It seizes and dwells upon those elements and features in human practice which are most essential and permanent, and it is small wonder that so much in it survives in our own ways of regarding conduct and speaking of it. Thus it still remains one of the classics of Moral Philosophy, nor is its value likely soon to be exhausted.

As was pointed out above, the proem (Book I, pp. 1–3) is a prelude to the treatment of the whole subject covered by the *Ethics* and the

Politics together. It sets forth the purpose of the enquiry, describes the spirit in which it is to be undertaken and what ought to be the expectation of the reader, and lastly states the necessary conditions of studying it with profit. The aim of it is the acquisition and propagation of a certain kind of knowledge (science), but this knowledge and the thinking which brings it about are subsidiary to a practical end. The knowledge aimed at is of what is best for man and of the conditions of its realisation. Such knowledge is that which in its consummate form we find in great statesmen, enabling them to organise and administer their states and regulate by law the life of the citizens to their advantage and happiness, but it is the same kind of knowledge which on a smaller scale secures success in the management of the family or of private life.

It is characteristic of such knowledge that it should be deficient in "exactness," in precision of statement, and closeness of logical concatenation. We must not look for a mathematics of conduct. The subject-matter of Human Conduct is not governed by necessary and uniform laws. But this does not mean that it is subject to no laws. There are general principles at work in it, and these can be formulated in "rules," which rules can be systematised or unified. It is all-important to remember that practical or moral rules are only general and always admit of exceptions, and that they arise not from the mere complexity of the facts, but from the liability of the facts to a certain unpredictable variation. At their very best, practical rules state probabilities, not certainties; a relative constancy of connection is all that exists, but it is enough to serve as a guide in life. Aristotle here holds the balance between a misleading hope of reducing the subject-matter of conduct to a few simple rigorous abstract principles, with conclusions necessarily issuing from them, and the view that it is the field of operation of inscrutable forces acting without predictable regularity. He does not pretend to find in it absolute uniformities, or to deduce the details from his principles. Hence, too, he insists on the necessity of experience as the source or test of all that he has to say. Moral experience—the actual possession and exercise of good character—is necessary truly to understand moral principles and profitably to apply them. The mere intellectual apprehension of them is not possible, or if possible, profitless.

The *Ethics* is addressed to students who are presumed both to have enough general education to appreciate these points, and also to have a solid foundation of good habits. More than that is not required for the profitable study of it.

If the discussion of the nature and formation of character be regarded as the central topic of the *Ethics*, the contents of Book I, pp. 3–16 may be considered as still belonging to the introduction and setting, but these chapters contain matter of profound importance and have exercised an enormous influence upon subsequent thought. They lay down a principle which governs all Greek thought about human life, viz. that it is only intelligible when viewed as directed towards some end or good. This is the Greek way of expressing that all human life involves an ideal element—something which it is not yet and which under certain conditions it is to be. In that sense Greek Moral Philosophy is essentially idealistic. Further, it is always assumed that all human practical activity is directed or "oriented" to a *single* end, and that that end is knowable or definable in advance of its realisation. To know it is not merely a matter of speculative interest, it is of the highest practical moment, for only in the light of it can life be duly guided, and particularly only so can the state be properly organised and administered. This explains the stress laid throughout by Greek Moral Philosophy upon the necessity of knowledge as a condition of the best life. This knowledge is not, though it includes, knowledge of the nature of man and his circumstances, it is knowledge of what is best—of man's supreme end or good.

But this end is not conceived as presented to him by a superior power, nor even as something which *ought* to be. The presentation of the Moral Ideal as Duty is almost absent. From the outset it is identified with the object of desire, or what we not merely judge desirable but actually do desire, or that which would, if realised, satisfy human desire. In fact it is what we all, wise and simple, agree in naming "Happiness" (Welfare or Well-being).

In what then does happiness consists? Aristotle summarily sets aside the more or less popular identifications of it with abundance of physical pleasures, with political power and honour, with the mere possession of such superior gifts or attainments as normally entitle men to these, with wealth. None of these can constitute the end or good of man as such. On the other hand, he rejects his master Plato's conception of a good which is the end of the whole universe, or at least dismisses it as irrelevant to his present enquiry. The good towards which all human desires and practical activities are directed must be one conformable to man's special nature and circumstances, and attainable by his efforts. There is in Aristotle's theory of human conduct no trace of Plato's "other worldliness"; he brings the moral ideal in Bacon's phrase down to "right earth"—and so closer to the facts and problems of actual human living. Turning from criticism of others he states his own positive view of Happiness, and, though he avowedly states it merely in outline, his account is pregnant with significance. Human Happiness lies in activity or energising, and that in a way peculiar to man with his given nature and his given circumstances; it is not theoretical, but practical: it is the activity not of reason, but still of a being who possesses reason and applies it, and it presupposes in that being the development, and not merely the natural possession, of certain relevant powers and capacities. The last is the prime condition of successful living and therefore of satisfaction, but Aristotle does not ignore other conditions, such as length of life, wealth and good luck, the absence or diminution of which render happiness not impossible, but difficult of attainment.

It is interesting to compare this account of Happiness with Mill's in *Utilitarianism*. Mill's is much the less consistent: at times he distinguishes and at times he identifies, happiness, pleasure, contentment, and satisfaction. He wavers between belief in its general attainability and an absence of hopefulness. He mixes up in an arbitrary way such ingredients as "not expecting more from life than it is capable of bestowing," "mental cultivation," "improved laws," etc., and in fact leaves the whole conception vague, blurred, and uncertain. Aristotle draws the outline with a firmer hand and presents a more definite ideal. He allows for the influence on happiness of conditions only partly, if at all, within the control of man, but he clearly makes the main positive determinant of man's happiness lie in himself, and more particularly in what he makes directly of his own nature, and so indirectly of his circumstances. "'Tis in ourselves that we are thus or thus." But once more this does not involve an artificial or abstract isolation of the individual moral agent from his relation to other persons or things, from his context in society and nature, nor ignore the relative dependence of his life upon a favourable environment.

The main factor which determines success or failure in human life is the acquisition of certain powers, for Happiness is just the exercise or putting forth of these in actual living; everything else is secondary and subordinate. These powers arise from the due development of certain natural aptitudes which belong (in various degrees) to human nature as such, and therefore to all normal human beings. In their developed form they are known as virtues (the Greek means simply "goodnesses," "perfections," "excellences," or "fitnesses"); some of them are physical, but others are psychical, and among the latter some, and these distinctively or peculiarly human, are "rational," *i.e.*, presuppose the possession and exercise of mind or intelligence. These last fall into two groups, which Aristotle distinguishes as Goodnesses of Intellect and Goodnesses of Character. They have in common that they all excite in us admiration and praise of their possessors, and that they are not natural endowments, but acquired characteristics. But they differ in important ways: (1) the former are excellences or developed powers of the reason as such — of that in us which sees and formulates laws, rules, regularities, systems, and is content in the vision of them, while the latter involve a submission or obedience to such rules of something in us which is in itself capricious and irregular, but capable of regulation, viz. our instincts and feelings; (2) the former are acquired by study and instruction, the latter by discipline. The latter constitute "character," each of them as a "moral virtue" (literally, "a goodness of character"), and upon them primarily depends the realisation of happiness. This is the case at least for the great majority of men, and for all men their possession is an indispensable basis of the best, *i.e.*, the most desirable life. They form the chief or central subject-matter of the *Ethics*.

Perhaps the truest way of conceiving Aristotle's meaning here is to regard a moral virtue as a form of obedience to a maxim or rule of conduct accepted by the agent as valid for a class of recurrent situations in human life. Such obedience requires knowledge of the rule and acceptance of it, *as the rule* of the agent's own actions, but not necessarily knowledge of its ground or of its systematic connexion with other similarly known and similarly accepted rules. (It may be remarked that the Greek word usually translated "reason," means in almost all cases in the *Ethics* such a rule, and not the faculty which apprehends, formulates, considers them).

The "moral virtues and vices" make up what we call character, and the important questions arise: (1) What is character? and (2) How is it formed? (for character in this sense is not a natural endowment; it is formed or produced). Aristotle deals with these questions in the reverse order. His answers are peculiar and distinctive — not that they are absolutely novel (for they are anticipated in Plato), but that by him they are for the first time distinctly and clearly formulated.

(1.) Character, good or bad, is produced by what Aristotle calls "habituation," that is, it is the result of the repeated doing of acts which have a similar or common quality. Such repetition acting upon natural aptitudes or propensities gradually fixes them in one or other of two opposite directions, giving them a bias towards good or evil. Hence the several acts which determine goodness or badness of character must be done in a certain way, and thus the formation of good character requires discipline and direction from without. Not that the agent himself contributes nothing to the formation of his character, but that at first he needs guidance. The point is not so much that the process cannot be safely left to Nature, but that it cannot be entrusted to merely intellectual instruction. The process is one of assimilation, largely by imitation and under direction and control. The result is a growing understanding of what is done, a choice of it for its own sake, a fixity and steadiness of purpose. Right acts and feelings become, through habit, easier and more pleasant, and the doing of them a "second nature." The agent acquires the power of doing them freely, willingly, more and more "of himself."

But what are "right" acts? In the first place, they are those that conform to a rule—to the right rule, and ultimately to reason. The Greeks never waver from the conviction that in the end moral conduct is essentially reasonable conduct. But there is a more significant way of describing their "rightness," and here for the first time Aristotle introduces his famous "Doctrine of the Mean." Reasoning from the analogy of "right" physical acts, he pronounces that rightness always means adaptation or adjustment to the special requirements of a situation. To this adjustment he gives a quantitative interpretation. To do (or to feel) what is right in a given situation is to do or to feel just the *amount* required—neither more nor less: to do wrong is to do or to feel too much or too little—to fall short of or over-shoot, "a mean" determined by the situation. The repetition of acts which lie in the mean is the cause of the formation of each and every "goodness of character," and for this "rules" can be given.

(2.) What then is a "moral virtue," the result of such a process duly directed? It is no mere mood of feeling, no mere liability to emotion, no mere natural aptitude or endowment; it is a permanent *state* of the agent's self, or, as we might in modern phrase put it, of his will; it consists in a steady self-imposed obedience to a rule of action in certain situations which frequently recur in human life. The rule prescribes the control and regulation within limits of the agent's natural impulses to act and feel thus and thus. The situations fall into groups which constitute the "fields" of the several "moral virtues"; for each there is a rule, conformity to which secures rightness in the individual acts. Thus the moral ideal appears as a code of rules, accepted by the agent, but as yet *to him* without rational justification and without system or unity. But the rules prescribe no mechanical uniformity: each within its limits permits variety, and the exactly right amount adopted to the requirements of the individual situation (and every actual situation is individual) must be determined by the intuition of the moment. There is no attempt to reduce the rich possibilities of right action to a single monotonous type. On the contrary, there are acknowledged to be many forms of moral virtue, and there is a long list of them, with their cor-relative vices, enumerated.

The Doctrine of the Mean here takes a form in which it has im-pressed subsequent thinkers, but which has less importance than is usually ascribed to it. In the "Table of the Virtues and Vices," each of the virtues is flanked by two opposite vices, which are respectively the excess and defect of that which in due measure constitutes the virtue. Aristotle tries to show that this is the case in regard to every virtue named and recognised as such, but his treatment is often forced and the endeavour is not very successful. Except as a convenient principle of arrangement of the various forms of praiseworthy or blameworthy characters, generally acknowledged as such by Greek opinion, this form of the doctrine is of no great significance.

Books III–V are occupied with a survey of the moral virtues and vices. These seem to have been undertaken in order to verify in detail the general account, but this aim is not kept steadily in view. Nor is there any well-considered principle of classification. What we find is a sort of portrait-gallery of the various types of moral excellence which the Greeks of the author's age admired and strove to encourage. The discussion is full of acute, interesting and sometimes profound obser-vations. Some of the types are those which are and will be admired at all times, but others are connected with peculiar features of Greek life which have now passed away. The most important is that of Justice or the Just Man, to which we may later return. But the discussion is pre-ceded by an attempt to elucidate some difficult and obscure points in the general account of moral virtue and action (Book III, pp. 34–42). This section is concerned with the notion of Responsibility. The dis-cussion designedly excludes what we may call the metaphysical issues of the problem, which here present themselves; it moves on the level of thought of the practical man, the statesman, and the legislator. Coercion and ignorance of relevant circumstances render acts invol-untary and exempt their doer from responsibility; otherwise the act is voluntary and the agent responsible; choice or preference of what is done, and inner consent to the deed, are to be presumed. Neither pas-sion nor ignorance of the right rule can extenuate responsibility. But there is a difference between acts done voluntarily and acts done of *set* choice or purpose. The latter imply Deliberation. Deliberation in-volves thinking, thinking out means to ends: in deliberate acts the whole nature of the agent consents to and enters into the act, and in a peculiar sense they are his, they *are* him in action, and the most signif-icant evidence of what he is. Aristotle is unable wholly to avoid allusion to the metaphysical difficulties, and what he does here say upon them is obscure and unsatisfactory. But he insists upon the importance in moral action of the agent's inner consent, and on the reality of his individual responsibility. For his present purpose the metaphysical difficulties are irrelevant.

The treatment of Justice in Book V has always been a source of great difficulty to students of the *Ethics*. Almost more than any other part of the work it has exercised influence upon mediæval and modern thought upon the subject. The distinctions and divisions have become part of the stock-in-trade of would-be philosophic jurists. And yet, oddly enough, most of these distinctions have been misunderstood and the whole purport of the discussion misconceived. Aristotle is here dealing with justice in a restricted sense, viz. as that special goodness of character which is required of every adult citizen and which can be produced by early discipline or habituation. It is the temper or habitual attitude demanded of the citizen for the due exercise of his functions as taking part in the administration of the civic community—as a member of the judicature and executive. The Greek citizen was only exceptionally, and at rare intervals, if ever, a law-maker, while at any moment he might be called upon to act as a judge (juryman or arbitrator) or as an administrator. For the work of a legislator far more than the moral virtue of justice or fairmindedness was necessary; these were requisite to the rarer and higher "intellectual virtue" of practical wisdom. Then here, too, the discussion moves on a low level, and the raising of fundamental problems is excluded. Hence "distributive justice" is concerned not with the large question of the distribution of political power and privileges among the constituent members or classes of the state, but with the smaller questions of the distribution among those of casual gains and even with the division among private claimants of a common fund or inheritance, while "corrective justice" is concerned solely with the management of legal redress. The whole treatment is confused by the unhappy attempt to give a precise mathematical form to the principles of justice in the various fields distinguished. Still it remains an interesting first endeavour to give greater exactness to some of the leading conceptions of jurisprudence.

Book VI appears to have in view two aims: (1) to describe goodness of intellect and discover its highest form or forms; (2) to show how this is related to goodness of character, and so to conduct generally. As all thinking is either theoretical or practical, goodness of intellect has *two* supreme forms—Theoretical and Practical Wisdom. The first, which apprehends the eternal laws of the universe, has no direct relation to human conduct: the second is identical with that master science of human life of which the whole treatise, consisting of the *Ethics* and the *Politics*, is an exposition. It is this science which supplies the right rules of conduct. Taking them as they emerge in and from practical experience, it formulates them more precisely and organises them into a system where they are all seen to converge upon happiness. The mode in which such knowledge manifests itself is in the power to show that such and such rules of action follow from the very nature of the end or good for man. It presupposes and starts from a clear conception of the end and the wish for it as conceived, and it proceeds by a deduction which is deliberation writ large. In the man of practical wisdom this process has reached its perfect result, and the code of right rules is apprehended as a system with a single principle and so as something wholly rational or reasonable. He has not on each occasion to seek and find the right rule applicable to the situation, he produces it at once from within himself, and can at need justify it by exhibiting its rationale, *i.e.*, its connection with the end. This is the consummate form of reason applied to conduct, but there are minor forms of it, less independent or original, but nevertheless of great value, such as the power to think out the proper cause of policy in novel circumstances, or the power to see the proper line of treatment to follow in a court of law.

The form of the thinking which enters into conduct is that which terminates in the production of a rule which declares some means to the end of life. The process presupposes (*a*) a clear and just apprehension of the nature of that end—such as the *Ethics* itself endeavours to supply; (*b*) a correct perception of the conditions of action. (*a*) at least is impossible except to a man whose character has been duly formed by discipline; it arises only in a man who has acquired moral virtue. For such action and feeling as forms bad character, blinds the eye of the soul and corrupts the moral principle, and the place of practical wisdom is taken by that parody of itself which Aristotle calls "cleverness"— the "wisdom" of the unscrupulous man of the world. Thus true practical wisdom and true goodness of character are interdependent; neither is genuinely possible or "completely" present without the other. This is Aristotle's contribution to the discussion of the question, so central in Greek Moral Philosophy, of the relation of the intellectual and the passionate factors in conduct.

Aristotle is not an intuitionist, but he recognises the implication in conduct of a direct and immediate apprehension both of the end and of the character of his circumstances under which it is from moment to moment realised. The directness of such apprehension makes it analogous to sensation or sense-perception; but it is on his view in the end due to the existence or activity in man of that power in him which is the highest thing in his nature, and akin to or identical with the divine nature—mind, or intelligence. It is this which reveals to us what is best for us—the ideal of a happiness which is the object of our real wish and the goal of all our efforts. But beyond and above the practical ideal of what is best *for man* begins to show itself another and still higher ideal—that of a life not distinctively human or in a narrow sense practical, yet capable of being participated in by man even under the actual circumstances of this world. For a time, however, this further and higher ideal is ignored.

The next book (Book VII), is concerned partly with moral conditions, in which the agent seems to rise above the level of moral virtue or fall below that of moral vice, but partly and more largely with conditions in which the agent occupies a middle position between the two. Aristotle's attention is here directed chiefly towards the phenomena of "Incontinence," weakness of will or imperfect self-control. This condition was to the Greeks a matter of only too frequent experience, but it appeared to them peculiarly difficult to understand. How can a man know what is good or best for him, and yet chronically fail to act upon his knowledge? Socrates was driven to the paradox of denying the possibility, but the facts are too strong for him. Knowledge of the right rule may be present, nay the rightfulness of its authority may be acknowledged, and yet time after time it may be disobeyed; the will may be good and yet overmastered by the force of desire, so that the act done is contrary to the agent's will. Nevertheless the act may be the agent's, and the will therefore divided against itself. Aristotle is aware of the seriousness and difficulty of the problem, but in spite of the vividness with which he pictures, and the acuteness with which he analyses, the situation in which such action occurs, it cannot be said that he solves the problem. It is time that he rises above the abstract view of it as a conflict between reason and passion, recognising that passion is involved in the knowledge which in conduct prevails or is overborne, and that the force which leads to the wrong act is not blind or ignorant passion, but always has some reason in it. But he tends to lapse back into the abstraction, and his final account is perplexed and obscure. He finds the source of the phenomenon in the nature of the desire for bodily pleasures, which is not irrational but has something rational in it. Such pleasures are not necessarily or inherently bad, as has sometimes been maintained; on the contrary, they are good, but only in certain amounts or under certain conditions, so that the will is often misled, hesitates, and is lost.

Books VIII and IX (on Friendship) are almost an interruption of the argument. The subject-matter of them was a favourite topic of ancient writers, and the treatment is smoother and more orderly than elsewhere in the *Ethics*. The argument is clear, and may be left without comment to the readers. These books contain a necessary and attractive complement to the somewhat dry account of Greek morality in the preceding books, and there are in them profound reflections on what may be called the metaphysics of friendship or love.

At the beginning of Book X we return to the topic of Pleasure, which is now regarded from a different point of view. In Book VII the antagonists were those who overemphasised the irrationality or badness of Pleasure: here it is rather those who so exaggerate its value as to confuse or identify it with the good or Happiness. But there is offered us in this section much more than criticism of the errors of others. Answers are given both to the psychological question, "What is Pleasure?" and to the ethical question, "What is its value?" Pleasure, we are told, is the natural concomitant and index of perfect activity, distinguishable but inseparable from it—"the activity of a subject at its best acting upon an object at its best." It is therefore always and in itself a good, but its value rises and falls with that of the activity with which it is conjoined, and which it intensifies and perfects. Hence it follows that the highest and best pleasures are those which accompany the highest and best activity.

Pleasure is, therefore, a necessary element in the best life, but it is not the whole of it nor the principal ingredient. The value of a life depends upon the nature and worth of the activity which it involves; given the maximum of full free action, the maximum of pleasure necessary follows. But on what sort of life is such activity possible? This leads us back to the question, What is Happiness? In what life can man find the fullest satisfaction for his desires? To this question Aristotle gives an answer which cannot but surprise us after what has preceded. True Happiness, great satisfaction, cannot be found by man in any form of "practical" life, no, not in the fullest and freest exercise possible of the "moral virtues," not in the life of the citizen or of the great soldier or statesman. To seek it there is to court failure and disappointment. It is to be found in the life of the onlooker, the disinterested spectator; or, to put it more distinctly, "in the life of the philosopher, the life of scientific and philosophic contemplation." The highest and most satisfying form of life possible to man is "the contemplative life"; it is only in a secondary sense and for those incapable of their life, that the practical or moral ideal is the best. It is time that such a life is not distinctively human, but it is the privilege of man to partake in it, and such participation, at however rare intervals and for however short a period, is the highest Happiness which human life can offer. All other activities have value only because and in so far as they render *this* life possible.

But it must not be forgotten that Aristotle conceives of this life as one of intense activity or energising: it is just this which gives it its supremacy. In spite of the almost religious fervour with which he speaks of it ("the most orthodox of his disciples" paraphrases his meaning by describing its content as "the service and vision of God"), it is clear that he identified it with the life of the philosopher, as he understood it, a life of ceaseless intellectual activity in which at least at times all the distractions and disturbances inseparable from practical life seemed to disappear and become as nothing. This ideal was partly an inheritance from the more ardent idealism of his master Plato, but partly it was the expression of personal experience.

The nobility of this ideal cannot be questioned; the conception of the end of man or a life lived for truth—of a life blissfully absorbed in the vision of truth—is a lofty and inspiring one. But we cannot resist certain criticisms upon its presentation by Aristotle: (1) the relation of it to the lower ideal of practice is left somewhat obscure; (2) it is described in such a way as renders its realisation possible only to a gifted few, and under exceptional circumstances; (3) it seems in various ways, as regards its content, to be unnecessarily and unjustifiably limited. But it must be borne in mind that this is a first endeavour to determine its principle, and that similar failures have attended the attempts to describe the "religious" or the "spiritual" ideals of life, which have continually been suggested by the apparently inherent limitations of the "practical" or "moral" life, which is the subject of Moral Philosophy. The Moral Ideal to those who have most deeply reflected on it leads to the thought of an Ideal beyond and above it, which alone gives it meaning, but which seems to escape from definite conception by man. The richness and variety of this Ideal ceaselessly invite, but as ceaselessly defy, our attempts to imprison it in a definite formula or portray it in detailed imagination. Yet the thought of it is and remains inexpungible from our minds.

This conception of the best life is not forgotten in the *Politics*. The end of life in the state is itself well-living and well-doing—a life which helps to produce the best life. The great agency in the production of such life is the State operating through Law, which is Reason backed by Force. For its greatest efficiency there is required the development of a science of legislation. The main drift of what he says here is that the most desirable thing would be that the best reason of the community should be embodied in its laws. But so far as that is not possible, it still is true that anyone who would make himself and others better must become a miniature legislator—must study the general principles of law, morality, and education. The conception of πολιτική with which he opened the *Ethics* would serve as a guide to a father educating his children as well as to the legislator legislating for the state. Finding in his predecessors no developed doctrine on this subject, Aristotle proposes himself to undertake the construction of it, and sketches in advance the programme of the *Politics* in the concluding sentence of the *Ethics.* His ultimate object is to answer the questions, What is the best form of Polity, how should each be constituted, and what laws and customs should it adopt and employ? Not till this answer is given will "the philosophy of human affairs" be complete.

On looking back it will be seen that the discussion of the central topic of the nature and formation of character has expanded into a Philosophy of Human Conduct, merging at its beginning and end into metaphysics. The result is a Moral Philosophy set against a background of Political Theory and general Philosophy. The most characteristic features of this Moral Philosophy are due to the fact of its essentially teleological view of human life and action: (1) Every human activity, but especially every human practical activity, is directed towards a simple End discoverable by reflection, and this End is conceived of as the object of universal human desire, as something to be enjoyed, not as something which ought to be done or enacted. Aristotle's Moral Philosophy is not hedonistic, but it is eudæmonistic; the end is the enjoyment of Happiness, not the fulfilment of Duty. (2) Every human practical activity derives its value from its efficiency as a means to that end; it is good or bad, right or wrong, as it conduces or fails to conduce to Happiness. Thus his Moral Philosophy is essentially utilitarian or prudential. Right action presupposes Thought or Thinking, partly on the development of a clearer and distincter conception of the end of desire, partly as the deduction from that of rules which state the normally effective conditions of its realisation. The thinking involved in right conduct is calculation—calculation of means to an end fixed by nature and foreknowable. Action itself is at its best just the realisation of a scheme preconceived and thought out beforehand, commending itself by its inherent attractiveness or promise of enjoyment.

This view has the great advantage of exhibiting morality as essentially reasonable, but the accompanying disadvantage of lowering it into a somewhat prosaic and unideal Prudentialism, nor is it saved from this by the tacking on to it, by a sort of after-thought, of the second and higher Ideal—an addition which ruins the coherence of the account without really transmuting its substance. The source of our dissatisfaction with the whole theory lies deeper than in its tendency to identify the end with the maximum of enjoyment or satisfaction, or to regard the goodness or badness of acts and feelings as lying solely in their efficacy to produce such a result. It arises from the application to morality of the distinction of means and end. For this distinction, for all its plausibility and usefulness in ordinary thought and speech, cannot finally be maintained. In morality—and this is vital to its character— everything is both means and end, and so neither in distinction or separation, and all thinking about it which presupposes the finality of this distinction wanders into misconception and error. The thinking which really matters in conduct is not a thinking which imaginatively forecasts ideals which promise to fulfil desire, or calculates means to their attainment—that is sometimes useful, sometimes harmful, and always subordinate, but thinking which reveals to the agent the situation in which he is to act, both, that is, the universal situation on which as man he always and everywhere stands, and the ever-varying and ever-novel situation in which he as this individual, here and now, finds himself. In such knowledge of given or historic fact lie the natural determinants of his conduct; in such knowledge alone lies the condition of his freedom and his good.

But this does not mean that Moral Philosophy has not still much to learn from Aristotle's *Ethics*. The work still remains one of the best introductions to a study of its important subject-matter; it spreads before us a view of the relevant facts, it reduces them to manageable compass and order, it raises some of the central problems, and makes acute and valuable suggestions towards their solution. Above all, it perpetually incites to renewed and independent reflection upon them.

J. A. SMITH

NICOMACHEAN ETHICS

BOOK I

EVERY art, and every science reduced to a teachable form, and in like manner every action and moral choice, aims, it is thought, at some good: for which reason a common and by no means a bad description of the Chief Good is, "that which all things aim at."

Now there plainly is a difference in the Ends proposed: for in some cases they are acts of working, and in others certain works or tangible results beyond and beside the acts of working: and where there are certain Ends beyond and beside the actions, the works are in their nature better than the acts of working. Again, since actions and arts and sciences are many, the Ends likewise come to be many: of the healing art, for instance, health; of the ship-building art, a vessel; of the military art, victory; and of domestic management, wealth; are respectively the Ends.

And whatever of such actions, arts, or sciences range under some one faculty (as under that of horsemanship the art of making bridles, and all that are connected with the manufacture of horse-furniture in general; this itself again, and every action connected with war, under the military art; and in the same way others under others), in all such, the Ends of the master-arts are more choice-worthy than those ranging under them, because it is with a view to the former that the latter are pursued.

(And in this comparison it makes no difference whether the acts of working are themselves the Ends of the actions, or something further beside them, as is the case in the arts and sciences we have been just speaking of.)

Since then of all things which may be done there is some one End which we desire for its own sake, and with a view to which we desire everything else; and since we do not choose in all instances with a further End in view (for then men would go on without limit, and so the desire would be unsatisfied and fruitless), this plainly must be the Chief Good, *i.e.* the best thing of all.

Surely then, even with reference to actual life and conduct, the knowledge of it must have great weight; and like archers, with a mark in view, we shall be more likely to hit upon what is right: and if so, we ought to try to describe, in outline at least, what it is and of which of the sciences and faculties it is the End.

Now one would naturally suppose it to be the End of that which is most commanding and most inclusive: and to this description, πολιτικὴ plainly answers: for this it is that determines which of the sciences should be in the communities, and which kind individuals are to learn, and what degree of proficiency is to be required. Again; we see also ranging under this the most highly esteemed faculties, such as the art military, and that of domestic management, and Rhetoric. Well then, since this uses all the other practical sciences, and moreover lays down rules as to what men are to do, and from what to abstain, the End of this must include the Ends of the rest, and so must be *The Good* of Man. And grant that this is the same to the individual and to the community, yet surely that of the latter is plainly greater and more perfect to discover and preserve: for to do this even for a single individual were a matter for contentment; but to do it for a whole nation, and for communities generally, were more noble and godlike.

Such then are the objects proposed by our treatise, which is of the nature of πολιτικὴ: and I conceive I shall have spoken on them satisfactorily, if they be made as distinctly clear as the nature of the subject-matter will admit: for exactness must not be looked for in all discussions alike, any more than in all works of handicraft. Now the notions of nobleness and justice, with the examination of which πολιτικὴ is concerned, admit of variation and error to such a degree, that they are supposed by some to exist conventionally only, and not in the nature of things: but then, again, the things which are allowed to be goods admit of a similar error, because harm comes to many from them: for before now some have perished through wealth, and others through valour.

We must be content then, in speaking of such things and from such data, to set forth the truth roughly and in outline; in other words, since we are speaking of general matter and from general data, to draw also conclusions merely general. And in the same spirit should each person receive what we say: for the man of education will seek exactness so far in each subject as the nature of the thing admits, it being plainly much the same absurdity to put up with a mathematician who tries to persuade instead of proving, and to demand strict demonstrative reasoning of a Rhetorician.

Now each man judges well what he knows, and of these things he is a good judge: on each particular matter then he is a good judge who has been instructed in *it*, and in a general way the man of general mental cultivation.

Hence the young man is not a fit student of Moral Philosophy, for he has no experience in the actions of life, while all that is said presupposes and is concerned with these: and in the next place, since he is apt to follow the impulses of his passions, he will hear as though he heard not, and to no profit, the end in view being practice and not mere knowledge.

And I draw no distinction between young in years, and youthful in temper and disposition: the defect to which I allude being no direct result of the time, but of living at the beck and call of passion, and following each object as it rises. For to them that are such the knowledge comes to be unprofitable, as to those of imperfect self-control: but, to those who form their desires and act in accordance with reason, to have knowledge on these points must be very profitable.

Let thus much suffice by way of preface on these three points, the student, the spirit in which our observations should be received, and the object which we propose.

And now, resuming the statement with which we commenced, since all knowledge and moral choice grasps at good of some kind or another, what good is that which we say πολιτικὴ aims at? or, in other words, what is the highest of all the goods which are the objects of action?

So far as name goes, there is a pretty general agreement: for HAPPINESS both the multitude and the refined few call it, and "living well" and "doing well" they conceive to be the same with "being happy;" but about the Nature of this Happiness, men dispute, and the multitude do not in their account of it agree with the wise. For some say it is some one of those things which are palpable and apparent, as pleasure or wealth or honour; in fact, some one thing, some another; nay, oftentimes the same man gives a different account of it; for when ill, he calls it health; when poor, wealth: and conscious of their own ignorance, men admire those who talk grandly and above their comprehension. Some again held it to be something by itself, other than and beside these many good things, which is in fact to all these the cause of their being good.

Now to sift all the opinions would be perhaps rather a fruitless task;

so it shall suffice to sift those which are most generally current, or are thought to have some reason in them.

And here we must not forget the difference between reasoning from principles, and reasoning to principles: for with good cause did Plato too doubt about this, and inquire whether the right road is from principles or to principles, just as in the racecourse from the judges to the further end, or *vice versa*.

Of course, we must begin with what is known; but then this is of two kinds, what we *do* know, and what we *may* know: perhaps then as individuals we must begin with what we *do* know. Hence the necessity that he should have been well trained in habits, who is to study, with any tolerable chance of profit, the principles of nobleness and justice and moral philosophy generally. For a principle is a matter of fact, and if the fact is sufficiently clear to a man there will be no need in addition of the reason for the fact. And he that has been thus trained either has principles already, or can receive them easily: as for him who neither has nor can receive them, let him hear his sentence from Hesiod:

> He is best of all who of himself conceiveth all things;
> Good again is he too who can adopt a good suggestion;
> But whoso neither of himself conceiveth nor hearing from another
> Layeth it to heart;—he is a useless man.

But to return from this digression.

Now of the Chief Good (*i.e.*, of Happiness) men seem to form their notions from the different modes of life, as we might naturally expect: the many and most low conceive it to be pleasure, and hence they are content with the life of sensual enjoyment. For there are three lines of life which stand out prominently to view, that just mentioned, and the life in society, and, thirdly, the life of contemplation.

Now the many are plainly quite slavish, choosing a life like that of brute animals: yet they obtain some consideration, because many of the great share the tastes of Sardanapalus. The refined and active again conceive it to be honour: for this may be said to be the end of the life in society: yet it is plainly too superficial for the object of our search, because it is thought to rest with those who pay rather than with him who receives it, whereas the Chief Good we feel instinctively must be something which is our own, and not easily to be taken from us.

And besides, men seem to pursue honour, that they may believe themselves to be good: for instance, they seek to be honoured by the wise, and by those among whom they are known, and for virtue: clearly then, in the opinion at least of these men, virtue is higher than honour. In truth, one would be much more inclined to think this to be the end of the life in society; yet this itself is plainly not sufficiently final: for it is conceived possible, that a man possessed of virtue might sleep or be inactive all through his life, or, as a third case, suffer the greatest evils and misfortunes: and the man who should live thus no one would call happy, except for mere disputation's sake.

And for these let thus much suffice, for they have been treated of at sufficient length in my Encyclia.

A third line of life is that of contemplation, concerning which we shall make our examination in the sequel.

As for the life of money-making, it is one of constraint, and wealth manifestly is not the good we are seeking, because it is for use, that is, for the sake of something further: and hence one would rather conceive the forementioned ends to be the right ones, for men rest content with them for their own sakes. Yet, clearly, they are not the objects of our search either, though many words have been wasted on them. So much then for these.

Again, the notion of one Universal Good (the same, that is, in all things), it is better perhaps we should examine, and discuss the meaning of it, though such an inquiry is unpleasant, because they are friends of ours who have introduced these εἴδη. Still perhaps it may appear better, nay to be our duty where the safety of the truth is concerned, to upset if need be even our own theories, specially as we are lovers of wisdom: for since both are dear to us, we are bound to prefer the truth. Now they who invented this doctrine of εἴδη, did not apply it to those things in which they spoke of priority and posteriority, and so they never made any ἰδέα of numbers; but good is predicated in the categories of Substance, Quality, and Relation; now that which exists of itself, i.e. Substance, is prior in the nature of things to that which is relative, because this latter is an off-shoot, as it were, and result of that which is; on their own principle then there cannot be a common ἰδέα in the case of these.

In the next place, since good is predicated in as many ways as there are modes of existence [for it is predicated in the category of Substance, as God, Intellect—and in that of Quality, as The Virtues—and in that of Quantity, as The Mean—and in that of Relation, as The Useful—and in that of Time, as Opportunity—and in that of Place, as Abode; and other such like things], it manifestly cannot be something common and universal and one in all: else it would not have been predicated in all the categories, but in one only.

Thirdly, since those things which range under one ἰδέα are also under the cognisance of one science, there would have been, on their theory, only one science taking cognisance of all goods collectively: but in fact there are many even for those which range under one category: for instance, of Opportunity or Seasonableness (which I have before mentioned as being in the category of Time), the science is, in war, generalship; in disease, medical science; and of the Mean (which I quoted before as being in the category of Quantity), in food, the medical science; and in labour or exercise, the gymnastic science. A person might fairly doubt also what in the world they mean by very-this that or the other, since, as they would themselves allow, the account of the humanity is one and the same in the very-Man, and in any individual Man: for so far as the individual and the very-Man are both Man, they will not differ at all: and if so, then very-good and any particular good will not differ, in so far as both are good. Nor will it do to say, that the eternity of the very-good makes it to be more good; for what has lasted white ever so long, is no whiter than what lasts but for a day.

No. The Pythagoreans do seem to give a more credible account of the matter, who place "One" among the goods in their double list of goods and bads: which philosophers, in fact, Speusippus seems to have followed.

But of these matters let us speak at some other time. Now there is plainly a loophole to object to what has been advanced, on the plea that the theory I have attacked is not by its advocates applied to all good: but those goods only are spoken of as being under one ἰδέα, which are pursued, and with which men rest content simply for their own sakes: whereas those things which have a tendency to produce or preserve them in any way, or to hinder their contraries, are called good because of these other goods, and after another fashion. It is manifest then that the goods may be so called in two senses, the one class for their own sakes, the other because of these.

Very well then, let us separate the independent goods from the instrumental, and see whether they are spoken of as under one ἰδέα. But the question next arises, what kind of goods are we to call independent? All such as are pursued even when separated from other goods, as, for instance, being wise, seeing, and certain pleasures and honours (for these, though we do pursue them with some further end in view, one would still place among the independent goods)? or does it come in fact to this, that we can call nothing independent good except the ἰδέα, and so the concrete of it will be nought?

If, on the other hand, these are independent goods, then we shall require that the account of the goodness be the same clearly in all, just as that of the whiteness is in snow and white lead. But how stands the fact? Why of honour and wisdom and pleasure the accounts are distinct and different in so far as they are good. The Chief Good then is not something common, and after one ἰδέα.

But then, how does the name come to be common (for it is not seemingly a case of fortuitous equivocation)? Are different individual things called good by virtue of being from one source, or all conducing to one end, or rather by way of analogy, for that intellect is to the soul as sight to the body, and so on? However, perhaps we ought to leave these questions now, for an accurate investigation of them is more properly the business of a different philosophy. And likewise respecting the ἰδέα: for even if there is some one good predicated in common of all things that are good, or separable and capable of existing independently, manifestly it cannot be the object of human action or attainable by Man; but we are in search now of something that is so.

It may readily occur to any one, that it would be better to attain a knowledge of it with a view to such concrete goods as are attainable and practical, because, with this as a kind of model in our hands, we shall the better know what things are good for us individually, and when we know them, we shall attain them.

Some plausibility, it is true, this argument possesses, but it is contradicted by the facts of the Arts and Sciences; for all these, though aiming at some good, and seeking that which is deficient, yet pretermit the knowledge of it: now it is not exactly probable that all artisans without exception should be ignorant of so great a help as this would be, and not even look after it; neither is it easy to see wherein a weaver or a carpenter will be profited in respect of his craft by knowing the very-good, or how a man will be the more apt to effect cures or to command an army for having seen the ἰδέα itself. For manifestly it is not health after this general and abstract fashion which is the subject of the physician's investigation, but the health of Man, or rather perhaps of this or that man; for he has to heal individuals.—Thus much on these points.

And now let us revert to the Good of which we are in search: what can it be? for manifestly it is different in different actions and arts: for it is different in the healing art and in the art military, and similarly in the rest. What then is the Chief Good in each? Is it not "that for the sake of which the other things are done?" and this in the healing art is health, and in the art military victory, and in that of housebuilding a house, and in any other thing something else; in short, in every action and moral choice the End, because in all cases men do everything else with a view of this. So that if there is some one End of all things which are and may be done, this must be the Good proposed by doing, or if more than one, then these.

Thus our discussion after some traversing about has come to the same point which we reached before. And this we must try yet more to clear up.

Now since the ends are plainly many, and of these we choose some with a view to others (wealth, for instance, musical instruments, and, in general, all instruments), it is clear that all are not final: but the Chief Good is manifestly something final; and so, if there is some one only which is final, this must be the object of our search: but if several, then the most final of them will be it.

Now that which is an object of pursuit in itself we call more final than that which is so with a view to something else; that again which is never an object of choice with a view to something else than those which are so both in themselves and with a view to this ulterior object: and so by the term "absolutely final," we denote that which is an object of choice always in itself, and never with a view to any other.

And of this nature Happiness is mostly thought to be, for this we choose always for its own sake, and never with a view to anything further: whereas honour, pleasure, intellect, in fact every excellence we choose for their own sakes, it is true (because we would choose each of these even if no result were to follow), but we choose them also with a view to happiness, conceiving that through their instrumentality we shall be happy: but no man chooses happiness with a view to them, nor in fact with a view to any other thing whatsoever.

The same result is seen to follow also from the notion of self-sufficiency, a quality thought to belong to the final good. Now by sufficient for Self, we mean not for a single individual living a solitary life, but for his parents also and children and wife, and, in general, friends and countrymen; for man is by nature adapted to a social existence. But of these, of course, some limit must be fixed: for if one extends it to parents and descendants and friends' friends, there is no end to it. This point, however, must be left for future investigation: for the present we define that to be self-sufficient "which taken alone makes life choice-worthy, and to be in want of nothing;" now of such kind we think Happiness to be: and further, to be most choice-worthy of all things; not being reckoned with any other thing, for if it were so reckoned, it is plain we must then allow it, with the addition of ever so small a good, to be more choice-worthy than it was before: because what is put to it becomes an addition of so much more good, and of goods the greater is ever the more choice-worthy.

So then Happiness is manifestly something final and self-sufficient, being the end of all things which are and may be done.

But, it may be, to call Happiness the Chief Good is a mere truism, and what is wanted is some clearer account of its real nature. Now this object may be easily attained, when we have discovered what is the work of man; for as in the case of flute-player, statuary, or artisan of any kind, or, more generally, all who have any work or course of action, their Chief Good and Excellence is thought to reside in their work, so it would seem to be with man, if there is any work belonging to him.

Are we then to suppose, that while carpenter and cobbler have certain works and courses of action, Man as Man has none, but is left by Nature without a work? or would not one rather hold, that as eye, hand, and foot, and generally each of his members, has manifestly some special work; so too the whole Man, as distinct from all these, has some work of his own?

What then can this be? not mere life, because that plainly is shared with him even by vegetables, and we want what is peculiar to him. We must separate off then the life of mere nourishment and growth, and next will come the life of sensation: but this again manifestly is common to horses, oxen, and every animal. There remains then a kind of life of the Rational Nature apt to act: and of this Nature there are two parts denominated Rational, the one as being obedient to Reason, the other as having and exerting it. Again, as this life is also spoken of in two ways, we must take that which is in the way of actual working, because this is thought to be most properly entitled to the name. If then the work of Man is a working of the soul in accordance with reason, or at least not independently of reason, and we say that the work of any given subject, and of that subject good of its kind, are the same in kind (as, for instance, of a harp-player and a good harp-player, and so on in every case, adding to the work eminence in the way of excellence; I mean the work of a harp-player is to play the harp, and of a good harp-player to play it well); if, I say, this is so, and we assume the work of Man to be life of a certain kind, that is to say a working of the soul, and actions with reason, and of a good man to do these things well and nobly, and in fact everything is finished off well in the way of the excellence which peculiarly belongs to it: if all this is so, then the Good of Man comes to be "a working of the Soul in the way of Excellence," or, if Excellence admits of degrees, in the way of the best and most perfect Excellence.

And we must add, in a complete life, for as it is not one swallow or one fine day that makes a spring, so it is not one day or a short time that makes a man blessed and happy.

Let this then be taken for a rough sketch of the Chief Good: since it is probably the right way to give first the outline, and fill it in afterwards. And it would seem that any man may improve and connect what is good in the sketch, and that time is a good discoverer and co-operator in such matters: it is thus in fact that all improvements in the various arts have been brought about, for any man may fill up a deficiency.

You must remember also what has been already stated, and not seek for exactness in all matters alike, but in each according to the subject-matter, and so far as properly belongs to the system. The carpenter and geometrician, for instance, inquire into the right line in different fashion: the former so far as he wants it for his work, the latter inquires into its nature and properties, because he is concerned with the truth.

So then should one do in other matters, that the incidental matters may not exceed the direct ones.

And again, you must not demand the reason either in all things alike, because in some it is sufficient that the fact has been well demonstrated, which is the case with first principles; and the fact is the first step, *i.e.* starting-point or principle.

And of these first principles some are obtained by induction, some by perception, some by a course of habituation, others in other different ways. And we must try to trace up each in their own nature, and take pains to secure their being well defined, because they have great influence on what follows: it is thought, I mean, that the starting-point or principle is more than half the whole matter, and that many of the points of inquiry come simultaneously into view thereby.

We must now inquire concerning Happiness, not only from our conclusion and the data on which our reasoning proceeds, but likewise from what is commonly said about it: because with what is true all things which really are are in harmony, but with that which is false the true very soon jars.

Now there is a common division of goods into three classes; one being called external, the other two those of the soul and body respectively, and those belonging to the soul we call most properly and specially good. Well, in our definition we assume that the actions and workings of the soul constitute Happiness, and these of course belong to the soul. And so our account is a good one, at least according to this opinion, which is of ancient date, and accepted by those who profess philosophy. Rightly too are certain actions and workings said to be the end, for thus it is brought into the number of the goods of the soul instead of the external. Agreeing also with our definition is the common notion, that the happy man lives well and does well, for it has been stated by us to be pretty much a kind of living well and doing well.

But further, the points required in Happiness are found in combination in our account of it.

For some think it is virtue, others practical wisdom, others a kind of scientific philosophy; others that it is these, or else some one of them, in combination with pleasure, or at least not independently of it; while others again take in external prosperity.

Of these opinions, some rest on the authority of numbers or antiquity, others on that of few, and those men of note: and it is not likely that either of these classes should be wrong in all points, but be right at least in some one, or even in most.

Now with those who assert it to be Virtue (Excellence), or some kind of Virtue, our account agrees: for working in the way of Excellence surely belongs to Excellence.

And there is perhaps no unimportant difference between conceiving of the Chief Good as in possession or as in use, in other words, as a mere state or as a working. For the state or habit may possibly exist in a subject without effecting any good, as, for instance, in him who is asleep, or in any other way inactive; but the working cannot so, for it will of necessity act, and act well. And as at the Olympic games it is not the finest and strongest men who are crowned, but they who enter the lists, for out of these the prize-men are selected; so too in life, of the honourable and the good, it is they who act who rightly win the prizes.

Their life too is in itself pleasant: for the feeling of pleasure is a mental sensation, and that is to each pleasant of which he is said to be fond: a horse, for instance, to him who is fond of horses, and a sight to him who is fond of sights: and so in like manner just acts to him who is fond of justice, and more generally the things in accordance with virtue to him who is fond of virtue. Now in the case of the multitude of men the things which they individually esteem pleasant clash, because they are not such by nature, whereas to the lovers of nobleness those things are pleasant which are such by nature: but the actions in accordance with virtue are of this kind, so that they are pleasant both to the individuals and also in themselves.

So then their life has no need of pleasure as a kind of additional appendage, but involves pleasure in itself. For, besides what I have just mentioned, a man is not a good man at all who feels no pleasure in noble actions, just as no one would call that man just who does not feel pleasure in acting justly, or liberal who does not in liberal actions, and similarly in the case of the other virtues which might be enumerated: and if this be so, then the actions in accordance with virtue must be in themselves pleasurable. Then again they are certainly good and noble, and each of these in the highest degree; if we are to take as right the judgment of the good man, for he judges as we have said.

Thus then Happiness is most excellent, most noble, and most pleasant, and these attributes are not separated as in the well-known Delian inscription —

> "Most noble is that which is most just, but best in health;
> And naturally most pleasant is the obtaining one's desires."

For all these co-exist in the best acts of working: and we say that Happiness is these, or one, that is, the best of them.

Still it is quite plain that it does require the addition of external goods, as we have said: because without appliances it is impossible, or at all events not easy, to do noble actions: for friends, money, and political influence are in a manner intruments whereby many things are done: some things there are again a deficiency in which mars blessedness; good birth, for instance, or fine offspring, or even personal beauty: for he is not at all capable of Happiness who is very ugly, or is ill-born, or solitary and childless; and still less perhaps supposing him to have very bad children or friends, or to have lost good ones by death. As we have said already, the addition of prosperity of this kind does seem necessary to complete the idea of Happiness; hence some rank good fortune, and others virtue, with Happiness.

And hence too a question is raised, whether it is a thing that can be learned, or acquired by habituation or discipline of some other kind, or whether it comes in the way of divine dispensation, or even in the way of chance.

Now to be sure, if anything else is a gift of the Gods to men, it is probable that Happiness is a gift of theirs too, and specially because of all human goods it is the highest. But this, it may be, is a question belonging more properly to an investigation different from ours: and it is quite clear, that on the supposition of its not being sent from the Gods direct, but coming to us by reason of virtue and learning of a certain kind, or discipline, it is yet one of the most Godlike things; because the prize and End of virtue is manifestly somewhat most excellent, nay divine and blessed.

It will also on this supposition be widely participated, for it may through learning and diligence of a certain kind exist in all who have not been maimed for virtue.

And if it is better we should be happy thus than as a result of chance, this is in itself an argument that the case is so; because those things which are in the way of nature, and in like manner of art, and of every cause, and specially the best cause, are by nature in the best way possible: to leave them to chance what is greatest and most noble would be very much out of harmony with all these facts.

The question may be determined also by a reference to our definition of Happiness, that it is a working of the soul in the way of excellence or virtue of a certain kind: and of the other goods, some we must have to begin with, and those which are co-operative and useful are given by nature as instruments.

These considerations will harmonise also with what we said at the commencement: for we assumed the End of πολιτική to be most excellent: now this bestows most care on making the members of the community of a certain character; good that is and apt to do what is honourable.

With good reason then neither ox nor horse nor any other brute animal do we call happy, for none of them can partake in such working: and for this same reason a child is not happy either, because by reason of his tender age he cannot yet perform such actions: if the term is applied, it is by way of anticipation.

For to constitute Happiness, there must be, as we have said, complete virtue and a complete life: for many changes and chances of all kinds arise during a life, and he who is most prosperous may become involved in great misfortunes in his old age, as in the heroic poems the tale is told of Priam: but the man who has experienced such fortune and died in wretchedness, no man calls happy.

Are we then to call no man happy while he lives, and, as Solon would have us, look to the end? And again, if we are to maintain this position, *is* a man then happy when he is dead? or is not this a complete absurdity, specially in us who say Happiness is a working of a certain kind?

If on the other hand we do not assert that the dead man is happy, and Solon does not mean this, but only that one would then be safe in pronouncing a man happy, as being thenceforward out of the reach of evils and misfortunes, this too admits of some dispute, since it is thought that the dead has somewhat both of good and evil (if, as we must allow, a man may have when alive but not aware of the circumstances), as honour and dishonour, and good and bad fortune of children and descendants generally.

Nor is this view again without its difficulties: for, after a man has lived in blessedness to old age and died accordingly, many changes may befall him in right of his descendants; some of them may be good and obtain positions in life accordant to their merits, others again quite the contrary: it is plain too that the descendants may at different intervals or grades stand in all manner of relations to the ancestors. Absurd indeed would be the position that even the dead man is to change about with them and become at one time happy and at another miserable. Absurd however it is on the other hand that the affairs of the descendants should in no degree and during no time affect the ancestors.

But we must revert to the point first raised, since the present question will be easily determined from that.

If then we are to look to the end and then pronounce the man blessed, not as being so but as having been so at some previous time, surely it is absurd that when he *is* happy the truth is not to be asserted of him, because we are unwilling to pronounce the living happy by reason of their liability to changes, and because, whereas we have conceived of happiness as something stable and no way easily changeable, the fact is that good and bad fortune are constantly circling about the same people: for it is quite plain, that if we are to depend upon the fortunes of men, we shall often have to call the same man happy, and a little while after miserable, thus representing our happy man

"Chameleon-like, and based on rottenness."

Is not this the solution? that to make our sentence dependent on the changes of fortune, is no way right: for not in them stands the well, or the ill, but though human life needs these as accessories (which we have allowed already), the workings in the way of virtue are what determine Happiness, and the contrary the contrary.

And, by the way, the question which has been here discussed, testifies incidentally to the truth of our account of Happiness. For to nothing does a stability of human results attach so much as it does to the workings in the way of virtue, since these are held to be more abiding even than the sciences: and of these last again the most precious are the most abiding, because the blessed live in them most and most continuously, which seems to be the reason why they are not forgotten. So then this stability which is sought will be in the happy man, and he will be such through life, since always, or most of all, he will be doing and contemplating the things which are in the way of virtue: and the various chances of life he will bear most nobly, and at all times and in all ways harmoniously, since he is the truly good man, or in the terms of our proverb "a faultless cube."

And whereas the incidents of chance are many, and differ in greatness and smallness, the small pieces of good or ill fortune evidently do not affect the balance of life, but the great and numerous, if happening for good, will make life more blessed (for it is their nature to contribute to ornament, and the using of them comes to be noble and excellent), but if for ill, they bruise as it were and maim the blessedness: for they bring in positive pain, and hinder many acts of working. But still, even in these, nobleness shines through when a man bears contentedly many and great mischances not from insensibility to pain but because he is noble and high-spirited.

And if, as we have said, the acts of working are what determine the character of the life, no one of the blessed can ever become wretched, because he will never do those things which are hateful and mean. For the man who is truly good and sensible bears all fortunes, we presume, becomingly, and always does what is noblest under the circumstances, just as a good general employs to the best advantage the force he has with him; or a good shoemaker makes the handsomest shoe he can out of the leather which has been given him; and all other good artisans likewise. And if this be so, wretched never can the happy man come to be: I do not mean to say he will be blessed should he fall into fortunes like those of Priam.

Nor, in truth, is he shifting and easily changeable, for on the one hand from his happiness he will not be shaken easily nor by ordinary mischances, but, if at all, by those which are great and numerous; and, on the other, after such mischances he cannot regain his happiness in a little time; but, if at all, in a long and complete period, during which he has made himself master of great and noble things.

Why then should we not call happy the man who works in the way of perfect virtue, and is furnished with external goods sufficient for acting his part in the drama of life: and this during no ordinary period but such as constitutes a complete life as we have been describing it.

Or we must add, that not only is he to live so, but his death must be in keeping with such life, since the future is dark to us, and Happiness we assume to be in every way an end and complete. And, if this be so, we shall call them among the living blessed who have and will have the things specified, but blessed *as Men*.

On these points then let it suffice to have defined thus much.

Now that the fortunes of their descendants, and friends generally, contribute nothing towards forming the condition of the dead, is plainly a very heartless notion, and contrary to the current opinions.

But since things which befall are many, and differ in all kinds of ways, and some touch more nearly, others less, to go into minute particular distinctions would evidently be a long and endless task: and so it may suffice to speak generally and in outline.

If then, as of the misfortunes which happen to one's self, some have a certain weight and turn the balance of life, while others are, so to speak, lighter; so it is likewise with those which befall all our friends alike; if further, whether they whom each suffering befalls be alive or dead makes much more difference than in a tragedy the presupposing or actual perpetration of the various crimes and horrors, we must take into our account this difference also, and still more perhaps the doubt concerning the dead whether they really partake of any good or evil; it seems to result from all these considerations, that if anything does pierce the veil and reach them, be the same good or bad, it must be something trivial and small, either in itself or to them; or at least of such a magnitude or such a kind as neither to make happy them that are not so otherwise, nor to deprive of their blessedness them that are.

It is plain then that the good or ill fortunes of their friends do affect the dead somewhat: but in such kind and degree as neither to make the happy unhappy nor produce any other such effect.

Having determined these points, let us examine with respect to Happiness, whether it belongs to the class of things praiseworthy or things precious; for to that of faculties it evidently does not.

Now it is plain that everything which is a subject of praise is praised for being of a certain kind and bearing a certain relation to something else: for instance, the just, and the valiant, and generally the good man, and virtue itself, we praise because of the actions and the results: and the strong man, and the quick runner, and so forth, we praise for being of a certain nature and bearing a certain relation to something good and excellent (and this is illustrated by attempts to praise the gods; for they are presented in a ludicrous aspect by being referred to our standard, and this results from the fact, that all praise does, as we have said, imply reference to a standard). Now if it is to such objects that praise belongs, it is evident that what is applicable to the best objects is not praise, but something higher and better: which is plain matter of fact, for not only do we call the gods blessed and happy, but of men also we pronounce those blessed who most nearly resemble the gods. And in like manner in respect of goods; no man thinks of praising Happiness as he does the principle of justice, but calls it blessed, as being somewhat more godlike and more excellent.

Eudoxus too is thought to have advanced a sound argument in support of the claim of pleasure to the highest prize: for the fact that, though it is one of the good things, it is not praised, he took for an indication of its superiority to those which are subjects of praise: a superiority he attributed also to a god and the Chief Good, on the ground that they form the standard to which everything besides is referred. For praise applies to virtue, because it makes men apt to do what is noble; but encomia to definite works of body or mind.

However, it is perhaps more suitable to a regular treatise on encomia to pursue this topic with exactness: it is enough for our purpose that from what has been said it is evident that Happiness belongs to the class of things precious and final. And it seems to be so also because of its being a starting-point; which it is, in that with a view to it we all do everything else that is done; now the starting-point and cause of good things we assume to be something precious and divine.

Moreover, since Happiness is a kind of working of the soul in the way of perfect Excellence, we must inquire concerning Excellence: for so probably shall we have a clearer view concerning Happiness; and again, he who is really a statesman is generally thought to have spent most pains on this, for he wishes to make the citizens good and obedient to the laws. (For examples of this class we have the lawgivers of the Cretans and Lacedæmonians and whatever other such there have been.) But if this investigation belongs properly to πολιτική then clearly the inquiry will be in accordance with our original design.

Well, we are to inquire concerning Excellence, *i.e.* Human Excellence of course, because it was the Chief Good of Man and the Happiness of Man that we were inquiring of just now.

By Human Excellence we mean not that of man's body but that of his soul; for we call Happiness a working of the Soul.

And if this is so, it is plain that some knowledge of the nature of the Soul is necessary for the statesman, just as for the Oculist a knowledge of the whole body, and the more so in proportion as πολιτική is more precious and higher than the healing art: and in fact physicians of the higher class do busy themselves much with the knowledge of the body.

So then the statesman is to consider the nature of the Soul: but he must do so with these objects in view, and so far only as may suffice for the objects of his special inquiry: for to carry his speculations to a greater exactness is perhaps a task more laborious than falls within his province.

In fact, the few statements made on the subject in my popular treatises are quite enough, and accordingly we will adopt them here: as,
that the Soul consists of two parts, the Irrational and the Rational (as to
whether these are actually divided, as are the parts of the body, and
everything that is capable of division; or are only metaphysically speaking two, being by nature inseparable, as are convex and concave cir-
cumferences, matters not in respect of our present purpose). And of the
Irrational, the one part seems common to other objects, and in fact vegetative; I mean the cause of nourishment and growth (for such a faculty of the Soul one would assume to exist in all things that receive
nourishment, even in embryos, and this the same as in the perfect creatures; for this is more likely than that it should be a different one).

Now the Excellence of this manifestly is not peculiar to the human
species but common to others: for this part and this faculty is thought
to work most in time of sleep, and the good and bad man are least distinguishable while asleep; whence it is a common saying that during
one half of life there is no difference between the happy and the
wretched; and this accords with our anticipations, for sleep is an inac-
tivity of the soul, in so far as it is denominated good or bad, except that
in some wise some of its movements find their way through the veil and
so the good come to have better dreams than ordinary men. But
enough of this: we must forgo any further mention of the nutritive part,
since it is not naturally capable of the Excellence which is peculiarly
human.

And there seems to be another Irrational Nature of the Soul, which
yet in a way partakes of Reason. For in the man who controls his appetites, and in him who resolves to do so and fails, we praise the Reason
or Rational part of the Soul, because it exhorts aright and to the best
course: but clearly there is in them, beside the Reason, some other natural principle which fights with and strains against the Reason. (For in
plain terms, just as paralysed limbs of the body when their owners
would move them to the right are borne aside in a contrary direction to
the left, so is it in the case of the Soul, for the impulses of men who
cannot control their appetites are to contrary points: the difference is
that in the case of the body we do see what is borne aside but in the
case of the soul we do not. But, it may be, not the less on that account
are we to suppose that there is in the Soul also somewhat besides the
Reason, which is opposed to this and goes against it; and to *how* it is different, that is irrelevant.)

But of Reason this too does evidently partake, as we have said: for instance, in the man of self-control it obeys Reason: and perhaps in the

man of perfected self-mastery, or the brave man, it is yet more obedient; in them it agrees entirely with the Reason.

So then the Irrational is plainly twofold: the one part, the merely vegetative, has no share of Reason, but that of desire, or appetition generally, does partake of it in a sense, in so far as it is obedient to it and capable of submitting to its rule. (So too in common phrase we say we have λόγος of our father or friends, and this in a different sense from that in which we say we have λόγος of mathematics.)

Now that the Irrational is in some way persuaded by the Reason, admonition, and every act of rebuke and exhortation indicate. If then we are to say that this also has Reason, then the Rational, as well as the Irrational, will be twofold, the one supremely and in itself, the other paying it a kind of filial regard.

The Excellence of Man then is divided in accordance with this difference: we make two classes, calling the one Intellectual, and the other Moral; pure science, intelligence, and practical wisdom—Intellectual: liberality, and perfected self-mastery—Moral: in speaking of a man's Moral character, we do not say he is a scientific or intelligent but a meek man, or one of perfected self-mastery: and we praise the man of science in right of his mental state; and of these such as are praiseworthy we call Excellences.

BOOK II

WELL: human Excellence is of two kinds, Intellectual and Moral: now the Intellectual springs originally, and is increased subsequently, from teaching (for the most part that is), and needs therefore experience and time; whereas the Moral comes from custom, and so the Greek term denoting it is but a slight deflection from the term denoting custom in that language.

From this fact it is plain that not one of the Moral Virtues comes to be in us merely by nature: because of such things as exist by nature, none can be changed by custom: a stone, for instance, by nature gravitating downwards, could never by custom be brought to ascend, not even if one were to try and accustom it by throwing it up ten thousand times; nor could fire again be brought to descend, nor in fact could anything whose nature is in one way be brought by custom to be in another. The Virtues then come to be in us neither by nature, nor in despite of nature, but we are furnished by nature with a capacity for receiving them, and are perfected in them through custom.

Again, in whatever cases we get things by nature, we get the faculties first and perform the acts of working afterwards; an illustration of which is afforded by the case of our bodily senses, for it was not from having often seen or heard that we got these senses, but just the reverse: we had them and so exercised them, but did not have them because we had exercised them. But the Virtues we get by first performing single acts of working, which, again, is the case of other things, as the arts for instance; for what we have to make when we have learned how, these we learn how to make by making: men come to be builders, for instance, by building; harp-players, by playing on the harp: exactly so, by doing just actions we come to be just; by doing the actions of self-mastery we come to be perfected in self-mastery; and by doing brave actions brave.

And to the truth of this testimony is borne by what takes place in communities: because the law-givers make the individual members good men by habituation, and this is the intention certainly of every

20

law-giver, and all who do not effect it well fail of their intent; and herein consists the difference between a good Constitution and a bad.

Again, every Virtue is either produced or destroyed from and by the very same circumstances: art too in like manner; I mean it is by playing the harp that both the good and the bad harp-players are formed: and similarly builders and all the rest; by building well men will become good builders; by doing it badly bad ones: in fact, if this had not been so, there would have been no need of instructors, but all men would have been at once good or bad in their several arts without them.

So too then is it with the Virtues: for by acting in the various relations in which we are thrown with our fellow men, we come to be, some just, some unjust: and by acting in dangerous positions and being habituated to feel fear or confidence, we come to be, some brave, others cowards.

Similarly is it also with respect to the occasions of lust and anger: for some men come to be perfected in self-mastery and mild, others destitute of all self-control and passionate; the one class by behaving in one way under them, the other by behaving in another. Or, in one word, the habits are produced from the acts of working like to them: and so what we have to do is to give a certain character to these particular acts, because the habits formed correspond to the differences of these.

So then, whether we are accustomed this way or that straight from childhood, makes not a small but an important difference, or rather I would say it makes all the difference.

Since then the object of the present treatise is not mere speculation, as it is of some others (for we are inquiring not merely that we may know what virtue is but that we may become virtuous, else it would have been useless), we must consider as to the particular actions how we are to do them, because, as we have just said, the quality of the habits that shall be formed depends on these.

Now, that we are to act in accordance with Right Reason is a general maxim, and may for the present be taken for granted: we will speak of it hereafter, and say both what Right Reason is, and what are its relations to the other virtues.

But let this point be first thoroughly understood between us, that all which can be said on moral action must be said in outline, as it were, and not exactly: for as we remarked at the commencement, such reasoning only must be required as the nature of the subject-matter admits of, and matters of moral action and expediency have no fixedness any more than matters of health. And if the subject in its general maxims is such, still less in its application to particular cases is exactness attainable: because these fall not under any art or system of rules, but it must be left in each instance to the individual agents to look to the exigencies of the particular case, as it is in the art of healing, or that of navigating a ship. Still, though the present subject is confessedly such, we must try and do what we can for it.

First then this must be noted, that it is the nature of such things to be spoiled by defect and excess; as we see in the case of health and strength (since for the illustration of things which cannot be seen we must use those that can), for excessive training impairs the strength as well as deficient: meat and drink, in like manner, in too great or too small quantities, impair the health: while in due proportion they cause, increase, and preserve it.

Thus it is therefore with the habits of perfected Self-Mastery and Courage and the rest of the Virtues: for the man who flies from and fears all things, and never stands up against anything, comes to be a coward; and he who fears nothing, but goes at everything, comes to be rash. In like manner too, he that tastes of every pleasure and abstains from none comes to lose all self-control; while he who avoids all, as do the dull and clownish, comes as it were to lose his faculties of perception: that is to say, the habits of perfected Self-Mastery and Courage are spoiled by the excess and defect, but by the mean state are preserved.

Furthermore, not only do the origination, growth, and marring of the habits come from and by the same circumstances, but also the acts of working after the habits are formed will be exercised on the same: for so it is also with those other things which are more directly matters of sight, strength for instance: for this comes by taking plenty of food and doing plenty of work, and the man who has attained strength is best able to do these: and so it is with the Virtues, for not only do we by abstaining from pleasures come to be perfected in Self-Mastery, but when we have come to be so we can best abstain from them: similarly too with Courage: for it is by accustoming ourselves to despise objects of fear and stand up against them that we come to be brave; and after we have come to be so we shall be best able to stand up against such objects.

And for a test of the formation of the habits we must take the pleasure or pain which succeeds the acts; for he is perfected in Self-Mastery who not only abstains from the bodily pleasures but is glad to do so; whereas he who abstains but is sorry to do it has not Self-Mastery: he again is brave who stands up against danger, either with positive pleasure or at least without any pain: whereas he who does it with pain is not brave.

For Moral Virtue has for its object-matter pleasures and pains, because by reason of pleasure we do what is bad, and by reason of pain decline doing what is right (for which cause, as Plato observes, men should have been trained straight from their childhood to receive pleasure and pain from proper objects, for this is the right education). Again: since Virtues have to do with actions and feelings, and on every feeling and every action pleasure and pain follow, here again is another proof that Virtue has for its object-matter pleasure and pain. The same is shown also by the fact that punishments are effected through the instrumentality of these; because they are of the nature of remedies, and it is the nature of remedies to be the contraries of the ills they cure. Again, to quote what we said before: every habit of the Soul by its very nature has relation to, and exerts itself upon, things of the same kind as those by which it is naturally deteriorated or improved: now such habits do come to be vicious by reason of pleasures and pains, that is, by men pursuing or avoiding respectively, either such as they ought not, or at wrong times, or in wrong manner, and so forth (for which reason, by the way, some people define the Virtues as certain states of impassibility and utter quietude, but they are wrong because they speak without modification, instead of adding "as they ought," "as they ought not," and "when," and so on). Virtue then is assumed to be that habit which is such, in relation to pleasures and pains, as to effect the best results, and Vice the contrary.

The following considerations may also serve to set this in a clear light. There are principally three things moving us to choice and three to avoidance, the honourable, the expedient, and pleasant; and their three contraries, the dishonourable, the hurtful, and the painful: now the good man is apt to go right, and the bad man wrong, with respect to all these of course, but most specially with respect to pleasure: because not only is this common to him with all animals but also it is a concomitant of all those things which move to choice, since both the honourable and the expedient give an impression of pleasure.

Again, it grows up with us all from infancy, and so it is a hard matter to remove from ourselves this feeling, engrained as it is into our very life.

Again, we adopt pleasure and pain (some of us more, and some less) as the measure even of actions: for this cause then our whole business must be with them, since to receive right or wrong impressions of pleasure and pain is a thing of no little importance in respect of the actions. Once more; it is harder, as Heraclitus says, to fight against pleasure than against anger: now it is about that which is more than commonly difficult that art comes into being, and virtue too, because in that which is difficult the good is of a higher order: and so for this reason too both virtue and moral philosophy generally must wholly busy themselves respecting pleasures and pains, because he that uses these well will be good, he that does so ill will be bad.

Let us then be understood to have stated, that Virtue has for its object-matter pleasures and pains, and that it is either increased or marred by the same circumstances (differently used) by which it is originally generated, and that it exerts itself on the same circumstances out of which it was generated.

Now I can conceive a person perplexed as to the meaning of our statement, that men must do just actions to become just, and those of self-mastery to acquire the habit of self-mastery; "for," he would say, "if men are doing the actions they have the respective virtues already, just as men are grammarians or musicians when they do the actions of either art." May we not reply by saying that it is not so even in the case of the arts referred to: because a man may produce something grammatical either by chance or the suggestion of another; but then only will he be a grammarian when he not only produces something grammatical but does so grammarian-wise; *i.e.* in virtue of the grammatical knowledge he himself possesses.

Again, the cases of the arts and the virtues are not parallel: because those things which are produced by the arts have their excellence in themselves, and it is sufficient therefore that these when produced should be in a certain state: but those which are produced in the way of the virtues, are, strictly speaking, actions of a certain kind (say of Justice or perfected Self-Mastery), not merely if in themselves they are in a certain state but if also he who does them does them being himself in a certain state, first if knowing what he is doing, next if with deliberate preference, and with such preference for the things' own sake; and thirdly if being himself stable and unapt to change. Now to constitute possession of the arts these requisites are not reckoned in, excepting the one point of knowledge: whereas for possession of the virtues knowledge avails little or nothing, but the other requisites avail not a little, but, in fact, are all in all, and these requisites as a matter of fact do come from oftentimes doing the actions of Justice and perfected Self-Mastery.

The facts, it is true, are called by the names of these habits when they are such as the just or perfectly self-mastering man would do; but he is not in possession of the virtues who merely does these facts, but he who also so does them as the just and self-mastering do them.

We are right then in saying, that these virtues are formed in a man by his doing the actions; but no one, if he should leave them undone, would be even in the way to become a good man. Yet people in general do not perform these actions, but taking refuge in talk they flatter themselves they are philosophising, and that they will so be good men: acting in truth very like those sick people who listen to the doctor with great attention but do nothing that he tells them: just as these then cannot be well bodily under such a course of treatment, so neither can those be mentally by such philosophising.

Next, we must examine what Virtue is. Well, since the things which come to be in the mind are, in all, of three kinds, Feelings, Capacities, States, Virtue of course must belong to one of the three classes.

By Feelings, I mean such as lust, anger, fear, confidence, envy, joy, friendship, hatred, longing, emulation, compassion, in short all such as are followed by pleasure or pain: by Capacities, those in right of which we are said to be capable of these feelings; as by virtue of which we are able to have been made angry, or grieved, or to have compassionated; by States, those in right of which we are in a certain relation good or bad to the aforementioned feelings; to having been made angry, for instance, we are in a wrong relation if in our anger we were too violent or too slack, but if we were in the happy medium we are in a right relation to the feeling. And so on of the rest.

Now Feelings neither the virtues nor vices are, because in right of the Feelings we are not denominated either good or bad, but in right of the virtues and vices we are.

Again, in right of the Feelings we are neither praised nor blamed (for a man is not commended for being afraid or being angry, nor blamed for being angry merely but for being so in a particular way), but in right of the virtues and vices we are.

Again, both anger and fear we feel without moral choice, whereas the virtues are acts of moral choice, or at least certainly not independent of it.

Moreover, in right of the Feelings we are said to be moved, but in right of the virtues and vices not to be moved, but disposed, in a certain way.

And for these same reasons they are not Capacities, for we are not called good or bad merely because we are able to feel, nor are we praised or blamed.

And again, Capacities we have by nature, but we do not come to be good or bad by nature, as we have said before.

Since then the virtues are neither Feelings nor Capacities, it remains that they must be States.

Now what the genus of Virtue is has been said; but we must not merely speak of it thus, that it is a state, but say also what kind of a state it is.

We must observe then that all excellence makes that whereof it is the excellence both to be itself in a good state and to perform its work well. The excellence of the eye, for instance, makes both the eye good and its work also: for by the excellence of the eye we see well. So too the excellence of the horse makes a horse good, and good in speed, and in carrying his rider, and standing up against the enemy. If then this is universally the case, the excellence of Man, i.e. Virtue, must be a state whereby Man comes to be good and whereby he will perform well his proper work. Now how this shall be it is true we have said already, but still perhaps it may throw light on the subject to see what is its characteristic nature.

In all quantity then, whether continuous or discrete, one may take the greater part, the less, or the exactly equal, and these either with reference to the thing itself, or relatively to us: and the exactly equal is a mean between excess and defect. Now by the mean of the thing, i.e. absolute mean, I denote that which is equidistant from either extreme (which of course is one and the same to all), and by the mean relatively to ourselves, that which is neither too much nor too little for the particular individual. This of course is not one nor the same to all: for instance, suppose ten is too much and two too little, people take six for the absolute mean; because it exceeds the smaller sum by exactly as much as it is itself exceeded by the larger, and this mean is according to arithmetical proportion.

But the mean relatively to ourselves must not be so found; for it does not follow, supposing ten minæ is too large a quantity to eat and two too small, that the trainer will order his man six; because for the person who is to take it this also may be too much or too little: for Milo it would be too little, but for a man just commencing his athletic exercises too much: similarly too of the exercises themselves, as running or wrestling.

So then it seems every one possessed of skill avoids excess and defect, but seeks for and chooses the mean, not the absolute but the relative.

Now if all skill thus accomplishes well its work by keeping an eye on the mean, and bringing the works to this point (whence it is common enough to say of such works as are in a good state, "one cannot add to or take ought from them," under the notion of excess or defect destroying goodness but the mean state preserving it), and good artisans, as we say, work with their eye on this, and excellence, like nature, is more exact and better than any art in the world, it must have an aptitude to aim at the mean.

It is moral excellence, *i.e.* Virtue, of course which I mean, because this it is which is concerned with feelings and actions, and in these there can be excess and defect and the mean: it is possible, for instance, to feel the emotions of fear, confidence, lust, anger, compassion, and pleasure and pain generally, too much or too little, and in either case wrongly; but to feel them when we ought, on what occasions, towards whom, why, and as, we should do, is the mean, or in other words the best state, and this is the property of Virtue.

In like manner too with respect to the actions, there may be excess and defect and the mean. Now Virtue is concerned with feelings and actions, in which the excess is wrong and the defect is blamed but the mean is praised and goes right; and both these circumstances belong to Virtue. Virtue then is in a sense a mean state, since it certainly has an aptitude for aiming at the mean.

Again, one may go wrong in many different ways (because, as the Pythagoreans expressed it, evil is of the class of the infinite, good of the finite), but right only in one; and so the former is easy, the latter difficult; easy to miss the mark, but hard to hit it: and for these reasons, therefore, both the excess and defect belong to Vice, and the mean state to Virtue; for, as the poet has it,

> "Men may be bad in many ways,
> But good in one alone."

Virtue then is "a state apt to exercise deliberate choice, being in the relative mean, determined by reason, and as the man of practical wisdom would determine."

It is a middle state between too faulty ones, in the way of excess on one side and of defect on the other: and it is so moreover, because the faulty states on one side fall short of, and those on the other exceed, what is right, both in the case of the feelings and the actions; but Virtue finds, and when found adopts, the mean.

And so, viewing it in respect of its essence and definition, Virtue is a mean state; but in reference to the chief good and to excellence it is the highest state possible.

But it must not be supposed that every action or every feeling is capable of subsisting in this mean state, because some there are which are so named as immediately to convey the notion of badness, as malevolence, shamelessness, envy; or, to instance in actions, adultery, theft, homicide; for all these and suchlike are blamed because they are in themselves bad, not the having too much or too little of them.

In these then you never can go right, but must always be wrong: nor in such does the right or wrong depend on the selection of a proper person, time, or manner (take adultery for instance), but simply doing any one soever of those things is being wrong.

You might as well require that there should be determined a mean state, an excess and a defect in respect of acting unjustly, being cowardly, or giving up all control of the passions: for at this rate there will be of excess and defect a mean state; of excess, excess; and of defect, defect.

But just as of perfected self-mastery and courage there is no excess and defect, because the mean is in one point of view the highest possible state, so neither of those faulty states can you have a mean state, excess, or defect, but howsoever done they are wrong: you cannot, in short, have of excess and defect a mean state, nor of a mean state excess and defect.

It is not enough, however, to state this in general terms, we must also apply it to particular instances, because in treatises on moral conduct general statements have an air of vagueness, but those which go into detail one of greater reality: for the actions after all must be in detail, and the general statements, to be worth anything, must hold good here.

We must take these details then from the Table.

I. In respect of fears and confidence or boldness:

The Mean state is Courage: men may exceed, of course, either in absence of fear or in positive confidence: the former has no name (which is a common case), the latter is called rash: again, the man who has too much fear and too little confidence is called a coward.

II. In respect of pleasures and pains (but not all, and perhaps fewer pains than pleasures):

The Mean state here is perfected Self-Mastery, the defect total absence of Self-control. As for defect in respect of pleasure, there are really no people who are chargeable with it, so, of course, there is really no name for such characters, but, as they are conceivable, we will give them one and call them insensible.

III. In respect of giving and taking wealth (a):

The mean state is Liberality, the excess Prodigality, the defect Stinginess: here each of the extremes involves really an excess and defect contrary to each other: I mean, the prodigal gives out too much and takes in too little, while the stingy man takes in too much and gives out too little. (It must be understood that we are now giving merely an outline and summary, intentionally: and we will, in a later part of the treatise, draw out the distinctions with greater exactness.)

IV. In respect of wealth (*b*):

There are other dispositions besides these just mentioned; a mean state called Munificence (for the munificent man differs from the liberal, the former having necessarily to do with great wealth, the latter with but small); the excess called by the names either of Want of taste or Vulgar Profusion, and the defect Paltriness (these also differ from the extremes connected with liberality, and the manner of their difference shall also be spoken of later).

V. In respect of honour and dishonour (*a*):

The mean state Greatness of Soul, the excess which may be called braggadocio, and the defect Littleness of Soul.

VI. In respect of honour and dishonour (*b*):

Now there is a state bearing the same relation to Greatness of Soul as we said just now Liberality does to Munificence, with the difference that is of being about a small amount of the same thing: this state having reference to small honour, as Greatness of Soul to great honour; a man may, of course, grasp at honour either more than he should or less; now he that exceeds in his grasping at it is called ambitious, he that falls short unambitious, he that is just as he should be has no proper name: nor in fact have the states, except that the disposition of the ambitious man is called ambition. For this reason those who are in either extreme lay claim to the mean as a debatable land, and we call the virtuous character sometimes by the name ambitious, sometimes by that of unambitious, and we commend sometimes the one and sometimes the other. Why we do it shall be said in the subsequent part of the treatise; but now we will go on with the rest of the virtues after the plan we have laid down.

VII. In respect of anger:

Here too there is excess, defect, and a mean state; but since they may be said to have really no proper names, as we call the virtuous character Meek, we will call the mean state Meekness, and of the extremes, let the man who is excessive be denominated Passionate, and the faulty state Passionateness, and him who is deficient Angerless, and the defect Angerlessness.

There are also three other mean states, having some mutual resemblance, but still with differences; they are alike in that they all have for their object-matter intercourse of words and deeds, and they differ in that one has respect to truth herein, the other two to what is pleasant; and this in two ways, the one in relaxation and amusement, the other in all things which occur in daily life. We must say a word or two about these also, that we may the better see that in all matters the mean is praiseworthy, while the extremes are neither right nor worthy of praise but of blame.

Now of these, it is true, the majority have really no proper names, but still we must try, as in the other cases, to coin some for them for the sake of clearness and intelligibleness.

I. In respect of truth:

The man who is in the mean state we will call Truthful, and his state Truthfulness, and as to the disguise of truth, if it be on the side of exaggeration, Braggadocia, and him that has it a Braggadocio; if on that of diminution, Reserve and Reserved shall be the terms.

II. In respect of what is pleasant in the way of relaxation or amusement:

The mean state shall be called Easy-pleasantry, and the character accordingly a man of Easy-pleasantry; the excess Buffoonery, and the man a Buffoon; the man deficient herein a Clown, and his state Clownishness.

III. In respect of what is pleasant in daily life:

He that is as he should be may be called Friendly, and his mean state Friendliness: he that exceeds, if it be without any interested motive, somewhat too Complaisant, if with such motive, a Flatterer: he that is deficient and in all instances unpleasant, Quarrelsome and Cross.

There are mean states likewise in feelings and matters concerning them. Shamefacedness, for instance, is no virtue, still a man is praised for being shamefaced: for in these too the one is denominated the man in the mean state, the other in the excess; the Dumbfoundered, for instance, who is overwhelmed with shame on all and any occasions: the man who is in the defect, *i.e.* who has no shame at all in his composition, is called Shameless: but the right character Shamefaced.

Indignation against successful vice, again, is a state in the mean between Envy and Malevolence: they all three have respect to pleasure and pain produced by what happens to one's neighbour: for the man who has this right feeling is annoyed at undeserved success of others, while the envious man goes beyond him and is annoyed at all success of others, and the malevolent falls so far short of feeling annoyance that he even rejoices [at misfortune of others].

But for the discussion of these also there will be another opportunity, as of Justice too, because the term is used in more senses than one. So after this we will go accurately into each and say how they are mean states: and in like manner also with respect to the Intellectual Excellences.

Now as there are three states in each case, two faulty either in the way of excess or defect, and one right, which is the mean state, of course all are in a way opposed to one another; the extremes, for instance, not only to the mean but also to one another, and the mean to the extremes: for just as the half is greater if compared with the less portion, and less if compared with the greater, so the mean states, compared with the defects, exceed, whether in feelings or actions, and *vice versâ*. The brave man, for instance, shows as rash when compared with the coward, and cowardly when compared with the rash; similarly too the man of perfected self-mastery, viewed in comparison with the man destitute of all perception, shows like a man of no self-control, but in comparison with the man who really has no self-control, he looks like one destitute of all perception: and the liberal man compared with the stingy seems prodigal, and by the side of the prodigal, stingy.

And so the extreme characters push away, so to speak, towards each other the man in the mean state; the brave man is called a rash man by the coward, and a coward by the rash man, and in the other cases accordingly. And there being this mutual opposition, the contrariety between the extremes is greater than between either and the mean, because they are further from one another than from the mean, just as the greater or less portion differ more from each other than either from the exact half.

Again, in some cases an extreme will bear a resemblance to the mean; rashness, for instance, to courage, and prodigality to liberality; but between the extremes there is the greatest dissimilarity. Now things which are furthest from one another are defined to be contrary, and so the further off the more contrary will they be.

Further: of the extremes in some cases the excess, and in others the defect, is most opposed to the mean: to courage, for instance, not rashness which is the excess, but cowardice which is the defect; whereas to perfected self-mastery not insensibility which is the defect but absence of all self-control which is the excess.

And for this there are two reasons to be given; one from the nature of the thing itself, because from the one extreme being nearer and more like the mean, we do not put this against it, but the other; as, for instance, since rashness is thought to be nearer to courage than cowardice is, and to resemble it more, we put cowardice against courage rather than rashness, because those things which are further from the mean are thought to be more contrary to it. This then is one reason arising from the thing itself; there is another arising from our own constitution and make: for in each man's own case those things give the impression of being more contrary to the mean to which we individually have a natural bias. Thus we have a natural bias towards pleasures, for which reason we are much more inclined to the rejection of all self-control, than to self-discipline.

These things then to which the bias is, we call more contrary, and so total want of self-control (the excess) is more contrary than the defect is to perfected self-mastery.

Now that Moral Virtue is a mean state, and how it is so, and that it lies between two faulty states, one in the way of excess and another in the way of defect, and that it is so because it has an aptitude to aim at the mean both in feelings and actions, all this has been set forth fully and sufficiently.

And so it is hard to be good: for surely hard it is in each instance to find the mean, just as to find the mean point or centre of a circle is not what any man can do, but only he who knows how: just so to be angry, to give money, and be expensive, is what any man can do, and easy: but to do these to the right person, in due proportion, at the right time, with a right object, and in the right manner, this is not as before what any man can do, nor is it easy; and for this cause goodness is rare, and praiseworthy, and noble.

Therefore he who aims at the mean should make it his first care to keep away from that extreme which is more contrary than the other to the mean; just as Calypso in Homer advises Ulysses,

"Clear of this smoke and surge thy barque direct;"

because of the two extremes the one is always more, and the other less, erroneous; and, therefore, since to hit exactly on the mean is difficult, one must take the least of the evils as the safest plan; and this a man will be doing, if he follows this method.

We ought also to take into consideration our own natural bias; which varies in each man's case, and will be ascertained from the pleasure and pain arising in us. Furthermore, we should force ourselves off in the contrary direction, because we shall find ourselves in the mean after we have removed ourselves far from the wrong side, exactly as men do in straightening bent timber.

But in all cases we must guard most carefully against what is pleasant, and pleasure itself, because we are not impartial judges of it.

We ought to feel in fact towards pleasure as did the old counsellors towards Helen, and in all cases pronounce a similar sentence; for so by sending it away from us, we shall err the less.

Well, to speak very briefly, these are the precautions by adopting which we shall be best able to attain the mean.

Still, perhaps, after all it is a matter of difficulty, and specially in the particular instances: it is not easy, for instance, to determine exactly in what manner, with what persons, for what causes, and for what length of time, one ought to feel anger: for we ourselves sometimes praise those who are defective in this feeling, and we call them meek; at another, we term the hot-tempered manly and spirited.

Then, again, he who makes a small deflection from what is right, be it on the side of too much or too little, is not blamed, only he who makes a considerable one; for he cannot escape observation. But to what point or degree a man must err in order to incur blame, it is not easy to determine exactly in words: nor in fact any of those points which are matter of perception by the Moral Sense: such questions are matters of detail, and the decision of them rests with the Moral Sense.

At all events thus much is plain, that the mean state is in all things praiseworthy, and that practically we must deflect sometimes towards excess sometimes towards defect, because this will be the easiest method of hitting on the mean, that is, on what is right.

BOOK III

Now since Virtue is concerned with the regulation of feelings and actions, and praise and blame arise upon such as are voluntary, while for the involuntary allowance is made, and sometimes compassion is excited, it is perhaps a necessary task for those who are investigating the nature of Virtue to draw out the distinction between what is voluntary and what involuntary; and it is certainly useful for legislators, with respect to the assigning of honours and punishments.

Involuntary actions then are thought to be of two kinds, being done either on compulsion, or by reason of ignorance.

An action is, properly speaking, compulsory, when the origination is external to the agent, being such that in it the agent (perhaps we may more properly say the patient) contributes nothing; as if a wind were to convey you anywhere, or men having power over your person.

But when actions are done, either from fear of greater evils, or from some honourable motive, as, for instance, if you were ordered to commit some base act by a despot who had your parents or children in his power, and they were to be saved upon your compliance or die upon your refusal, in such cases there is room for a question whether the actions are voluntary or involuntary.

A similar question arises with respect to cases of throwing goods overboard in a storm: abstractedly no man throws away his property willingly, but with a view to his own and his shipmates' safety any one would who had any sense.

The truth is, such actions are of a mixed kind, but are most like voluntary actions; for they are choiceworthy at the time when they are being done, and the end or object of the action must be taken with reference to the actual occasion. Further, we must denominate an action voluntary or involuntary at the time of doing it: now in the given case the man acts voluntarily, because the originating of the motion of his limbs in such actions rests with himself; and where the origination is in himself it rests with himself to do or not to do.

34

Such actions then are voluntary, though in the abstract perhaps involuntary because no one would choose any of such things in and by itself.

But for such actions men sometimes are even praised, as when they endure any disgrace or pain to secure great and honourable equivalents; if *vice versa*, then they are blamed, because it shows a base mind to endure things very disgraceful for no honourable object, or for a trifling one.

For some again no praise is given, but allowance is made; as where a man does what he should not by reason of such things as overstrain the powers of human nature, or pass the limits of human endurance.

Some acts perhaps there are for which compulsion cannot be pleaded, but a man should rather suffer the worst and die; how absurd, for instance, are the pleas of compulsion with which Alcmæon in Euripides' play excuses his matricide!

But it is difficult sometimes to decide what kind of thing should be chosen instead of what, or what endured in preference to what, and much moreso to abide by one's decisions: for in general the alternatives are painful, and the actions required are base, and so praise or blame is awarded according as persons have been compelled or no.

What kind of actions then are to be called compulsory? may we say, simply and abstractedly whenever the cause is external and the agent contributes nothing; and that where the acts are in themselves such as one would not wish but choice-worthy at the present time and in preference to such and such things, and where the origination rests with the agent, the actions are in themselves involuntary but at the given time and in preference to such and such things voluntary; and they are more like voluntary than involuntary, because the actions consist of little details, and these are voluntary.

But what kind of things one ought to choose instead of what, it is not easy to settle, for there are many differences in particular instances.

But suppose a person should say, things pleasant and honourable exert a compulsive force (for that they are external and do compel); at that rate every action is on compulsion, because these are universal motives of action.

Again, they who act on compulsion and against their will do so with pain; but they who act by reason of what is pleasant or honourable act with pleasure.

It is truly absurd for a man to attribute his actions to external things instead of to his own capacity for being easily caught by them; or, again, to ascribe the honourable to himself, and the base ones to pleasure.

So then that seems to be compulsory "whose origination is from without, the party compelled contributing nothing."

Now every action of which ignorance is the cause is not-voluntary, but that only is involuntary which is attended with pain and remorse; for clearly the man who has done anything by reason of ignorance, but is not annoyed at his own action, cannot be said to have done it *with* his will because he did not know he was doing it, nor again *against* his will because he is not sorry for it.

So then of the class "acting by reason of ignorance," he who feels regret afterwards is thought to be an involuntary agent, and him that has no such feeling, since he certainly is different from the other, we will call a not-voluntary agent; for as there is a real difference it is better to have a proper name.

Again, there seems to be a difference between acting *because of* ignorance and acting *with* ignorance: for instance, we do not usually assign ignorance as the cause of the actions of the drunken or angry man, but either the drunkenness or the anger, yet they act not knowingly but with ignorance.

Again, every bad man is ignorant what he ought to do and what to leave undone, and by reason of such error men become unjust and wholly evil.

Again, we do not usually apply the term involuntary when a man is ignorant of his own true interest; because ignorance which affects moral choice constitutes depravity but not involuntariness: nor does any ignorance of principle (because for this men are blamed) but ignorance in particular details, wherein consists the action and wherewith it is concerned, for in these there is both compassion and allowance, because he who acts in ignorance of any of them acts in a proper sense involuntarily.

It may be as well, therefore, to define these particular details; what they are, and how many; viz. who acts, what he is doing, with respect to what or in what, sometimes with what, as with what instrument, and with what result (as that of preservation, for instance), and how, as whether softly or violently.

All these particulars, in one and the same case, no man in his senses could be ignorant of; plainly not of the agent, being himself. But what he is doing a man may be ignorant, as men in speaking say a thing escaped them unawares; or as Æschylus did with respect to the Mysteries, that he was not aware that it was unlawful to speak of them; or as in the case of that catapult accident the other day the man said he discharged it merely to display its operation. Or a person might suppose a son to be an enemy, as Merope did; or that the spear really pointed was rounded off; or that the stone was a pumice; or in striking with a view to save might kill or might strike when merely wishing to show another, as people do in sham-fighting.

Now since ignorance is possible in respect to all these details in which the action consists, he that acted in ignorance of any of them is thought to have acted involuntarily, and he most so who was in ignorance as regards the most important, which are thought to be those in which the action consists, and the result.

Further, not only must the ignorance be of this kind, to constitute an action involuntary, but it must be also understood that the action is followed by pain and regret.

Now since all involuntary action is either upon compulsion or by reason of ignorance, Voluntary Action would seem to be "that whose origination is in the agent, he being aware of the particular details in which the action consists."

For, it may be, men are not justified by calling those actions involuntary, which are done by reason of Anger or Lust.

Because, in the first place, if this be so no other animal but man, and not even children, can be said to act voluntarily. Next, is it meant that we never act voluntarily when we act from Lust or Anger, or that we act voluntarily in doing what is right and involuntarily in doing what is discreditable? The latter supposition is absurd, since the cause is one and the same. Then as to the former, it is a strange thing to maintain actions to be involuntary which we are bound to grasp at: now there are occasions on which anger is a duty, and there are things which we are bound to lust after, health, for instance, and learning.

Again, whereas actions strictly involuntary are thought to be attended with pain, those which are done to gratify lust are thought to be pleasant.

Again: how does the involuntariness make any difference between wrong actions done from deliberate calculation, and those done by reason of anger? for both ought to be avoided, and the irrational feelings are thought to be just as natural to man as reason, and so of course must be such actions of the individual as are done from Anger and Lust. It is absurd then to class these actions among the involuntary.

Having thus drawn out the distinction between voluntary and involuntary action our next step is to examine into the nature of Moral Choice, because this seems most intimately connected with Virtue and to be a more decisive test of moral character than a man's acts are.

Now Moral Choice is plainly voluntary, but the two are not co-extensive, voluntary being the more comprehensive term; for first, children and all other animals share in voluntary action but not in Moral Choice; and next, sudden actions we call voluntary but do not ascribe them to Moral Choice.

Nor do they appear to be right who say it is lust or anger, or wish, or opinion of a certain kind; because, in the first place, Moral Choice is not shared by the irrational animals while Lust and Anger are. Next: the man who fails of self-control acts from Lust but not from Moral Choice; the man of self-control, on the contrary, from Moral Choice, not from Lust. Again: whereas Lust is frequently opposed to Moral Choice, Lust is not to Lust.

Lastly: the object-matter of Lust is the pleasant and the painful, but of Moral Choice neither the one nor the other. Still less can it be Anger, because actions done from Anger are thought generally to be least of all consequent on Moral Choice.

Nor is it Wish either, though appearing closely connected with it; because, in the first place, Moral Choice has not for its objects impossibilities, and if a man were to say he chose them he would be thought to be a fool; but Wish may have impossible things for its objects, immortality for instance.

Wish again may be exercised on things in the accomplishment of which one's self could have nothing to do, as the success of any particular actor or athlete; but no man chooses things of this nature, only such as he believes he may himself be instrumental in procuring.

Further: Wish has for its object the End rather, but Moral Choice the means to the End; for instance, we wish to be healthy but we choose the means which will make us so; or happiness again we wish for, and commonly say so, but to say we choose is not an appropriate term, because, in short, the province of Moral Choice seems to be those things which are in our own power.

Neither can it be Opinion; for Opinion is thought to be unlimited in its range of objects, and to be exercised as well upon things eternal and impossible as on those which are in our own power: again, Opinion is logically divided into true and false, not into good and bad as Moral Choice is.

However, nobody perhaps maintains its identity with Opinion simply; but it is not the same with opinion of any kind, because by choosing good and bad things we are constituted of a certain character, but by having opinions on them we are not.

Again, we choose to take or avoid, and so on, but we opine what a thing is, or for what it is serviceable, or how; but we do not opine to take or avoid.

Further, Moral Choice is commended rather for having a right object than for being judicious, but Opinion for being formed in accordance with truth.

Again, we choose such things as we pretty well know to be good, but we form opinions respecting such as we do not know at all.

And it is not thought that choosing and opining best always go together, but that some opine the better course and yet by reason of viciousness choose not the things which they should.

It may be urged, that Opinion always precedes or accompanies Moral Choice; be it so, this makes no difference, for this is not the point in question, but whether Moral Choice is the same as Opinion of a certain kind.

Since then it is none of the aforementioned things, what is it, or how is it characterised? Voluntary it plainly is, but not all voluntary action is an object of Moral Choice. May we not say then, it is "that voluntary which has passed through a stage of previous deliberation?" because Moral Choice is attended with reasoning and intellectual process. The etymology of its Greek name seems to give a hint of it, being when analysed "chosen in preference to somewhat else."

Well then; do men deliberate about everything, and is anything soever the object of Deliberation, or are there some matters with respect to which there is none? (It may be as well perhaps to say, that by "object of Deliberation" is meant such matter as a sensible man would deliberate upon, not what any fool or madman might.)

Well: about eternal things no one deliberates; as, for instance, the universe, or the incommensurability of the diameter and side of a square.

Nor again about things which are in motion but which always happen in the same way either necessarily, or naturally, or from some other cause, as the solstices or the sunrise.

Nor about those which are variable, as drought and rains; nor fortuitous matters, as finding of treasure.

Nor in fact even about all human affairs; no Lacedæmonian, for instance, deliberates as to the best course for the Scythian government to adopt; because in such cases we have no power over the result.

But we do deliberate respecting such practical matters as are in our own power (which are what are left after all our exclusion).

I have adopted this division because causes seem to be divisible into nature, necessity, chance, and moreover intellect, and all human powers.

And as man in general deliberates about what man in general can effect, so individuals do about such practical things as can be effected through their own instrumentality.

Again, we do not deliberate respecting such arts or sciences as are exact and independent: as, for instance, about written characters, because we have no doubt how they should be formed; but we do deliberate on all such things as are usually done through our own instrumentality, but not invariably in the same way; as, for instance, about matters connected with the healing art, or with money-making; and, again, more about piloting ships than gymnastic exercises, because the former has been less exactly determined, and so forth; and more about arts than sciences, because we more frequently doubt respecting the former.

So then Deliberation takes place in such matters as are under general laws, but still uncertain how in any given case they will issue, *i.e.* in which there is some indefiniteness; and for great matters we associate coadjutors in counsel, distrusting our ability to settle them alone.

Further, we deliberate not about Ends, but Means to Ends. No physician, for instance, deliberates whether he will cure, nor orator whether he will persuade, nor statesman whether he will produce a good constitution, nor in fact any man in any other function about his particular End; but having set before them a certain End they look how and through what means it may be accomplished: if there is a choice of means, they examine further which are easiest and most creditable; or, if there is but one means of accomplishing the object, then how it may be through this, this again through what, till they come to the first cause; and this will be the last found; for a man engaged in a process of deliberation seems to seek and analyse, as a man, to solve a problem, analyses the figure given him. And plainly not every search is Deliberation, those in mathematics to wit, but every Deliberation is a search, and the last step in the analysis is the first in the constructive process. And if in the course of their search men come upon an impossibility, they give it up; if money, for instance, be necessary, but cannot be got: but if the thing appears possible they then attempt to do it.

And by possible I mean what may be done through our own instrumentality (of course what may be done through our friends is through our own instrumentality in a certain sense, because the origination in such cases rests with us). And the object of search is sometimes the necessary instruments, sometimes the method of using them; and similarly in the rest sometimes through what, and sometimes how or through what.

So it seems, as has been said, that Man is the originator of his actions; and Deliberation has for its object whatever may be done through one's own instrumentality, and the actions are with a view to other things; and so it is, not the End, but the Means to Ends on which Deliberation is employed.

Nor, again, is it employed on matters of detail, as whether the substance before me is bread, or has been properly cooked; for these come under the province of sense, and if a man is to be always deliberating, he may go on *ad infinitum.*

Further, exactly the same matter is the object both of Deliberation and Moral Choice; but that which is the object of Moral Choice is thenceforward separated off and definite, because by object of Moral Choice is denoted that which after Deliberation has been preferred to something else: for each man leaves off searching how he shall do a thing when he has brought the origination up to himself, *i.e.* to the governing principle in himself, because it is this which makes the choice. A good illustration of this is furnished by the old regal constitutions which Homer drew from, in which the Kings would announce to the commonalty what they had determined before.

Now since that which is the object of Moral Choice is something in our own power, which is the object of deliberation and the grasping of the Will, Moral Choice must be "a grasping after something in our own power consequent upon Deliberation:" because after having deliberated we decide, and then grasp by our Will in accordance with the result of our deliberation.

Let this be accepted as a sketch of the nature and object of Moral Choice, that object being "Means to Ends."

That Wish has for its object-matter the End, has been already stated; but there are two opinions respecting it; some thinking that its object is real good, others whatever impresses the mind with a notion of good.

Now those who maintain that the object of Wish is real good are beset by this difficulty, that what is wished for by him who chooses wrongly is not really an object of Wish (because, on their theory, if it is an object of wish, it must be good, but it is, in the case supposed, evil). Those who maintain, on the contrary, that that which impresses the mind with a notion of good is properly the object of Wish, have to meet this difficulty, that there is nothing naturally an object of Wish but to each individual whatever seems good to him; now different people have different notions, and it may chance contrary ones.

But, if these opinions do not satisfy us, may we not say that, abstractedly and as a matter of objective truth, the really good is the object of Wish, but to each individual whatever impresses his mind with the notion of good. And so to the good man that is an object of Wish which is really and truly so, but to the bad man anything may be; just as physically those things are wholesome to the healthy which are really so, but other things to the sick. And so too of bitter and sweet, and hot and heavy, and so on. For the good man judges in every instance correctly, and in every instance the notion conveyed to his mind is the true one.

For there are fair and pleasant things peculiar to, and so varying with, each state; and perhaps the most distinguishing characteristic of the good man is his seeing the truth in every instance, he being, in fact, the rule and measure of these matters.

The multitude of men seem to be deceived by reason of pleasure, because though it is not really a good it impresses their minds with the notion of goodness, so they choose what is pleasant as good and avoid pain as an evil.

Now since the End is the object of Wish, and the means to the End of Deliberation and Moral Choice, the actions regarding these matters must be in the way of Moral Choice, *i.e.* voluntary: but the acts of working out the virtues are such actions, and therefore Virtue is in our power.

And so too is Vice: because wherever it is in our power to do it is also in our power to forbear doing, and *vice versa*: therefore if the doing (being in a given case creditable) is in our power, so too is the forbearing (which is in the same case discreditable), and *vice versa*.

But if it is in our power to do and to forbear doing what is creditable or the contrary, and these respectively constitute the being good or bad, then the being good or vicious characters is in our power.

As for the well-known saying, "No man voluntarily is wicked or involuntarily happy," it is partly true, partly false; for no man is happy against his will, of course, but wickedness is voluntary. Or must we dispute the statements lately made, and not say that Man is the originator or generator of his actions as much as of his children?

But if this is matter of plain manifest fact, and we cannot refer our actions to any other originations beside those in our own power, those things must be in our own power, and so voluntary, the originations of which are in ourselves.

Moreover, testimony seems to be borne to these positions both privately by individuals, and by law-givers too, in that they chastise and punish those who do wrong (unless they do so on compulsion, or by reason of ignorance which is not self-caused), while they honour those who act rightly, under the notion of being likely to encourage the latter and restrain the former. But such things as are not in our own power, *i.e.* not voluntary, no one thinks of encouraging us to do, knowing it to be of no avail for one to have been persuaded not to be hot (for instance), or feel pain, or be hungry, and so forth, because we shall have those sensations all the same.

And what makes the case stronger is this: that they chastise for the very fact of ignorance, when it is thought to be self-caused; to the drunken, for instance, penalties are double, because the origination in such case lies in a man's own self: for he might have helped getting drunk, and this is the cause of his ignorance.

Again, those also who are ignorant of legal regulations which they are bound to know, and which are not hard to know, they chastise; and similarly in all other cases where neglect is thought to be the cause of the ignorance, under the notion that it was in their power to prevent their ignorance, because they might have paid attention.

But perhaps a man is of such a character that he cannot attend to such things: still men are themselves the causes of having become such characters by living carelessly, and also of being unjust or destitute of self-control, the former by doing evil actions, the latter by spending their time in drinking and such-like; because the particular acts of working form corresponding characters, as is shown by those who are practising for any contest or particular course of action, for such men persevere in the acts of working.

As for the plea, that a man did not know that habits are produced from separate acts of working, we reply, such ignorance is a mark of excessive stupidity.

Furthermore, it is wholly irrelevant to say that the man who acts unjustly or dissolutely does not *wish* to attain the habits of these vices: for if a man wittingly does those things whereby he must become unjust he is to all intents and purposes unjust voluntarily; but he cannot with a wish cease to be unjust and become just. For, to take the analogous case, the sick man cannot with a wish be well again, yet in a supposable case he is voluntarily ill because he has produced his sickness by living intemperately and disregarding his physicians. There was a time then when he might have helped being ill, but now he has let himself go he cannot any longer; just as he who has let a stone out of his hand cannot recall it, and yet it rested with him to aim and throw it, because the origination was in his power. Just so the unjust man, and he who has lost all self-control, might originally have helped being what they are, and so they are voluntarily what they are; but now that they are become so they no longer have the power of being otherwise.

And not only are mental diseases voluntary, but the bodily are so in some men, whom we accordingly blame: for such as are naturally deformed no one blames, only such as are so by reason of want of exercise, and neglect: and so too of weakness and maiming: no one would think of upbraiding, but would rather compassionate, a man who is blind by nature, or from disease, or from an accident; but every one would blame him who was so from excess of wine, or any other kind of intemperance. It seems, then, that in respect of bodily diseases, those which depend on ourselves are censured, those which do not are not censured; and if so, then in the case of the mental disorders, those which are censured must depend upon ourselves.

But suppose a man to say, "that (by our own admission) all men aim at that which conveys to their minds an impression of good, and that men have no control over this impression, but that the End impresses each with a notion correspondent to his own individual character; that to be sure if each man is in a way the cause of his own moral state, so he will be also of the kind of impression he receives: whereas, if this is not so, no one is the cause to himself of doing evil actions, but he does them by reason of ignorance of the true End, supposing that through their means he will secure the Chief Good. Further, that this aiming at the End is no matter of one's own choice, but one must be born with a power of mental vision, so to speak, whereby to judge fairly and choose that which is really good; and he is blessed by nature who has this naturally well: because it is the most important thing and the fairest, and what a man cannot get or learn from another but will have such as nature has given it; and for this to be so given well and fairly would be excellence of nature in the highest and truest sense."

If all this be true, how will Virtue be a whit more voluntary than Vice? Alike to the good man and the bad, the End gives its impression and is fixed by nature or howsoever you like to say, and they act so and so, referring everything else to this End.

Whether then we suppose that the End impresses each man's mind with certain notions not merely by nature, but that there is somewhat also dependent on himself; or that the End is given by nature, and yet Virtue is voluntary because the good man does all the rest voluntarily, Vice must be equally so, because his own agency equally attaches to the bad man in the actions, even if not in the selection of the End.

If then, as is commonly said, the Virtues are voluntary (because we at least co-operate in producing our moral states, and we assume the End to be of a certain kind according as we are ourselves of certain characters), the Vices must be voluntary also, because the cases are exactly similar.

Well now, we have stated generally respecting the Moral Virtues, the genus (in outline), that they are mean states, and that they are habits, and how they are formed, and that they are of themselves calculated to act upon the circumstances out of which they were formed, and that they are in our own power and voluntary, and are to be done so as right Reason may direct.

But the particular actions and the habits are not voluntary in the same sense; for of the actions we are masters from beginning to end (supposing of course a knowledge of the particular details), but only of the origination of the habits, the addition by small particular accessions not being cognisable (as is the case with sicknesses): still they are voluntary because it rested with us to use our circumstances this way or that.

Here we will resume the particular discussion of the Moral Virtues, and say what they are, what is their object-matter, and how they stand respectively related to it: of course their number will be thereby shown.

First, then, of Courage. Now that it is a mean state, in respect of fear and boldness, has been already said: further, the objects of our fears are obviously things fearful or, in a general way of statement, evils; which accounts for the common definition of fear, viz. "expectation of evil."

Of course we fear evils of all kinds: disgrace, for instance, poverty, disease, desolateness, death; but not all these seem to be the object-matter of the Brave man, because there are things which to fear is right and noble, and not to fear is base; disgrace, for example, since he who fears this is a good man and has a sense of honour, and he who does not fear it is shameless (though there are those who call him Brave by analogy, because he somewhat resembles the Brave man who agrees with him in being free from fear); but poverty, perhaps, or disease, and in fact whatever does not proceed from viciousness, nor is attributable to his own fault, a man ought not to fear: still, being fearless in respect of these would not constitute a man Brave in the proper sense of the term.

Yet we do apply the term in light of the similarity of the cases; for there are men who, though timid in the dangers of war, are liberal men and are stout enough to face loss of wealth.

And, again, a man is not a coward for fearing insult to his wife or children, or envy, or any such thing; nor is he a Brave man for being bold when going to be scourged.

What kind of fearful things then do constitute the object-matter of the Brave man? first of all, must they not be the greatest, since no man is more apt to withstand what is dreadful. Now the object of the greatest dread is death, because it is the end of all things, and the dead man is thought to be capable neither of good nor evil. Still it would seem that the Brave man has not for his object-matter even death in every circumstance; on the sea, for example, or in sickness: in what circumstances then? must it not be in the most honourable? now such is death in war, because it is death in the greatest and most honourable danger; and this is confirmed by the honours awarded in communities, and by monarchs.

He then may be most properly denominated Brave who is fearless in respect of honourable death and such sudden emergencies as threaten death; now such specially are those which arise in the course of war.

It is not meant but that the Brave man will be fearless also on the sea (and in sickness), but not in the same way as sea-faring men; for these are light-hearted and hopeful by reason of their experience, while landsmen though Brave are apt to give themselves up for lost and shudder at the notion of such a death: to which it should be added that Courage is exerted in circumstances which admit of doing something to help one's self, or in which death would be honourable; now neither of these requisites attach to destruction by drowning or sickness.

Again, fearful is a term of relation, the same thing not being so to all, and there is according to common parlance somewhat so fearful as to be beyond human endurance: this of course would be fearful to every man of sense, but those objects which are level to the capacity of man differ in magnitude and admit of degrees, so too the objects of confidence or boldness.

Now the Brave man cannot be frighted from his propriety (but of course only so far as he is man); fear such things indeed he will, but he will stand up against them as he ought and as right reason may direct, with a view to what is honourable, because this is the end of the virtue.

Now it is possible to fear these things too much, or too little, or again to fear what is not really fearful as if it were such. So the errors come to be either that a man fears when he ought not to fear at all, or that he fears in an improper way, or at a wrong time, and so forth; and so too in respect of things inspiring confidence. He is Brave then who withstands, and fears, and is bold, in respect of right objects, from a right motive, in right manner, and at right times: since the Brave man suffers or acts as he ought and as right reason may direct.

Now the end of every separate act of working is that which accords with the habit, and so to the Brave man Courage; which is honourable; therefore such is also the End, since the character of each is determined by the End.

So honour is the motive from which the Brave man withstands things fearful and performs the acts which accord with Courage.

Of the characters on the side of Excess, he who exceeds in utter absence of fear has no appropriate name (I observed before that many states have none), but he would be a madman or inaccessible to pain if he feared nothing, neither earthquake, nor the billows, as they tell of the Celts.

He again who exceeds in confidence in respect of things fearful is rash. He is thought moreover to be a braggart, and to advance unfounded claims to the character of Brave: the relation which the Brave man really bears to objects of fear this man wishes to appear to bear, and so imitates him in whatever points he can; for this reason most of them exhibit a curious mixture of rashness and cowardice; because, affecting rashness in these circumstances, they do not withstand what is truly fearful.

The man moreover who exceeds in feeling fear is a coward, since there attach to him the circumstances of fearing wrong objects, in wrong ways, and so forth. He is deficient also in feeling confidence, but he is most clearly seen as exceeding in the case of pains; he is a faint-hearted kind of man, for he fears all things: the Brave man is just the contrary, for boldness is the property of the light-hearted and hopeful.

So the coward, the rash, and the Brave man have exactly the same object-matter, but stand differently related to it: the two first-mentioned respectively exceed and are deficient, the last is in a mean state and as he ought to be. The rash again are precipitate, and, being eager before danger, when actually in it fall away, while the Brave are quick and sharp in action, but before are quiet and composed.

Well then, as has been said, Courage is a mean state in respect of objects inspiring boldness or fear, in the circumstances which have been stated, and the Brave man chooses his line and withstands danger either because to do so is honourable, or because not to do so is base. But dying to escape from poverty, or the pangs of love, or anything that is simply painful, is the act not of a Brave man but of a coward; because it is mere softness to fly from what is toilsome, and the suicide braves the terrors of death not because it is honourable but to get out of the reach of evil.

Courage proper is somewhat of the kind I have described, but there are dispositions, differing in five ways, which also bear in common parlance the name of Courage.

We will take first that which bears most resemblance to the true, the Courage of Citizenship, so named because the motives which are thought to actuate the members of a community in braving danger are the penalties and disgrace held out by the laws to cowardice, and the dignities conferred on the Brave; which is thought to be the reason why those are the bravest people among whom cowards are visited with disgrace and the Brave held in honour.

Such is the kind of Courage Homer exhibits in his characters; Diomed and Hector for example. The latter says,

> "Polydamas will be the first to fix
> Disgrace upon me."

Diomed again,

> "For Hector surely will hereafter say,
> Speaking in Troy, Tydides by my hand" —

This I say most nearly resembles the Courage before spoken of, because it arises form virtue, from a feeling of shame, and a desire of what is noble (that is, of honour), and avoidance of disgrace which is base.

In the same rank one would be inclined to place those also who act under compulsion from their commanders; yet are they really lower, because not a sense of honour but fear is the motive from which they act, and what they seek to avoid is not that which is base but that which is simply painful: commanders do in fact compel their men sometimes, as Hector says (to quote Homer again),

> "But whomsoever I shall find cowering afar from the fight,
> The teeth of dogs he shall by no means escape."

Those commanders who station staunch troops by doubtful ones, or who beat their men if they flinch, or who draw their troops up in line with the trenches, or other similar obstacles, in their rear, do in effect the same as Hector, for they all use compulsion.

But a man is to be Brave, not on compulsion but from a sense of honour.

In the next place, Experience and Skill in the various particulars is thought to be a species of Courage: whence Socrates also thought that Courage was knowledge.

This quality is exhibited of course by different men under different circumstances, but in warlike manners, with which we are now concerned, it is exhibited by the soldiers ("the regulars"): for there are, it would seem, many things in war of no real importance which these have been constantly used to see; so they have a show of Courage because other people are not aware of the real nature of these things.

Then again by reason of their skill they are better able than any others to inflict without suffering themselves, because they are able to use their arms and have such as are most serviceable both with a view to offence and defence: so that their case is parallel to that of armed men fighting with unarmed or trained athletes with amateurs, since in contests of this kind those are the best fighters, not who are the bravest men, but who are the strongest and are in the best condition.

In fact, the regular troops come to be cowards whenever the danger is greater than their means of meeting it; supposing, for example, that they are inferior in numbers and resources: then they are the first to fly, but the mere militia stand and fall on the ground (which as you know really happened at the Hermæum), for in the eyes of these flight was disgraceful and death preferable to safety bought at such a price: while "the regulars" originally went into the danger under a notion of their own superiority, but on discovering their error they took to flight, having greater fear of death than of disgrace; but this is not the feeling of the Brave man.

Thirdly, mere Animal Spirit is sometimes brought under the term Courage: they are thought to be Brave who are carried on by mere Animal Spirit, as are wild beasts against those who have wounded them, because in fact the really Brave have much Spirit, there being nothing like it for going at danger of any kind; whence those frequent expressions in Homer, "infused strength into his spirit," "roused his strength and spirit," or again, "and keen strength in his nostrils," "his blood boiled:" for all these seem to denote the arousing and impetuosity of the Animal Spirit.

Now they that are truly Brave act from a sense of honour, and this Animal Spirit co-operates with them; but wild beasts from pain, that is because they have been wounded, or are frightened; since if they are quietly in their own haunts, forest or marsh, they do not attack men. Surely they are not Brave because they rush into danger when goaded on by pain and mere Spirit, without any view of the danger: else would asses be Brave when they are hungry, for though beaten they will not then leave their pasture: profligate men besides do many bold actions by reason of their lust. We may conclude then that they are not Brave who are goaded on to meet danger by pain and mere Spirit; but still this temper which arises from Animal Spirit appears to be most natural, and would be Courage of the true kind if it could have added to it moral choice and the proper motive.

So men also are pained by a feeling of anger, and take pleasure in revenge; but they who fight from these causes may be good fighters, but they are not truly Brave (in that they do not act from a sense of honour, nor as reason directs, but merely from the present feeling), still they bear some resemblance to that character.

Nor, again, are the Sanguine and Hopeful therefore Brave: since their boldness in dangers arises from their frequent victories over numerous foes. The two characters are alike, however, in that both are confident; but then the Brave are so from the afore-mentioned causes, whereas these are so from a settled conviction of their being superior and not likely to suffer anything in return (they who are intoxicated do much the same, for they become hopeful when in that state); but when the event disappoints their expectations they run away: now it was said to be the character of a Brave man to withstand things which are fearful to man or produce that impression, because it is honourable so to do and the contrary is dishonourable.

For this reason it is thought to be a greater proof of Courage to be fearless and undisturbed under the pressure of sudden fear than under that which may be anticipated, because Courage then comes rather from a fixed habit, or less from preparation: since as to foreseen dangers a man might take his line even from calculation and reasoning, but in those which are sudden he will do so according to his fixed habit of mind.

Fifthly and lastly, those who are acting under Ignorance have a show of Courage and are not very far from the Hopeful; but still they are inferior inasmuch as they have no opinion of themselves; which the others have, and therefore stay and contest a field for some little time; but they who have been deceived fly the moment they know things to be otherwise than they supposed, which the Argives experienced when they fell on the Lacedæmonians, taking them for the men of Sicyon.

We have described then what kind of men the Brave are, and what they who are thought to be, but are not really, Brave.

It must be remarked, however, that though Courage has for its object-matter boldness and fear it has not both equally so, but objects of fear much more than the former; for he that under pressure of these is undisturbed and stands related to them as he ought is better entitled to the name of Brave than he who is properly affected towards objects of confidence. So then men are termed Brave for withstanding painful things.

It follows that Courage involves pain and is justly praised, since it is a harder matter to withstand things that are painful than to abstain from such as are pleasant.

It must not be thought but that the End and object of Courage is pleasant, but it is obscured by the surrounding circumstances: which happens also in the gymnastic games; to the boxers the End is pleasant with a view to which they act, I mean the crown and the honours; but the receiving the blows they do is painful and annoying to flesh and blood, and so is all the labour they have to undergo; and, as these drawbacks are many, the object in view being small appears to have no pleasantness in it.

If then we may say the same of Courage, of course death and wounds must be painful to the Brave man and against his will: still he endures these because it is honourable so to do or because it is dishonourable not to do so. And the more complete his virtue and his happiness so much the more will he be pained at the notion of death: since to such a man as he is it is best worth while to live, and he with full consciousness is deprived of the greatest goods by death, and this is a painful idea. But he is not the less Brave for feeling it to be so, nay rather it may be he is shown to be more so because he chooses the honour that may be reaped in war in preference to retaining safe possession of these other goods. The fact is that to act with pleasure does not belong to all the virtues, except so far as a man realises the End of his actions.

But there is perhaps no reason why not such men should make the best soldiers, but those who are less truly Brave but have no other good to care for: these being ready to meet danger and bartering their lives against small gain.

Let thus much be accepted as sufficient on the subject of Courage; the true nature of which it is not difficult to gather, in outline at least, from what has been said.

Next let us speak of Perfected Self-Mastery, which seems to claim the next place to Courage, since these two are the Excellences of the Irrational part of the Soul.

That it is a mean state, having for its object-matter Pleasures, we have already said (Pains being in fact its object-matter in a less degree and dissimilar manner), the state of utter absence of self-control has plainly the same object-matter; the next thing then is to determine what kind of Pleasures.

Let Pleasures then be understood to be divided into mental and bodily: instances of the former being love of honour or of learning: it being plain that each man takes pleasure in that of these two objects which he has a tendency to like, his body being no way affected but rather his intellect. Now men are not called perfectly self-mastering or wholly destitute of self-control in respect of pleasures of this class: nor in fact in respect of any which are not bodily; those for example who love to tell long stories, and are prosy, and spend their days about mere chance matters, we call gossips but not wholly destitute of self-control, nor again those who are pained at the loss of money or friends.

It is bodily Pleasures then which are the object-matter of Perfected Self-Mastery, but not even all these indifferently: I mean, that they who take pleasure in objects perceived by the Sight, as colours, and forms, and painting, are not denominated men of Perfected Self-Mastery, or wholly destitute of self-control; and yet it would seem that one may take pleasure even in such objects, as one ought to do, or excessively, or too little.

So too of objects perceived by the sense of Hearing; no one applies the terms before quoted respectively to those who are excessively pleased with musical tunes or acting, or to those who take such pleasure as they ought.

Nor again to those persons whose pleasure arises from the sense of Smell, except incidentally: I mean, we do not say men have no self-control because they take pleasure in the scent of fruit, or flowers, or incense, but rather when they do so in the smells of unguents and sauces: since men destitute of self-control take pleasure herein, because hereby the objects of their lusts are recalled to their imagination (you may also see other men take pleasure in the smell of food when they are hungry): but to take pleasure in such is a mark of the character before named since these are objects of desire to him.

Now not even brutes receive pleasure in right of these senses, except incidentally. I mean, it is not the scent of hares' flesh but the eating it which dogs take pleasure in, perception of which pleasure is caused by the sense of Smell. Or again, it is not the lowing of the ox but eating him which the lion likes; but of the fact of his nearness the lion is made sensible by the lowing, and so he appears to take pleasure in this. In like manner, he has no pleasure in merely seeing or finding a stag or wild goat, but in the prospect of a meal.

The habits of Perfect Self-Mastery and entire absence of self-control have then for their object-matter such pleasures as brutes also share in, for which reason they are plainly servile and brutish: they are Touch and Taste.

But even Taste men seem to make little or no use of; for to the sense of Taste belongs the distinguishing of flavours; what men do, in fact, who are testing the quality of wines or seasoning "made dishes."

But men scarcely take pleasure at all in these things, at least those whom we call destitute of self-control do not, but only in the actual enjoyment which arises entirely from the sense of Touch, whether in eating or in drinking, or in grosser lusts. This accounts for the wish said to have been expressed once by a great glutton, "that his throat had been formed longer than a crane's neck," implying that his pleasure was derived from the Touch.

The sense then with which is connected the habit of absence of self-control is the most common of all the senses, and this habit would seem to be justly a matter of reproach, since it attaches to us not in so far as we are men but in so far as we are animals. Indeed it is brutish to take pleasure in such things and to like them best of all; for the most respectable of the pleasures arising from the touch have been set aside; those, for instance, which occur in the course of gymnastic training from the rubbing and the warm bath: because the touch of the man destitute of self-control is not indifferently of *any* part of the body but only of particular parts.

Now of lusts or desires some are thought to be universal, others peculiar and acquired; thus desire for food is natural since every one who really needs desires also food, whether solid or liquid, or both (and, as Homer says, the man in the prime of youth needs and desires intercourse with the other sex); but when we come to this or that particular kind, then neither is the desire universal nor in all men is it directed to the same objects. And therefore the conceiving of such desires plainly attaches to us as individuals. It must be admitted, however, that there is something natural in it: because different things are pleasant to different men and a preference of some particular objects to chance ones is universal. Well then, in the case of the desires which are strictly and properly natural few men go wrong and all in one direction, that is, on the side of too much: I mean, to eat and drink of such food as happens to be on the table till one is overfilled is exceeding in quantity the natural limit, since the natural desire is simply a supply of a real deficiency.

For this reason these men are called belly-mad, as filling it beyond what they ought, and it is the slavish who become of this character.

But in respect of the peculiar pleasures many men go wrong and in many different ways; for whereas the term "fond of so and so" implies either taking pleasure in wrong objects, or taking pleasure excessively, or as the mass of men do, or in a wrong way, they who are destitute of all self-control exceed in all these ways; that is to say, they take pleasure in some things in which they ought not to do so (because they are properly objects of detestation), and in such as it is right to take pleasure in they do so more than they ought and as the mass of men do.

Well then, that excess with respect to pleasures is absence of self-control, and blameworthy, is plain. But viewing these habits on the side of pains, we find that a man is not said to have the virtue for withstanding them (as in the case of Courage), nor the vice for not withstanding them; but the man destitute of self-control is such, because he is pained more than he ought to be at not obtaining things which are pleasant (and thus his pleasure produces pain to him), and the man of Perfected Self-Mastery is such in virtue of not being pained by their absence, that is, by having to abstain from what is pleasant.

Now the man destitute of self-control desires either all pleasant things indiscriminately or those which are specially pleasant, and he is impelled by his desire to choose these things in preference to all others; and this involves pain, not only when he misses the attainment of his objects but, in the very desiring them, since all desire is accompanied by pain. Surely it is a strange case this, being pained by reason of pleasure.

As for men who are defective on the side of pleasure, who take less pleasure in things than they ought, they are almost imaginary characters, because such absence of sensual perception is not natural to man: for even the other animals distinguish between different kinds of food, and like some kinds and dislike others. In fact, could a man be found who takes no pleasure in anything and to whom all things are alike, he would be far from being human at all: there is no name for such a character because it is simply imaginary.

But the man of Perfected Self-Mastery is in the mean with respect to these objects: that is to say, he neither takes pleasure in the things which delight the vicious man, and in fact rather dislikes them, nor at all in improper objects; nor to any great degree in any object of the class; nor is he pained at their absence; nor does he desire them; or, if he does, only in moderation, and neither more than he ought, nor at improper times, and so forth; but such things as are conducive to health and good condition of body, being also pleasant, these he will grasp at in moderation and as he ought to do, and also such other pleasant things as do not hinder these objects, and are not unseemly or disproportionate to his means; because he that should grasp at such would be liking such pleasures more than is proper; but the man of Perfected Self-Mastery is not of this character, but regulates his desires by the dictates of right reason.

Now the vice of being destitute of all Self-Control seems to be more truly voluntary than Cowardice, because pleasure is the cause of the former and pain of the latter, and pleasure is an object of choice, pain of avoidance. And again, pain deranges and spoils the natural disposition of its victim, whereas pleasure has no such effect and is more voluntary and therefore more justly open to reproach.

It is so also for the following reason; that it is easier to be inured by habit to resist the objects of pleasure, there being many things of this kind in life and the process of habituation being unaccompanied by danger; whereas the case is the reverse as regards the objects of fear.

Again, Cowardice as a confirmed habit would seem to be voluntary in a different way from the particular instances which form the habit; because it is painless, but these derange the man by reason of pain so that he throws away his arms and otherwise behaves himself unseemly, for which reason they are even thought by some to exercise a power of compulsion.

But to the man destitute of Self-Control the particular instances are on the contrary quite voluntary, being done with desire and direct exertion of the will, but the general result is less voluntary: since no man desires to form the habit.

The name of this vice (which signifies etymologically unchastenedness) we apply also to the faults of children, there being a certain resemblance between the cases: to which the name is primarily applied, and to which secondarily or derivatively, is not relevant to the present subject, but it is evident that the later in point of time must get the name from the earlier. And the metaphor seems to be a very good one; for whatever grasps after base things, and is liable to great increase, ought to be chastened; and to this description desire and the child answer most truly, in that children also live under the direction of desire and the grasping after what is pleasant is most prominently seen in these.

Unless then the appetite be obedient and subjected to the governing principle it will become very great: for in the fool the grasping after what is pleasant is insatiable and undiscriminating; and every acting out of the desire increases the kindred habit, and if the desires are great and violent in degree they even expel Reason entirely; therefore they ought to be moderate and few, and in no respect to be opposed to Reason. Now when the appetite is in such a state we denominate it obedient and chastened.

In short, as the child ought to live with constant regard to the orders of its educator, so should the appetitive principle with regard to those of Reason.

So then in the man of Perfected Self-Mastery, the appetitive principle must be accordant with Reason: for what is right is the mark at which both principles aim: that is to say, the man of perfected self-mastery desires what he ought in right manner and at right times, which is exactly what Reason directs. Let this be taken for our account of Perfected Self-Mastery.

BOOK IV

WE will next speak of Liberality. Now this is thought to be the mean state, having for its object-matter Wealth: I mean, the Liberal man is praised not in the circumstances of war, nor in those which constitute the character of perfected self-mastery, nor again in judicial decisions, but in respect of giving and receiving Wealth, chiefly the former. By the term Wealth I mean "all those things whose worth is measured by money."

Now the states of excess and defect in regard of Wealth are respectively Prodigality and Stinginess: the latter of these terms we attach invariably to those who are over careful about Wealth, but the former we apply sometimes with a complex notion; that is to say, we give the name to those who fail of self-control and spend money on the unrestrained gratification of their passions; and this is why they are thought to be most base, because they have many vices at once.

It must be noted, however, that this is not a strict and proper use of the term, since its natural etymological meaning is to denote him who has one particular evil, viz. the wasting his substance: he is unsaved (as the term literally denotes) who is wasting away by his own fault; and this he really may be said to be; the destruction of his substance is thought to be a kind of wasting of himself, since these things are the means of living. Well, this is our acceptation of the term Prodigality.

Again. Whatever things are for use may be used well or ill, and Wealth belongs to this class. He uses each particular thing best who has the virtue to whose province it belongs: so that he will use Wealth best who has the virtue respecting Wealth, that is to say, the Liberal man.

Expenditure and giving are thought to be the using of money, but receiving and keeping one would rather call the possessing of it. And so the giving to proper persons is more characteristic of the Liberal man, than the receiving from proper quarters and forbearing to receive from the contrary. In fact generally, doing well by others is more characteristic of virtue than being done well by, and doing things positively ho-

56

nourable than forbearing to do things dishonourable; and any one may see that the doing well by others and doing things positively honourable attaches to the act of giving, but to that of receiving only the being done well by or forbearing to do what is dishonourable.

Besides, thanks are given to him who gives, not to him who merely forbears to receive, and praise even more. Again, forbearing to receive is easier than giving, the case of being too little freehanded with one's own being commoner than taking that which is not one's own.

And again, it is they who give that are denominated Liberal, while they who forbear to receive are commended, not on the score of Liberality but of just dealing, while for receiving men are not, in fact, praised at all.

And the Liberal are liked almost best of all virtuous characters, because they are profitable to others, and this their profitableness consists in their giving.

Furthermore: all the actions done in accordance with virtue are honourable, and done from the motive of honour: and the Liberal man, therefore, will give from a motive of honour, and will give rightly; I mean, to proper persons, in right proportion, at right times, and whatever is included in the term "right giving:" and this too with positive pleasure, or at least without pain, since whatever is done in accordance with virtue is pleasant or at least not unpleasant, most certainly not attended with positive pain.

But the man who gives to improper people, or not from a motive of honour but from some other cause, shall be called not Liberal but something else. Neither shall he be so denominated who does it with pain: this being a sign that he would prefer his wealth to the honourable action, and this is no part of the Liberal man's character; neither will such an one receive from improper sources, because the so receiving is not characteristic of one who values not wealth: nor again will he be apt to ask, because one who does kindnesses to others does not usually receive them willingly; but from proper sources (his own property, for instance) he will receive, doing this not as honourable but as necessary, that he may have somewhat to give: neither will he be careless of his own, since it is his wish through these to help others in need: nor will he give to chance people, that he may have wherewith to give to those to whom he ought, at right times, and on occasions when it is honourable so to do.

Again, it is a trait in the Liberal man's character even to exceed very much in giving so as to leave too little for himself, it being characteristic of such an one not to have a thought of self.

Now Liberality is a term of relation to a man's means, for the Liberalness depends not on the amount of what is given but on the moral state of the giver which gives in proportion to his means. There is then no reason why he should not be the more Liberal man who gives the less amount, if he has less to give out of.

Again, they are thought to be more Liberal who have inherited, not acquired for themselves, their means; because, in the first place, they have never experienced want, and next, all people love most their own works, just as parents do and poets.

It is not easy for the Liberal man to be rich, since he is neither apt to receive nor to keep but to lavish, and values not wealth for its own sake but with a view to giving it away. Hence it is commonly charged upon fortune that they who most deserve to be rich are least so. Yet this happens reasonably enough: it is impossible he should have wealth who does not take any care to have it, just as in any similar case.

Yet he will not give to improper people, nor at wrong times, and so on: because he would not then be acting in accordance with Liberality, and, if he spent upon such objects, would have nothing to spend on those on which he ought: for, as I have said before, he is Liberal who spends in proportion to his means, and on proper objects, while he who does so in excess is prodigal (this is the reason why we never call despots prodigal, because it does not seem to be easy for them by their gifts and expenditure to go beyond their immense possessions).

To sum up then. Since Liberality is a mean state in respect of the giving and receiving of wealth, the Liberal man will give and spend on proper objects, and in proper proportion, in great things and in small alike, and all this with pleasure to himself; also he will receive from right sources, and in right proportion: because, as the virtue is a mean state in respect of both, he will do both as he ought, and, in fact, upon proper giving follows the correspondent receiving, while that which is not such is contrary to it. (Now those which follow one another come to co-exist in the same person, those which are contraries plainly do not.)

Again, should it happen to him to spend money beyond what is needful, or otherwise than is well, he will be vexed, but only moderately and as he ought; for feeling pleasure and pain at right objects, and in right manner, is a property of Virtue.

The Liberal man is also a good man to have for a partner in respect of wealth: for he can easily be wronged, since he values not wealth, and is more vexed at not spending where he ought to have done so than at spending where he ought not, and he relishes not the maxim of Simonides.

But the Prodigal man goes wrong also in these points, for he is neither pleased nor pained at proper objects or in proper manner, which will become more plain as we proceed.

We have said already that Prodigality and Stinginess are respectively states of excess and defect, and this in two things, giving and receiving (expenditure of course we class under giving). Well now, Prodigality exceeds in giving and forbearing to receive and is deficient in receiving; while Stinginess is deficient in giving and exceeds in receiving, but it is in small things.

The two parts of Prodigality, to be sure, do not commonly go together; it is not easy, I mean, to give to all if you receive from none, because private individuals thus giving will soon find their means run short, and such are in fact thought to be prodigal. He that should combine both would seem to be no little superior to the Stingy man: for he may be easily cured, both by advancing in years, and also by the want of means, and he may come thus to the mean: he has, you see, already the *facts* of the Liberal man, he gives and forbears to receive, only he does neither in right manner or well: so if he could be wrought upon by habituation in this respect, or change in any other way, he would be a real Liberal man, for he will give to those to whom he should, and will forbear to receive whence he ought not. This is the reason too why he is thought not to be low in moral character, because to exceed in giving and in forbearing to receive is no sign of badness or meanness, but only of folly.

Well then, he who is prodigal in this fashion is thought far superior to the Stingy man for the aforementioned reasons, and also because he does good to many; but the Stingy man to no one, not even to himself. But most Prodigals, as has been said, combine with their other faults that of receiving from improper sources, and on this point are Stingy: and they become grasping, because they wish to spend and cannot do this easily, since their means soon run short and they are then necessitated to get from some other quarter: and then again, because they care not for what is honourable, they receive recklessly, and from all sources indifferently, because they desire to give but care not how or whence.

And for this reason their givings are not Liberal, inasmuch as they are not honourable, nor purely disinterested, nor done in right fashion; but they oftentimes make those rich who should be poor, and to those who are quiet respectable kind of people they will give nothing, but to flatterers, or those who subserve their pleasures in any way, they will give much. And therefore most of them are utterly devoid of self-restraint; for as they are open-handed they are liberal in expenditure upon the unrestrained gratification of their passions, and turn off to their pleasures because they do not live with reference to what is honourable.

Thus then the Prodigal, if unguided, slides into these faults; but if he could get care bestowed on him he might come to the mean and to what is right.

Stinginess, on the contrary, is incurable: old age, for instance, and incapacity of any kind, is thought to make people Stingy; and it is more congenial to human nature than Prodigality, the mass of men being fond of money rather than apt to give: moreover it extends far and has many phases, the modes of stinginess being thought to be many. For as it consists of two things, defect of giving and excess of receiving, everybody does not have it entire, but it is sometimes divided, and one class of persons exceed in receiving, the other are deficient in giving. I mean those who are designated by such appellations as sparing, close-fisted, niggards, are all deficient in giving; but other men's property they neither desire nor are willing to receive, in some instances from a real moderation and shrinking from what is base.

There are some people whose motive, either supposed or alleged, for keeping their property is this, that they may never be driven to do anything dishonourable: to this class belongs the skinflint, and every one of similar character, so named from the excess of not-giving. Others again decline to receive their neighbour's goods from a motive of fear; their notion being that it is not easy to take other people's things yourself without their taking yours: so they are content neither to receive nor give.

The other class again who are Stingy in respect of receiving exceed in that they receive anything from any source; such as they who work at illiberal employments, brothel keepers, and such-like, and usurers who lend small sums at large interest: for all these receive from improper sources, and improper amounts. Their common characteristic is base-gaining, since they all submit to disgrace for the sake of gain and that small; because those who receive great things neither whence they ought, nor what they ought (as for instance despots who sack cities and plunder temples), we denominate wicked, impious, and unjust, but not Stingy.

Now the dicer and bath-plunderer and the robber belong to the class of the Stingy, for they are given to base gain: both busy themselves and submit to disgrace for the sake of gain, and the one class incur the greatest dangers for the sake of their booty, while the others make gain of their friends to whom they ought to be giving.

So both classes, as wishing to make gain from improper sources, are given to base gain, and all such receivings are Stingy. And with good reason is Stinginess called the contrary of Liberality: both because it is a greater evil than Prodigality, and because men err rather in this direction than in that of the Prodigality which we have spoken of as properly and completely such.

Let this be considered as what we have to say respecting Liberality and the contrary vices.

Next in order would seem to come a dissertation on Magnificence, this being thought to be, like liberality, a virtue having for its object-matter Wealth; but it does not, like that, extend to all transactions in respect of Wealth, but only applies to such as are expensive, and in these circumstances it exceeds liberality in respect of magnitude, because it is (what the very name in Greek hints at) fitting expense on a large scale: this term is of course relative: I mean, the expenditure of equipping and commanding a trireme is not the same as that of giving a public spectacle: "fitting" of course also is relative to the individual, and the matter wherein and upon which he has to spend. And a man is not denominated Magnificent for spending as he should do in small or ordinary things, as, for instance,

"Oft to the wandering beggar did I give,"

but for doing so in great matters: that is to say, the Magnificent man is liberal, but the liberal is not thereby Magnificent. The falling short of such a state is called Meanness, the exceeding it Vulgar Profusion, Want of Taste, and so on; which are faulty, not because they are on an excessive scale in respect of right objects but, because they show off in improper objects, and in improper manner: of these we will speak presently. The Magnificent man is like a man of skill, because he can see what is fitting, and can spend largely in good taste; for, as we said at the commencement, the confirmed habit is determined by the separate acts of working, and by its object-matter.

Well, the expenses of the Magnificent man are great and fitting: such also are his works (because this secures the expenditure being not great merely, but befitting the work). So then the work is to be proportionate to the expense, and this again to the work, or even above it: and the Magnificent man will incur such expenses from the motive of honour, this being common to all the virtues, and besides he will do it with pleasure and lavishly; excessive accuracy in calculation being Mean. He will consider also how a thing may be done most beautifully and fittingly, rather, than for how much it may be done, and how at the least expense.

So the Magnificent man must be also a liberal man, because the liberal man will also spend what he ought, and in right manner: but it is the Great, that is to say the large scale, which is distinctive of the Magnificent man, the object-matter of liberality being the same, and without spending more money than another man he will make the work more magnificent. I mean, the excellence of a possession and of a work is not the same: as a piece of property that thing is most valuable which is worth most, gold for instance; but as a work that which is great and beautiful, because the contemplation of such an object is admirable, and so is that which is Magnificent. So the excellence of a work is Magnificence on a large scale. There are cases of expenditure which we call honourable, such as are dedicatory offerings to the gods, and the furnishing their temples, and sacrifices, and in like manner everything that has reference to the Deity, and all such public matters as are objects of honourable ambition, as when men think in any case that it is their duty to furnish a chorus for the stage splendidly, or fit out and maintain a trireme, or give a general public feast.

Now in all these, as has been already stated, respect is had also to the rank and the means of the man who is doing them: because they should be proportionate to these, and befit not the work only but also the doer of the work. For this reason a poor man cannot be a Magnificent man, since he has not means wherewith to spend largely and yet becomingly; and if he attempts it he is a fool, inasmuch as it is out of proportion and contrary to propriety, whereas to be in accordance with virtue a thing must be done rightly.

Such expenditure is fitting moreover for those to whom such things previously belong, either through themselves or through their ancestors or people with whom they are connected, and to the high-born or people of high repute, and so on: because all these things imply greatness and reputation.

So then the Magnificent man is pretty much as I have described him, and Magnificence consists in such expenditures: because they are the greatest and most honourable: and of private ones such as come but once for all, marriage to wit, and things of that kind; and any occasion which engages the interest of the community in general, or of those who are in power; and what concerns receiving and despatching strangers; and gifts, and repaying gifts: because the Magnificent man is not apt to spend upon himself but on the public good, and gifts are pretty much in the same case as dedicatory offerings.

It is characteristic also of the Magnificent man to furnish his house suitably to his wealth, for this also in a way reflects credit; and, again, to spend rather upon such works as are of long duration, these being most honourable. And again, propriety in each case, because the same things are not suitable to gods and men, nor in a temple and a tomb. And again, in the case of expenditures, each must be great of its kind, and great expense on a great object is most magnificent, that is in any case what is great in these particular things.

There is a difference too between greatness of a work and greatness of expenditure: for instance, a very beautiful ball or cup is magnificent as a present to a child, while the price of it is small and almost mean. Therefore it is characteristic of the Magnificent man to do magnificently whatever he is about: for whatever is of this kind cannot be easily surpassed, and bears a proper proportion to the expenditure.

Such then is the Magnificent man.

The man who is in the state of excess, called one of Vulgar Profusion, is in excess because he spends improperly, as has been said. I mean in cases requiring small expenditure he lavishes much and shows off out of taste; giving his club a feast fit for a wedding-party, or if he has to furnish a chorus for a comedy, giving the actors purple to wear in the first scene, as did the Megarians. And all such things he will do, not with a view to that which is really honourable, but to display his wealth, and because he thinks he shall be admired for these things; and he will spend little where he ought to spend much, and much where he should spend little.

The Mean man will be deficient in every case, and even where he has spent the most he will spoil the whole effect for want of some trifle; he is procrastinating in all he does, and contrives how he may spend the least, and does even that with lamentations about the expense, and thinking that he does all things on a greater scale than he ought.

Of course, both these states are faulty, but they do not involve disgrace because they are neither hurtful to others nor very unseemly.

The very name of Great-mindedness implies, that great things are its object-matter; and we will first settle what kind of things. It makes no difference, of course, whether we regard the moral state in the abstract or as exemplified in an individual.

Well then, he is thought to be Great-minded who values himself highly and at the same time justly, because he that does so without grounds is foolish, and no virtuous character is foolish or senseless.

Well, the character I have described is Great-minded. The man who estimates himself lowly, and at the same time justly, is modest; but not Great-minded, since this latter quality implies greatness, just as beauty implies a large bodily conformation while small people are neat and well made but not beautiful.

Again, he who values himself highly without just grounds is a Vain man: though the name must not be applied to every case of unduly high self-estimation. He that values himself below his real worth is Small-minded, and whether that worth is great, moderate, or small, his own estimate falls below it. And he is the strongest case of this error who is really a man of great worth, for what would he have done had his worth been less?

The Great-minded man is then, as far as greatness is concerned, at the summit, but in respect of propriety he is in the mean, because he estimates himself at his real value (the other characters respectively are in excess and defect). Since then he justly estimates himself at a high, or rather at the highest possible rate, his character will have respect specially to one thing: this term "rate" has reference of course to external goods: and of these we should assume that to be the greatest which we attribute to the gods, and which is the special object of desire to those who are in power, and which is the prize proposed to the most honourable actions: now honour answers to these descriptions, being the greatest of external goods. So the Great-minded man bears himself as he ought in respect of honour and dishonour. In fact, without need of words, the Great-minded plainly have honour for their object-matter: since honour is what the great consider themselves specially worthy of, and according to a certain rate.

The Small-minded man is deficient, both as regards himself, and also as regards the estimation of the Great-minded: while the Vain man is in excess as regards himself, but does not get beyond the Great-minded man. Now the Great-minded man, being by the hypothesis worthy of the greatest things, must be of the highest excellence, since the better a man is the more is he worth, and he who is best is worth the most: it follows then, that to be truly Great-minded a man must be good, and whatever is great in each virtue would seem to belong to the Great-minded. It would no way correspond with the character of the Great-minded to flee spreading his hands all abroad; nor to injure any one; for with what object in view will he do what is base, in whose eyes nothing is great? In short, if one were to go into particulars, the Great-minded man would show quite ludicrously unless he were a good man:

he would not be in fact deserving of honour if he were a bad man, honour being the prize of virtue and given to the good.

This virtue, then, of Great-mindedness seems to be a kind of ornament of all the other virtues, in that it makes them better and cannot be without them; and for this reason it is a hard matter to be really and truly Great-minded; for it cannot be without thorough goodness and nobleness of character.

Honour then and dishonour are specially the object-matter of the Great-minded man: and at such as is great, and given by good men, he will be pleased moderately as getting his own, or perhaps somewhat less for no honour can be quite adequate to perfect virtue: but still he will accept this because they have nothing higher to give him. But such as is given by ordinary people and on trifling grounds he will entirely despise, because these do not come up to his deserts: and dishonour likewise, because in his case there cannot be just ground for it.

Now though, as I have said, honour is specially the object-matter of the Great-minded man, I do not mean but that likewise in respect of wealth and power, and good or bad fortune of every kind, he will bear himself with moderation, fall out how they may, and neither in prosperity will he be overjoyed nor in adversity will he be unduly pained. For not even in respect of honour does he so bear himself; and yet it is the greatest of all such objects, since it is the cause of power and wealth being choice-worthy, for certainly they who have them desire to receive honour through them. So to whom honour even is a small thing to him will all other things also be so; and this is why such men are thought to be supercilious.

It seems too that pieces of good fortune contribute to form this character of Great-mindedness: I mean, the nobly born, or men of influence, or the wealthy, are considered to be entitled to honour, for they are in a position of eminence and whatever is eminent by good is more entitled to honour: and this is why such circumstances dispose men rather to Great-mindedness, because they receive honour at the hands of some men.

Now really and truly the good man alone is entitled to honour; only if a man unites in himself goodness with these external advantages he is thought to be more entitled to honour: but they who have them without also having virtue are not justified in their high estimate of themselves, nor are they rightly denominated Great-minded; since perfect virtue is one of the indispensable conditions to such a character.

Further, such men become supercilious and insolent, it not being easy to bear prosperity well without goodness; and not being able to bear it, and possessed with an idea of their own superiority to others, they despise them, and do just whatever their fancy prompts; for they mimic the Great-minded man, though they are not like him, and they do this in such points as they can, so without doing the actions which can only flow from real goodness they despise others. Whereas the Great-minded man despises on good grounds (for he forms his opinions truly), but the mass of men do it at random.

Moreover, he is not a man to incur little risks, nor does he court danger, because there are but few things he has a value for; but he will incur great dangers, and when he does venture he is prodigal of his life as knowing that there are terms on which it is not worth his while to live. He is the sort of man to do kindnesses, but he is ashamed to receive them; the former putting a man in the position of superiority, the latter in that of inferiority; accordingly he will greatly overpay any kindness done to him, because the original actor will thus be laid under obligation and be in the position of the party benefited. Such men seem likewise to remember those they have done kindnesses to, but not those from whom they have received them: because he who has received is inferior to him who has done the kindness and our friend wishes to be superior; accordingly he is pleased to hear of his own kind acts but not of those done to himself (and this is why, in Homer, Thetis does not mention to Jupiter the kindnesses she had done him, nor did the Lacedæmonians to the Athenians but only the benefits they had received).

Further, it is characteristic of the Great-minded man to ask favours not at all, or very reluctantly, but to do a service very readily; and to bear himself loftily towards the great or fortunate, but towards people of middle station affably; because to be above the former is difficult and so a grand thing, but to be above the latter is easy; and to be high and mighty towards the former is not ignoble, but to do it towards those of humble station would be low and vulgar; it would be like parading strength against the weak.

And again, not to put himself in the way of honour, nor to go where others are the chief men; and to be remiss and dilatory, except in the case of some great honour or work; and to be concerned in few things, and those great and famous. It is a property of him also to be open, both in his dislikes and his likings, because concealment is a consequent of fear. Likewise to be careful for reality rather than appearance, and talk and act openly (for his contempt for others makes him a bold man, for which same reason he is apt to speak the truth, except where the principle of reserve comes in), but to be reserved towards the generality of men.

And to be unable to live with reference to any other but a friend; because doing so is servile, as may be seen in that all flatterers are low and men in low estate are flatterers. Neither is his admiration easily excited, because nothing is great in his eyes; nor does he bear malice, since remembering anything, and specially wrongs, is no part of Greatmindedness, but rather overlooking them; nor does he talk of other men; in fact, he will not speak either of himself or of any other; he neither cares to be praised himself nor to have others blamed; nor again does he praise freely, and for this reason he is not apt to speak ill even of his enemies except to show contempt and insolence.

And he is by no means apt to make laments about things which cannot be helped, or requests about those which are trivial; because to be thus disposed with respect to these things is consequent only upon real anxiety about them. Again, he is the kind of man to acquire what is beautiful and unproductive rather than what is productive and profitable: this being rather the part of an independent man.

Also slow motion, deep-toned voice, and deliberate style of speech, are thought to be characteristic of the Great-minded man: for he who is earnest about few things is not likely to be in a hurry, nor he who esteems nothing great to be very intent: and sharp tones and quickness are the result of these.

This then is my idea of the Great-minded man; and he who is in the defect is a Small-minded man, he who is in the excess a Vain man. However, as we observed in respect of the last character we discussed, these extremes are not thought to be vicious exactly, but only mistaken, for they do no harm.

The Small-minded man, for instance, being really worthy of good deprives himself of his deserts, and seems to have somewhat faulty from not having a sufficiently high estimate of his own desert, in fact from self-ignorance: because, but for this, he would have grasped after what he really is entitled to, and that is good. Still such characters are not thought to be foolish, but rather laggards. But the having such an opinion of themselves seems to have a deteriorating effect on the character: because in all cases men's aims are regulated by their supposed desert, and thus these men, under a notion of their own want of desert, stand aloof from honourable actions and courses, and similarly from external goods.

But the Vain are foolish and self-ignorant, and that palpably: because they attempt honourable things, as though they were worthy, and then they are detected. They also set themselves off, by dress, and carriage, and such-like things, and desire that their good circumstances may be seen, and they talk of them under the notion of receiving honour thereby. Small-mindedness rather than Vanity is opposed to Great-mindedness, because it is more commonly met with and is worse.

Well, the virtue of Great-mindedness has for its object great Honour, as we have said: and there seems to be a virtue having Honour also for its object (as we stated in the former book), which may seem to bear to Great-mindedness the same relation that Liberality does to Magnificence: that is, both these virtues stand aloof from what is great but dispose us as we ought to be disposed towards moderate and small matters. Further: as in giving and receiving of wealth there is a mean state, an excess, and a defect, so likewise in grasping after Honour there is the more or less than is right, and also the doing so from right sources and in right manner.

For we blame the lover of Honour as aiming at Honour more than he ought, and from wrong sources; and him who is destitute of a love of Honour as not choosing to be honoured even for what is noble. Sometimes again we praise the lover of Honour as manly and having a love for what is noble, and him who has no love for it as being moderate and modest (as we noticed also in the former discussion of these virtues).

It is clear then that since "Lover of so and so" is a term capable of several meanings, we do not always denote the same quality by the term "Lover of Honour;" but when we use it as a term of commendation we denote more than the mass of men are; when for blame more than a man should be.

And the mean state having no proper name the extremes seem to dispute for it as unoccupied ground: but of course where there is excess and defect there must be also the mean. And in point of fact, men do grasp at Honour more than they should, and less, and sometimes just as they ought; for instance, this state is praised, being a mean state in regard of Honour, but without any appropriate name. Compared with what is called Ambition it shows like a want of love for Honour, and compared with this it shows like Ambition, or compared with both, like both faults: nor is this a singular case among the virtues. Here the extreme characters appear to be opposed, because the mean has no name appropriated to it.

Meekness is a mean state, having for its object-matter Anger: and as the character in the mean has no name, and we may almost say the same of the extremes, we give the game of Meekness (leaning rather to the defect, which has no name either) to the character in the mean.

The excess may be called an over-aptness to Anger: for the passion is Anger, and the producing causes many and various. Now he who is angry at what and with whom he ought, and further, in right manner and time, and for proper length of time, is praised, so this Man will be Meek since Meekness is praised. For the notion represented by the term Meek man is the being imperturbable, and not being led away by passion, but being angry in that manner, and at those things, and for that length of time, which Reason may direct. This character however is thought to err rather on the side of defect, inasmuch as he is not apt to take revenge but rather to make allowances and forgive. And the defect, call it Angerlessness or what you will, is blamed: I mean, they who are not angry at things at which they ought to be angry are thought to be foolish, and they who are angry not in right manner, nor in right time, nor with those with whom they ought; for a man who labours under this defect is thought to have no perception, nor to be pained, and to have no tendency to avenge himself, inasmuch as he feels no anger: now to bear with scurrility in one's own person, and patiently see one's own friends suffer it, is a slavish thing.

As for the excess, it occurs in all forms; men are angry with those with whom, and at things with which, they ought not to be, and more than they ought, and too hastily, and for too great a length of time. I do not mean, however, that these are combined in any one person: that would in fact be impossible, because the evil destroys itself, and if it is developed in its full force it becomes unbearable.

Now those whom we term the Passionate are soon angry, and with people with whom and at things at which they ought not, and in an excessive degree, but they soon cool again, which is the best point about them. And this results from their not repressing their anger, but repaying their enemies (in that they show their feelings by reason of their vehemence), and then they have done with it.

The Choleric again are excessively vehement, and are angry at everything, and on every occasion; whence comes their Greek name signifying that their choler lies high.

The Bitter-tempered are hard to reconcile and keep their anger for a long while, because they repress the feeling: but when they have revenged themselves then comes a lull; for the vengeance destroys their anger by producing pleasure in lieu of pain. But if this does not happen they keep the weight on their minds: because, as it does not show itself, no one attempts to reason it away, and digesting anger within one's self takes time. Such men are very great nuisances to themselves and to their best friends.

Again, we call those Cross-grained who are angry at wrong objects, and in excessive degree, and for too long a time, and who are not appeased without vengeance or at least punishing the offender.

To Meekness we oppose the excess rather than the defect, because it is of more common occurrence: for human nature is more disposed to take than to forgo revenge. And the Cross-grained are worse to live with [than they who are too phlegmatic].

Now, from what has been here said, that is also plain which was said before. I mean, it is no easy matter to define how, and with what persons, and at what kind of things, and how long one ought to be angry, and up to what point a person is right or is wrong. For he that transgresses the strict rule only a little, whether on the side of too much or too little, is not blamed: sometimes we praise those who are deficient in the feeling and call them Meek, sometimes we call the irritable Spirited as being well qualified for government. So it is not easy to lay down, in so many words, for what degree or kind of transgression a man is blameable: because the decision is in particulars, and rests therefore with the Moral Sense. Thus much, however, is plain, that the mean state is praiseworthy, in virtue of which we are angry with those with whom, and at those things with which, we ought to be angry, and in right manner, and so on; while the excesses and defects are blameable, slightly so if only slight, more so if greater, and when considerable very blameable.

It is clear, therefore, that the mean state is what we are to hold to.

This then is to be taken as our account of the various moral states which have Anger for their object-matter.

Next, as regards social intercourse and interchange of words and acts, some men are thought to be Over-Complaisant who, with a view solely to giving pleasure, agree to everything and never oppose, but think their line is to give no pain to those they are thrown amongst: they, on the other hand, are called Cross and Contentious who take exactly the contrary line to these, and oppose in everything, and have no care at all whether they give pain or not.

Now it is quite clear of course, that the states I have named are blameable, and that the mean between them is praiseworthy, in virtue of which a man will let pass what he ought as he ought, and also will object in like manner. However, this state has no name appropriated, but it is most like Friendship; since the man who exhibits it is just the kind of man whom we would call the amiable friend, with the addition of strong earnest affection; but then this is the very point in which it differs from Friendship, that it is quite independent of any feeling or strong affection for those among whom the man mixes: I mean, that he takes everything as he ought, not from any feeling of love or hatred, but simply because his natural disposition leads him to do so; he will do it alike to those whom he does know and those whom he does not, and those with whom he is intimate and those with whom he is not; only in each case as propriety requires, because it is not fitting to care alike for intimates and strangers, nor again to pain them alike.

It has been stated in a general way that his social intercourse will be regulated by propriety, and his aim will be to avoid giving pain and to contribute to pleasure, but with a constant reference to what is noble and expedient.

His proper object-matter seems to be the pleasures and pains which arise out of social intercourse, but whenever it is not honourable or even hurtful to him to contribute to pleasure, in these instances he will run counter and prefer to give pain.

Or if the things in question involve unseemliness to the doer, and this not inconsiderable, or any harm, whereas his opposition will cause some little pain, here he will not agree but will run counter.

Again, he will regulate differently his intercourse with great men and with ordinary men, and with all people according to the knowledge he has of them; and in like manner, taking in any other differences which ·may exist, giving to each his due, and in itself preferring to give pleasure and cautious not to give pain, but still guided by the results, I mean by what is noble and expedient according as they preponderate.

Again, he will inflict trifling pain with a view to consequent pleasure.

Well, the man bearing the mean character is pretty well such as I have described him, but he has no name appropriated to him: of those who try to give pleasure, the man who simply and disinterestedly tries to be agreeable is called Over-Complaisant, he who does it with a view to secure some profit in the way of wealth, or those things which wealth may procure, is a Flatterer: I have said before, that the man who is "always non-content" is Cross and Contentious. Here the extremes have the appearance of being opposed to one another, because the mean has no appropriate name.

The mean state which steers clear of Exaggeration has pretty much the same object-matter as the last we described, and likewise has no name appropriated to it. Still it may be as well to go over these states: because, in the first place, by a particular discussion of each we shall be better acquainted with the general subject of moral character, and next we shall be the more convinced that the virtues are mean states by seeing that this is universally the case.

In respect then of living in society, those who carry on this intercourse with a view to pleasure and pain have been already spoken of; we will now go on to speak of those who are True or False, alike in their words and deeds and in the claims which they advance.

Now the Exaggerator is thought to have a tendency to lay claim to things reflecting credit on him, both when they do not belong to him at all and also in greater degree than that in which they really do: whereas the Reserved man, on the contrary, denies those which really belong to him or else depreciates them, while the mean character being a Plain-matter-of-fact person is Truthful in life and word, admitting the existence of what does really belong to him and making it neither greater nor less than the truth.

It is possible of course to take any of these lines either with or without some further view: but in general men speak, and act, and live, each according to his particular character and disposition, unless indeed a man is acting from any special motive.

Now since falsehood is in itself low and blameable, while truth is noble and praiseworthy, it follows that the Truthful man (who is also in the mean) is praiseworthy, and the two who depart from strict truth are both blameable, but especially the Exaggerator.

We will now speak of each, and first of the Truthful man: I call him Truthful, because we are not now meaning the man who is true in his agreements nor in such matters as amount to justice or injustice (this would come within the province of a different virtue), but, in such as do not involve any such serious difference as this, the man we are describing is true in life and word simply because he is in a certain moral state.

And he that is such must be judged to be a good man: for he that has a love for Truth as such, and is guided by it in matters indifferent, will be so likewise even more in such as are not indifferent; for surely he will have a dread of falsehood as base, since he shunned it even in itself: and he that is of such a character is praiseworthy, yet he leans rather to that which is below the truth, this having an appearance of being in better taste because exaggerations are so annoying.

As for the man who lays claim to things above what really belongs to him *without* any special motive, he is like a base man because he would not otherwise have taken pleasure in falsehood, but he shows as a fool rather than as a knave. But if a man does this *with* a special motive, suppose for honour or glory, as the Braggart does, then he is not so

very blameworthy, but if, directly or indirectly, for pecuniary considerations, he is more unseemly.

Now the Braggart is such not by his power but by his purpose, that is
to say, in virtue of his moral state, and because he is a man of a certain
kind; just as there are liars who take pleasure in falsehood for its own
sake while others lie from a desire of glory or gain. They who exaggerate with a view to glory pretend to such qualities as are followed by
praise or highest congratulation: they who do it with a view to gain assume those which their neighbours can avail themselves of, and the absence of which can be concealed, as a man's being a skilful soothsayer
or physician; and accordingly most men pretend to such things and exaggerate in this direction, because the faults I have mentioned are in
them.

The Reserved, who depreciate their own qualities, have the appearance of being more refined in their characters, because they are not
thought to speak with a view to gain but to avoid grandeur: one very
common trait in such characters is their denying common current
opinions, as Socrates used to do. There are people who lay claim falsely
to small things and things the falsity of their pretensions to which is obvious; these are called Factotums and are very despicable.

This very Reserve sometimes shows like Exaggeration; take, for instance, the excessive plainness of dress affected by the Lacedæmonians:
in fact, both excess and the extreme of deficiency partake of the nature
of Exaggeration. But they who practise Reserve in moderation, and in
cases in which the truth is not very obvious and plain, give an impression of refinement. Here it is the Exaggerator (as being the worst character) who appears to be opposed to the Truthful Man.

Next, as life has its pauses and in them admits of pastime combined
with Jocularity, it is thought that in this respect also there is a kind of
fitting intercourse, and that rules may be prescribed as to the kind of
things one should say and the manner of saying them; and in respect
of hearing likewise (and there will be a difference between the saying
and hearing such and such things). It is plain that in regard to these
things also there will be an excess and defect and a mean.

Now they who exceed in the ridiculous are judged to be Buffoons
and Vulgar, catching at it in any and every way and at any cost, and
aiming rather at raising laughter than at saying what is seemly and at
avoiding to pain the object of their wit. They, on the other hand, who
would not for the world make a joke themselves and are displeased with
such as do are thought to be Clownish and Stern. But they who are
Jocular in good taste are denominated by a Greek term expressing

properly ease of movement, because such are thought to be, as one may say, motions of the moral character; and as bodies are judged of by their motions so too are moral characters.

Now as the ridiculous lies on the surface, and the majority of men take more pleasure than they ought in Jocularity and Jesting, the Buffoons too get this name of Easy Pleasantry, as if refined and gentlemanlike; but that they differ from these, and considerably too, is plain from what has been said.

One quality which belongs to the mean state is Tact: it is characteristic of a man of Tact to say and listen to such things as are fit for a good man and a gentleman to say and listen to: for there are things which are becoming for such a one to say and listen to in the way of Jocularity, and there is a difference between the Jocularity of the Gentleman and that of the Vulgarian; and again, between that of the educated and uneducated man. This you may see from a comparison of the Old and New Comedy: in the former obscene talk made the fun; in the latter it is rather innuendo: and this is no slight difference *as regards decency*.

Well then, are we to characterise him who jests well by his saying what is becoming a gentleman, or by his avoiding to pain the object of his wit, or even by his giving him pleasure? or will not such a definition be vague, since different things are hateful and pleasant to different men?

Be this as it may, whatever he says such things will he also listen to, since it is commonly held that a man will do what he will bear to hear: this must, however, be limited; a man will not do quite all that he will hear: because jesting is a species of scurrility and there are some points of scurrility forbidden by law; it may be certain points of jesting should have been also so forbidden. So then the refined and gentlemanlike man will bear himself thus as being a law to himself. Such is the mean character, whether denominated the man of Tact or of Easy Pleasantry.

But the Buffoon cannot resist the ridiculous, sparing neither himself nor any one else so that he can but raise his laugh, saying things of such kind as no man of refinement would say and some which he would not even tolerate if said by others in his hearing.

The Clownish man is for such intercourse wholly useless: inasmuch as contributing nothing jocose of his own he is savage with all who do.

Yet some pause and amusement in life are generally judged to be indispensable.

The three mean states which have been described do occur in life, and the object-matter of all is interchange of words and deeds. They differ, in that one of them is concerned with truth, and the other two with the pleasurable: and of these two again, the one is conversant with the jocosities of life, the other with all other points of social intercourse.

To speak of Shame as a Virtue is incorrect, because it is much more like a feeling than a moral state. It is defined, we know, to be "a kind of fear of disgrace," and its effects are similar to those of the fear of danger, for they who feel Shame grow red and they who fear death turn pale. So both are evidently in a way physical, which is thought to be a mark of a feeling rather than a moral state.

Moreover, it is a feeling not suitable to every age, but only to youth: we do think that the young should be Shame-faced, because since they live at the beck and call of passion they do much that is wrong and Shame acts on them as a check. In fact, we praise such young men as are Shame-faced, but no one would ever praise an old man for being given to it, inasmuch as we hold that he ought not to do things which cause Shame; for Shame, since it arises at low bad actions, does not at all belong to the good man, because such ought not to be done at all: nor does it make any difference to allege that some things are disgraceful really, others only because they are thought so; for neither should be done, so that a man ought not to be in the position of feeling Shame. In truth, to be such a man as to do anything disgraceful is the part of a faulty character. And for a man to be such that he would feel Shame if he should do anything disgraceful, and to think that this constitutes him a good man, is absurd: because Shame is felt at voluntary actions only, and a good man will never voluntarily do what is base.

True it is, that Shame may be good on a certain supposition, as "if a man should do such things, he would feel Shame:" but then the Virtues are good in themselves, and not merely in supposed cases. And, granted that impudence and the not being ashamed to do what is disgraceful is base, it does not the more follow that it is good for a man to do such things and feel Shame.

Nor is Self-Control properly a Virtue, but a kind of mixed state: however, all about this shall be set forth in a future Book.

BOOK V

Now the points for our inquiry in respect of Justice and Injustice are, what kind of actions are their object-matter, and what kind of a mean state Justice is, and between what points the abstract principle of it, *i.e.* the Just, is a mean. And our inquiry shall be, if you please, conducted in the same method as we have observed in the foregoing parts of this treatise.

We see then that all men mean by the term Justice a moral state such that in consequence of it men have the capacity of doing what is just, and actually do it, and wish it: similarly also with respect to Injustice, a moral state such that in consequence of it men do unjustly and wish what is unjust: let us also be content then with these as a ground-work sketched out.

I mention the two, because the same does not hold with regard to States whether of mind or body as with regard to Sciences or Faculties: I mean that whereas it is thought that the same Faculty or Science embraces contraries, a State will not: from health, for instance, not the contrary acts are done but the healthy ones only; we say a man walks healthily when he walks as the healthy man would.

However, of the two contrary states the one may be frequently known from the other, and oftentimes the states from their subject-matter: if it be seen clearly what a good state of body is, then is it also seen what a bad state is, and from the things which belong to a good state of body the good state itself is seen, and *vice versa*. If, for instance, the good state is firmness of flesh it follows that the bad state is flabbiness of flesh; and whatever causes firmness of flesh is connected with the good state.

It follows moreover in general, that if of two contrary terms the one is used in many senses so also will the other be; as, for instance, if "the Just," then also "the Unjust." Now Justice and Injustice do seem to be used respectively in many senses, but, because the line of demarcation between these is very fine and minute, it commonly escapes notice that

76

they are thus used, and it is not plain and manifest as where the various significations of terms are widely different: for in these last the visible difference is great; for instance, the word κλεὶς used equivocally to denote the bone which is under the neck of animals and the instrument with which people close doors.

Let it be ascertained then in how many senses the term "Unjust man" is used. Well, he who violates the law, and he who is a grasping man, and the unequal man, are all thought to be Unjust: and so manifestly the Just man will be, the man who acts according to law, and the equal man. "The Just" then will be the lawful and the equal, and "the Unjust" the unlawful and the unequal.

Well, since the Unjust man is also a grasping man, he will be so, of course, with respect to good things, but not of every kind, only those which are the subject-matter of good and bad fortune and which are in themselves always good but not always to the individual. Yet men pray for and pursue these things: this they should not do but pray that things which are in the abstract good may be so also to them, and choose what is good for themselves.

But the Unjust man does not always choose actually the greater part, but even sometimes the less; as in the case of things which are simply evil: still, since the less evil is thought to be in a manner a good and the grasping is after good, therefore even in this case he is thought to be a grasping man, *i.e.* one who strives for more good than fairly falls to his share: of course he is also an unequal man, this being an inclusive and common term.

We said that the violator of Law is Unjust, and the keeper of the Law Just: further, it is plain that all Lawful things are in a manner Just, because by Lawful we understand what have been defined by the legislative power and each of these we say is Just. The Laws too give directions on all points, aiming either at the common good of all, or that of the best, or that of those in power (taking for the standard real goodness or adopting some other estimate); in one way we mean by Just, those things which are apt to produce and preserve happiness and its ingredients for the social community.

Further, the Law commands the doing the deeds not only of the brave man (as not leaving the ranks, nor flying, nor throwing away one's arms), but those also of the perfectly self-mastering man, as abstinence from adultery and wantonness; and those of the meek man, as refraining from striking others or using abusive language: and in like manner in respect of the other virtues and vices commanding some things and forbidding others, rightly if it is a good law, in a way somewhat inferior if it is one extemporised.

Now this Justice is in fact perfect Virtue, yet not simply so but as exercised towards one's neighbour: and for this reason Justice is thought oftentimes to be the best of the Virtues, and

> "neither Hesper nor the Morning-star
> So worthy of our admiration:"

and in a proverbial saying we express the same;

> "All virtue is in Justice comprehended."

And it is in a special sense perfect Virtue because it is the practice of perfect Virtue. And perfect it is because he that has it is able to practise his virtue towards his neighbour and not merely on himself; I mean, there are many who can practise virtue in the regulation of their own personal conduct who are wholly unable to do it in transactions with their neighbour. And for this reason that saying of Bias is thought to be a good one,

> "Rule will show what a man is;"

for he who bears Rule is necessarily in contact with others, *i.e.* in a community. And for this same reason Justice alone of all the Virtues is thought to be a good to others, because it has immediate relation to some other person, inasmuch as the Just man does what is advantageous to another, either to his ruler or fellow-subject. Now he is the basest of men who practises vice not only in his own person but towards his friends also; but he the best who practises virtue not merely in his own person but towards his neighbour, for this is a matter of some difficulty.

However, Justice in this sense is not a part of Virtue but is co-extensive with Virtue; nor is the Injustice which answers to it a part of Vice but co-extensive with Vice. Now wherein Justice in this sense differs from Virtue appears from what has been said: it is the same really, but the point of view is not the same: in so far as it has respect to one's neighbour it is Justice, in so far as it is such and such a moral state it is simply Virtue.

But the object of our inquiry is Justice, in the sense in which it is a part of Virtue (for there is such a thing, as we commonly say), and likewise with respect to particular Injustice. And of the existence of this last the following consideration is a proof: there are many vices by practising which a man acts unjustly, of course, but does not grasp at more than his share of good; if, for instance, by reason of cowardice he throws away his shield, or by reason of ill-temper he uses abusive language, or by reason of stinginess does not give a friend pecuniary assistance; but whenever he does a grasping action, it is often in the way of none of these vices, certainly not in all of them, still in the way of some vice or other (for we blame him), and in the way of Injustice. There is then some kind of Injustice distinct from that co-extensive with Vice and related to it as a part to a whole, and some "Unjust" related to that which is co-extensive with violation of the law as a part to a whole.

Again, suppose one man seduces a man's wife with a view to gain and actually gets some advantage by it, and another does the same from impulse of lust, at an expense of money and damage; this latter will be thought to be rather destitute of self-mastery than a grasping man, and the former Unjust but not destitute of self-mastery: now why? plainly because of his gaining.

Again, all other acts of Injustice we refer to some particular depravity, as, if a man commits adultery, to abandonment to his passions; if he deserts his comrade, to cowardice; if he strikes another, to anger: but if he gains by the act to no other vice than to Injustice.

Thus it is clear that there is a kind of Injustice different from and besides that which includes all Vice, having the same name because the definition is in the same genus; for both have their force in dealings with others, but the one acts upon honour, or wealth, or safety, or by whatever one name we can include all these things, and is actuated by pleasure attendant on gain, while the other acts upon all things which constitute the sphere of the good man's action.

Now that there is more than one kind of Justice, and that there is one which is distinct from and besides that which is co-extensive with, Virtue, is plain: we must next ascertain what it is, and what are its characteristics.

Well, the Unjust has been divided into the unlawful and the unequal, and the Just accordingly into the lawful and the equal: the aforementioned Injustice is in the way of the unlawful. And as the unequal and the more and not the same, but differing as part to whole (because all more is unequal, but not all unequal more), so the Unjust and the Injustice we are now in search of are not the same with, but other than, those before mentioned, the one being the parts, the other the wholes; for this particular Injustice is a part of the Injustice co-extensive with

Vice, and likewise this Justice of the Justice co-extensive with Virtue. So that what we have now to speak of is the particular Justice and Injustice, and likewise the particular Just and Unjust.

Here then let us dismiss any further consideration of the Justice ranking as co-extensive with Virtue (being the practice of Virtue in all its bearings towards others), and of the co-relative Injustice (being similarly the practice of Vice). It is clear too, that we must separate off the Just and the Unjust involved in these: because one may pretty well say that most lawful things are those which naturally result in action from Virtue in its fullest sense, because the law enjoins the living in accordance with each Virtue and forbids living in accordance with each Vice. And the producing causes of Virtue in all its bearings are those enactments which have been made respecting education for society.

By the way, as to individual education, in respect of which a man is simply good without reference to others, whether it is the province of πολιτική or some other science we must determine at a future time: for it may be it is not the same thing to be a good man and a good citizen in every case.

Now of the Particular Justice, and the Just involved in it, one species is that which is concerned in the distributions of honour, or wealth, or such other things as are to be shared among the members of the social community (because in these one man as compared with another may have either an equal or an unequal share), and the other is that which is Corrective in the various transactions between man and man.

And of this latter there are two parts: because of transactions some are voluntary and some involuntary; voluntary, such as follow; selling, buying, use, bail, borrowing, deposit, hiring: and this class is called voluntary because the origination of these transactions is voluntary.

The involuntary again are either such as effect secrecy; as theft, adultery, poisoning, pimping, kidnapping of slaves, assassination, false witness; or accompanied with open violence; as insult, bonds, death, plundering, maiming, foul language, slanderous abuse.

Well, the unjust man we have said is unequal, and the abstract "Unjust" unequal: further, it is plain that there is some mean of the unequal, that is to say, the equal or exact half (because in whatever action there is the greater and the less there is also the equal, *i.e.* the exact half). If then the Unjust is unequal the Just is equal, which all must allow without further proof: and as the equal is a mean the Just must be also a mean. Now the equal implies two terms at least: it follows then that the Just is both a mean and equal, and these to certain persons; and, in so far as it is a mean, between certain things (that is, the greater and the less), and, so far as it is equal, between two, and in so far as it is just it is so to certain persons. The Just then must imply four terms at least, for those to which it is just are two, and the terms representing the things are two.

And there will be the same equality between the terms representing the persons, as between those representing the things: because as the latter are to one another so are the former: for if the persons are not equal they must not have equal shares; in fact this is the very source of all the quarrelling and wrangling in the world, when either they who are equal have and get awarded to them things not equal, or being not equal those things which are equal. Again, the necessity of this equality of ratios is shown by the common phrase "according to rate," for all agree that the Just in distributions ought to be according to some rate: but what that rate is to be, all do not agree; the democrats are for freedom, oligarchs for wealth, others for nobleness of birth, and the aristocratic party for virtue.

The Just, then, is a certain proportionable thing. For proportion does not apply merely to number in the abstract, but to number generally, since it is equality of ratios, and implies four terms at least (that this is the case in what may be called discrete proportion is plain and obvious, but it is true also in continual proportion, for this uses the one term as two, and mentions it twice; thus $A:B:C$ may be expressed $A:B::B:C$. In the first, B is named twice; and so, if, as in the second, B is actually written twice, the proportionals will be four): and the Just likewise implies four terms at the least, and the ratio between the two pair of terms is the same, because the persons and the things are divided similarly. It will stand then thus, $A:B::C:D$, and then permutando $A:C::B:D$, and then (supposing C and D to represent the things) $A+C:B+D::A:B$. The distribution in fact consisting in putting together these terms thus: and if they are put together so as to preserve this same ratio, the distribution puts them together justly. So then the joining together of the first and third and second and fourth proportionals is the Just in the distribution, and this Just is the mean relatively to that which violates the proportionate, for the proportionate is a mean and the Just is proportionate. Now mathematicians call this kind of proportion geometrical: for in geometrical proportion the whole is to the whole as each part to each part. Furthermore this proportion is not continual, because the person and thing do not make up one term.

The Just then is this proportionate, and the Unjust that which violates the proportionate; and so there comes to be the greater and the less: which in fact is the case in actual transactions, because he who acts unjustly has the greater share and he who is treated unjustly has the less of what is good: but in the case of what is bad this is reversed: for the less evil compared with the greater comes to be reckoned for good, because the less evil is more choice-worthy than the greater, and what is choice-worthy is good, and the more so the greater good.

This then is the one species of the Just.

And the remaining one is the Corrective, which arises in voluntary as well as involuntary transactions. Now this Just has a different form from the afore-mentioned; for that which is concerned in distribution of common property is always according to the afore-mentioned proportion: I mean that, if the division is made out of common property, the shares will bear the same proportion to one another as the original contributions did: and the Unjust which is opposite to this Just is that which violates the proportionate.

But the Just which arises in transactions between men is an equal in a certain sense, and the Unjust an unequal, only not in the way of that proportion but of arithmetical. Because it makes no difference whether a robbery, for instance, is committed by a good man on a bad or by a bad man on a good, nor whether a good or a bad man has committed adultery: the law looks only to the difference created by the injury and treats the men as previously equal, where the one does and the other suffers injury, or the one has done and the other suffered harm. And so this Unjust, being unequal, the judge endeavours to reduce to equality again, because really when the one party has been wounded and the other has struck him, or the one kills and the other dies, the suffering and the doing are divided into unequal shares; well, the judge tries to restore equality by penalty, thereby taking from the gain.

For these terms gain and loss are applied to these cases, though perhaps the term in some particular instance may not be strictly proper, as gain, for instance, to the man who has given a blow, and loss to him who has received it: still, when the suffering has been estimated, the one is called loss and the other gain.

And so the equal is a mean between the more and the less, which represent gain and loss in contrary ways (I mean, that the more of good and the less of evil is gain, the less of good and the more of evil is loss): between which the equal was stated to be a mean, which equal we say is Just: and so the Corrective Just must be the mean between loss and gain. And this is the reason why, upon a dispute arising, men have recourse to the judge: going to the judge is in fact going to the Just, for the judge is meant to be the personification of the Just. And men seek a judge as one in the mean, which is expressed in a name given by some to judges (μεσίδιοι, or middle-men) under the notion that if they can hit on the mean they shall hit on the Just. The Just is then surely a mean since the judge is also.

So it is the office of a judge to make things equal, and the line, as it were, having been unequally divided, he takes from the greater part that by which it exceeds the half, and adds this on to the less. And when the whole is divided into two exactly equal portions then men say they have their own, when they have gotten the equal; and the equal is a mean between the greater and the less according to arithmetical equality.

This, by the way, accounts for the etymology of the term by which we in Greek express the ideas of Just and Judge; (δίκαιον quasi δίχαιον, that is in two parts, and δικάστης quasi διχάστης, he who divides into two parts). For when from one of two equal magnitudes somewhat has been taken and added to the other, this latter exceeds the former by twice that portion: if it had been merely taken from the former and not added to the latter, then the latter would have exceeded the former only by that one portion; but in the other case, the greater exceeds the mean by one, and the mean exceeds also by one that magnitude from which the portion was taken. By this illustration, then, we obtain a rule to determine what one ought to take from him who has the greater, and what to add to him who has the less. The excess of the mean over the less must be added to the less, and the excess of the greater over the mean be taken from the greater.

Thus let there be three straight lines equal to one another. From one of them cut off a portion, and add as much to another of them. The whole line thus made will exceed the remainder of the first-named line, by twice the portion added, and will exceed the untouched line by that portion. And these terms loss and gain are derived from voluntary exchange: that is to say, the having more than what was one's own is called gaining, and the having less than one's original stock is called losing; for instance, in buying or selling, or any other transactions, which are guaranteed by law: but when the result is neither more nor less, but exactly the same as there was originally, people say they have their own, and neither lose nor gain.

So then the Just we have been speaking of is a mean between loss and gain arising in involuntary transactions; that is, it is the having the same after the transaction as one had before it took place.

There are people who have a notion that Reciprocation is simply just, as the Pythagoreans said: for they defined the Just simply and without qualification as "That which reciprocates with another." But this simple Reciprocation will not fit on either to the Distributive Just, or the Corrective (and yet this is the interpretation they put on the Rhadamanthian rule of Just,

> "If a man should suffer what he hath done, then there would be straightforward justice");

for in many cases differences arise: as, for instance, suppose one in authority has struck a man, he is not to be struck in turn; or if a man has struck one in authority, he must not only be struck but punished also. And again, the voluntariness or involuntariness of actions makes a great difference.

But in dealings of exchange such a principle of Justice as this Reciprocation forms the bond of union; but then it must be Reciprocation according to proportion and not exact equality, because by proportionate reciprocity of action the social community is held together. For either Reciprocation of evil is meant, and if this be not allowed it is thought to be a servile condition of things: or else Reciprocation of good, and if this be not effected then there is no admission to participation which is the very bond of their union.

And this is the moral of placing the Temple of the Graces (χάριτες) in the public streets; to impress the notion that there may be requital, this being peculiar to χάρις, because a man ought to require with a good turn the man who has done him a favour and then to become himself the originator of another χάρις, by doing him a favour.

Now the acts of mutual giving in due proportion may be represented by the diameters of a parallelogram, at the four angles of which the parties and their wares are so placed that the side connecting the parties be opposite to that connecting the wares, and each party be connected by one side with his own ware, as in the accompanying diagram.

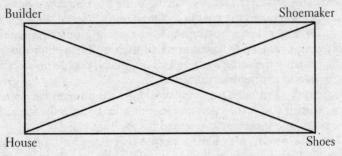

The builder is to receive from the shoemaker of his ware, and to give him of his own: if then there be first proportionate equality, and *then* the Reciprocation takes place, there will be the just result which we are speaking of: if not, there is not the equal, nor will the connection stand: for there is no reason why the ware of the one may not be better than that of the other, and therefore before the exchange is made they must have been equalised. And this is so also in the other arts: for they would have been destroyed entirely if there were not a correspondence in point of quantity and quality between the producer and the consumer. For, we must remember, no dealing arises between two of the same kind, two physicians, for instance; but say between a physician and agriculturist, or, to state it generally, between those who are different and not equal, but these of course must have been equalised before the exchange can take place.

It is therefore indispensable that all things which can be exchanged should be capable of comparison, and for this purpose money has come in, and comes to be a kind of medium, for it measures all things and so likewise the excess and defect; for instance, how many shoes are equal to a house or a given quantity of food. As then the builder to the shoemaker, so many shoes must be to the house (or food, if instead of a builder an agriculturist be the exchanging party); for unless there is this proportion there cannot be exchange or dealing, and this proportion cannot be unless the terms are in some way equal; hence the need, as was stated above, of some one measure of all things. Now this is really and truly the Demand for them, which is the common bond of all such dealings. For if the parties were not in want at all or not similarly of one another's wares, there would either not be any exchange, or at least not the same.

And money has come to be, by general agreement, a representative of Demand: and the account of its Greek name νομισμα is this, that it is what it is not naturally but by custom or law (νόμος), and it rests with us to change its value, or make it wholly useless.

Very well then, there will be Reciprocation when the terms have been equalised so as to stand in this proportion; Agriculturist : Shoemaker :: wares of Shoemaker : wares of Agriculturist; but you must bring them to this form of proportion when they exchange, otherwise the one extreme will combine both exceedings of the mean: but when they have exactly their own then they are equal and have dealings, because the same equality can come to be in their case. Let A represent an agriculturist, C, food, B a shoemaker, D his wares equalised with A's. Then the proportion will be correct, A:B::C:D; *now*

Reciprocation will be practicable, if it were not, there would have been no dealing.

Now that what connects men in such transactions is Demand, as being some one thing, is shown by the fact that, when either one does not want the other or neither want one another, they do not exchange at all: whereas they do when one wants what the other man has, wine for instance, giving in return corn for exportation.

And further, money is a kind of security to us in respect of exchange at some future time (supposing that one wants nothing now that we shall have it when we do): the theory of money being that whenever one brings it one can receive commodities in exchange: of course this too is liable to depreciation, for its purchasing power is not always the same, but still it is of a more permanent nature than the commodities it represents. And this is the reason why all things should have a price set upon them, because thus there may be exchange at any time, and if exchange then dealing. So money, like a measure, making all things commensurable equalises them: for if there was not exchange there would not have been dealing, nor exchange if there were not equality, nor equality if there were not the capacity of being commensurate: it is impossible that things so greatly different should be really commensurate, but we can approximate sufficiently for all practical purposes in reference to Demand. The common measure must be some one thing, and also from agreement (for which reason it is called νόμισμα), for this makes all things commensurable: in fact, all things are measured by money. Let B represent ten minæ, A a house worth five minæ, or in other words half B, C a bed worth ⅒ of B: it is clear then how many beds are equal to one house, namely, five.

It is obvious also that exchange was thus conducted before the existence of money: for it makes no difference whether you give for a house five beds or the price of five beds.

We have now said then what the abstract Just and Unjust are, and these having been defined it is plain that just acting is a mean between acting unjustly and being acted unjustly towards: the former being equivalent to having more, and the latter to having less.

But Justice, it must be observed, is a mean state not after the same manner as the forementioned virtues, but because it aims at producing the mean, while Injustice occupies *both* the extremes.

And Justice is the moral state in virtue of which the just man is said to have the aptitude for practising the Just in the way of moral choice, and for making division between himself and another, or between two other men, not so as to give to himself the greater and to his neighbour the less share of what is choice-worthy and contrariwise of what is hurtful, but what is proportionably equal, and in like manner when adjudging the rights of two other men.

Injustice is all this with respect to the Unjust: and since the Unjust is excess or defect of what is good or hurtful respectively, in violation of the proportionate, therefore Injustice is both excess and defect because it aims at producing excess and defect; excess, that is, in a man's own case of what is simply advantageous, and defect of what is hurtful: and in the case of other men in like manner generally speaking, only that the proportionate is violated not always in one direction as before but whichever way it happens in the given case. And of the Unjust act the less is being acted unjustly towards, and the greater the acting unjustly towards others.

Let this way of describing the nature of Justice and Injustice, and likewise the Just and the Unjust generally, be accepted as sufficient.

Again, since a man may do unjust acts and not yet have formed a character of injustice, the question arises whether a man is unjust in each particular form of injustice, say a thief, or adulterer, or robber, by doing acts of a given character.

We may say, I think, that this will not of itself make any difference; a man may, for instance, have had connection with another's wife, knowing well with whom he was sinning, but he may have done it not of deliberate choice but from the impulse of passion: of course he acts unjustly, but he has not necessarily formed an unjust character: that is, he may have stolen yet not be a thief; or committed an act of adultery but still not be an adulterer, and so on in other cases which might be enumerated.

Of the relation which Reciprocation bears to the Just we have already spoken: and here it should be noticed that the Just which we are investigating is both the Just in the abstract and also as exhibited in Social Relations, which latter arises in the case of those who live in communion with a view to independence and who are free and equal either proportionately or numerically.

It follows then that those who are not in this position have not among themselves the Social Just, but still Just of some kind and resembling that other. For Just implies mutually acknowledged law, and law the possibility of injustice, for adjudication is the act of distinguishing between the Just and the Unjust.

And among whomsoever there is the possibility of injustice among these there is that of acting unjustly; but it does not hold conversely that injustice attaches to all among whom there is the possibility of acting unjustly, since by the former we mean giving one's self the larger share of what is abstractedly good and the less of what is abstractedly evil.

This, by the way, is the reason why we do not allow a man to govern, but Principle, because a man governs for himself and comes to be a despot: but the office of a ruler is to be guardian of the Just and therefore of the Equal. Well, then, since he seems to have no peculiar personal advantage, supposing him a Just man, for in this case he does not allot to himself the larger share of what is abstractedly good unless it falls to his share proportionately (for which reason he really governs for others, and so Justice, men say, is a good not to one's self so much as to others, as was mentioned before), therefore some compensation must be given him, as there actually is in the shape of honour and privilege; and wherever these are not adequate there rulers turn into despots.

But the Just which arises in the relations of Master and Father, is not identical with, but similar to, these; because there is no possibility of injustice towards those things which are absolutely one's own; and a slave or child (so long as this last is of a certain age and not separated into an independent being), is, as it were, part of a man's self, and no man chooses to hurt himself, for which reason there cannot be injustice towards one's own self: therefore neither is there the social Unjust or Just, which was stated to be in accordance with law and to exist between those among whom law naturally exists, and these were said to be they to whom belongs equality of ruling and being ruled.

Hence also there is Just rather between a man and his wife than between a man and his children or slaves; this is in fact the Just arising in domestic relations: and this too is different from the Social Just.

Further, this last-mentioned Just is of two kinds, natural and conventional; the former being that which has everywhere the same force and does not depend upon being received or not; the latter being that which originally may be this way or that indifferently but not after enactment: for instance, the price of ransom being fixed at a mina, or the sacrificing a goat instead of two sheep; and again, all cases of special enactment, as the sacrificing to Brasidas as a hero; in short, all matters of special decree.

But there are some men who think that all the Justs are of this latter kind, and on this ground: whatever exists by nature, they say, is unchangeable and has everywhere the same force; fire, for instance, burns not here only but in Persia as well, but the Justs they see changed in various places.

Now this is not really so, and yet it is in a way (though among the gods perhaps by no means): still even amongst ourselves there is some-what existing by nature: allowing that everything is subject to change, still there is that which does exist by nature, and that which does not.

Nay, we may go further, and say that it is practically plain what among things which can be otherwise does exist by nature, and what does not but is dependent upon enactment and conventional, even granting that both are alike subject to be changed: and the same dis-tinctive illustration will apply to this and other cases; the right hand is naturally the stronger, still some men may become equally strong in both.

A parallel may be drawn between the Justs which depend upon con-vention and expedience, and measures; for wine and corn measures are not equal in all places, but where men buy they are large, and where these same sell again they are smaller: well, in like manner the Justs which are not natural, but of human invention, are not everywhere the same, for not even the forms of government are, and yet there is one only which by nature would be best in all places.

Now of Justs and Lawfuls each bears to the acts which embody and exemplify it the relation of a universal to a particular; the acts being many, but each of the principles only singular because each is a uni-versal. And so there is a difference between an unjust act and the ab-stract Unjust, and the just act and the abstract Just: I mean, a thing is unjust in itself, by nature or by ordinance; well, when this has been em-bodied in act, there is an unjust act, but not till then, only some unjust thing. And similarly of a just act. (Perhaps δικαιοπράγημα is more correctly the common or generic term for just act, the word δικαίωμα, which I have here used, meaning generally and properly the act cor-rective of the unjust act.) Now as to each of them, what kinds there are, and how many, and what is their object-matter, we must examine af-terwards.

For the present we proceed to say that, the Justs and the Unjusts being what have been mentioned, a man is said to act unjustly or justly when he embodies these abstracts in voluntary actions, but when in in-voluntary, then he neither acts unjustly or justly except accidentally; I mean that the being just or unjust is really only accidental to the agents in such cases.

So both unjust and just actions are limited by the being voluntary or the contrary: for when an embodying of the Unjust is voluntary, then it is blamed and is at the same time also an unjust action: but, if volun-tariness does not attach, there will be a thing which is in itself unjust but not yet an unjust action.

By voluntary, I mean, as we stated before, whatsoever of things in his own power a man does with knowledge, and the absence of ignorance as to the person to whom, or the instrument with which, or the result with which he does; as, for instance, whom he strikes, what he strikes him with, and with what probable result; and each of these points again, not accidentally nor by compulsion; as supposing another man were to seize his hand and strike a third person with it, here, of course, the owner of the hand acts not voluntarily, because it did not rest with him to do or leave undone: or again, it is conceivable that the person struck may be his father, and he may know that it is a man, or even one of the present company, whom he is striking, but not know that it is his father. And let these same distinctions be supposed to be carried into the case of the result and in fact the whole of any given action. In fine then, that is involuntary which is done through ignorance, or which, not resulting from ignorance, is not in the agent's control or is done on compulsion.

I mention these cases, because there are many natural things which we do and suffer knowingly but still no one of which is either voluntary or involuntary, growing old, or dying, for instance.

Again, accidentality may attach to the unjust in like manner as to the just acts. For instance, a man may have restored what was deposited with him, but against his will and from fear of the consequences of a refusal: we must not say that he either does what is just, or does justly, except accidentally: and in like manner the man who through compulsion and against his will fails to restore a deposit, must be said to do unjustly, or to do what is unjust, accidentally only.

Again, voluntary actions we do either from deliberate choice or without it; from it, when we act from previous deliberation; without it, when without any previous deliberation. Since then hurts which may be done in transactions between man and man are threefold, those mistakes which are attended with ignorance are, when a man either does a thing not to the man to whom he meant to do it, or not the thing he meant to do, or not with the instrument, or not with the result which he intended: either he did not think he should hit him at all, or not with this, or this is not the man he thought he should hit, or he did not think this would be the result of the blow but a result has followed which he did not anticipate; as, for instance, he did it not to wound but merely to prick him; or it is not the man whom, or the way in which, he meant.

Now when the hurt has come about contrary to all reasonable expectation, it is a Misadventure; when though not contrary to expectation yet without any viciousness, it is a Mistake; for a man makes a mistake when the origination of the cause rests with himself, he has a misadventure when it is external to himself. When again he acts with knowledge, but not from previous deliberation, it is an unjust action; for instance, whatever happens to men from anger or other passions which are necessary or natural: for when doing these hurts or making these mistakes they act unjustly of course and their actions are unjust, still they are not yet confirmed unjust or wicked persons by reason of these, because the hurt did not arise from depravity in the doer of it: but when it does arise from deliberate choice, then the doer is a confirmed unjust and depraved man.

And on this principle acts done from anger are fairly judged not to be from malice prepense, because it is not the man who acts in wrath who is the originator really but he who caused his wrath. And again, the question at issue in such cases is not respecting the fact but respecting the justice of the case, the occasion of anger being a notion of injury. I mean, that the parties do not dispute about the fact, as in questions of contract (where one of the two must be a rogue, unless real forgetfulness can be pleaded), but, admitting the fact, they dispute on which side the justice of the case lies (the one who plotted against the other, *i.e.* the real aggressor, of course, cannot be ignorant), so that the one thinks there is injustice committed while the other does not.

Well then, a man acts unjustly if he has hurt another of deliberate purpose, and he who commits such acts of injustice is *ipso facto* an unjust character when they are in violation of the proportionate or the equal; and in like manner also a man is a just character when he acts justly of deliberate purpose, and he does act justly if he acts voluntarily.

Then as for involuntary acts of harm, they are either such as are excusable or such as are not: under the former head come all errors done not merely in ignorance but from ignorance; under the latter all that are done not from ignorance but in ignorance caused by some passion which is neither natural nor fairly attributable to human infirmity.

Now a question may be raised whether we have spoken with sufficient distinctness as to being unjustly dealt with, and dealing unjustly towards others.

First, whether the case is possible which Euripides has put, saying somewhat strangely,

> "My mother he hath slain; the tale is short,
> Either he willingly did slay her willing,
> Or else with her will but against his own."

I mean then, is it really possible for a person to be unjustly dealt with with his own consent, or must every case of being unjustly dealt with be against the will of the sufferer as every act of unjust dealing is voluntary?

And next, are cases of being unjustly dealt with to be ruled all one way as every act of unjust dealing is voluntary? or may we say that some cases are voluntary and some involuntary?

Similarly also as regards being justly dealt with: all just acting is voluntary, so that it is fair to suppose that the being dealt with unjustly or justly must be similarly opposed, as to being either voluntary or involuntary.

Now as for being justly dealt with, the position that every case of this is voluntary is a strange one, for some are certainly justly dealt with without their will. The fact is a man may also fairly raise this question, whether in every case he who has suffered what is unjust is therefore unjustly dealt with, or rather that the case is the same with suffering as it is with acting; namely that in both it is possible to participate in what is just, but only accidentally. Clearly the case of what is unjust is similar: for doing things in themselves unjust is not identical with acting unjustly, nor is suffering them the same as being unjustly dealt with. So too of acting justly and being justly dealt with, since it is impossible to be unjustly dealt with unless some one else acts unjustly or to be justly dealt with unless some one else acts justly.

Now if acting unjustly is simply "hurting another voluntarily" (by which I mean, knowing whom you are hurting, and wherewith, and how you are hurting him), and the man who fails of self-control voluntarily hurts himself, then this will be a case of being voluntarily dealt unjustly with, and it will be possible for a man to deal unjustly with himself. (This by the way is one of the questions raised, whether it is possible for a man to deal unjustly with himself.) Or again, a man may, by reason of failing of self-control, receive hurt from another man acting voluntarily, and so here will be another case of being unjustly dealt with voluntarily.

The solution, I take it, is this: the definition of being unjustly dealt with is not correct, but we must add, to the hurting with the knowledge of the person hurt and the instrument and the manner of hurting him, the fact of its being against the wish of the man who is hurt.

So then a man may be hurt and suffer what is in itself unjust voluntarily, but unjustly dealt with voluntarily no man can be: since no man wishes to be hurt, not even he who fails of self-control, who really acts contrary to his wish: for no man wishes for that which he does not *think* to be good, and the man who fails of self-control does not what he thinks he ought to do.

And again, he that gives away his own property (as Homer says Glaucus gave to Diomed, "armour of gold for brass, armour worth a hundred oxen for that which was worth but nine") is not unjustly dealt with, because the giving rests entirely with himself; but being unjustly dealt with does not, there must be some other person who is dealing unjustly towards him.

With respect to being unjustly dealt with then, it is clear that it is not voluntary.

There remain yet two points on which we purposed to speak: first, is he chargeable with an unjust act who in distribution has *given* the larger share to one party contrary to the proper rate, or he that *has* the larger share? next, can a man deal unjustly by himself?

In the first question, if the first-named alternative is possible and it is the distributor who acts unjustly and not he who has the larger share, then supposing that a person knowingly and willingly gives more to another than to himself here is a case of a man dealing unjustly by himself; which, in fact, moderate men are thought to do, for it is a characteristic of the equitable man to take less than his due.

Is not this the answer? that the case is not quite fairly stated, because of some other good, such as credit or the abstract honourable, in the supposed case the man did get the larger share. And again, the difficulty is solved by reference to the definition of unjust dealing: for the man suffers nothing contrary to his own wish, so that, on this score at least, he is not unjustly dealt with, but, if anything, he is hurt only.

It is evident also that it is the distributor who acts unjustly and not the man who has the greater share: because the mere fact of the abstract Unjust attaching to what a man does, does not constitute unjust action, but the doing this voluntarily: and voluntariness attaches to that quarter whence is the origination of the action, which clearly is in the distributor not in the receiver. And again the term doing is used in several senses; in one sense inanimate objects kill, or the hand, or the slave by his master's bidding; so the man in question does not act unjustly but does things which are in themselves unjust.

Again, suppose that a man has made a wrongful award in ignorance; in the eye of the law he does not act unjustly nor is his awarding unjust, but yet he is in a certain sense: for the Just according to law and primary or natural Just are not coincident: but, if he knowingly decided unjustly, then he himself as well as the receiver got the larger share, that is, either of favour from the receiver or private revenge against the other party: and so the man who decided unjustly from these motives gets a larger share, in exactly the same sense as a man would who received part of the actual matter of the unjust action: because in this case the man who wrongly adjudged, say a field, did not actually get land but money by his unjust decision.

Now men suppose that acting Unjustly rests entirely with themselves, and conclude that acting Justly is therefore also easy. But this is not really so; to have connection with a neighbour's wife, or strike one's neighbour, or give the money with one's hand, is of course easy and rests with one's self: but the doing these acts with certain inward dispositions neither is easy nor rests entirely with one's self. And in like way, the knowing what is Just and what Unjust men think no great instance of wisdom because it is not hard to comprehend those things of which the laws speak. They forget that these are not Just actions, except accidentally: to be Just they must be done and distributed in a certain manner: and this is a more difficult task than knowing what things are wholesome; for in this branch of knowledge it is an easy matter to know honey, wine, hellebore, cautery, or the use of the knife, but the knowing how one should administer these with a view to health, and to whom and at what time, amounts in fact to being a physician.

From this very same mistake they suppose also, that acting Unjustly is equally in the power of the Just man, for the Just man no less, nay even more, than the Unjust, may be able to do the particular acts; he may be able to have intercourse with a woman or strike a man; or the brave man to throw away his shield and turn his back and run this way or that. True: but then it is not the mere doing these things which constitutes acts of cowardice or injustice (except accidentally), but the doing them with certain inward dispositions: just as it is not the mere using or not using the knife, administering or not administering certain drugs, which constitutes medical treatment or curing, but doing these things in a certain particular way.

Again the abstract principles of Justice have their province among those who partake of what is abstractedly good, and can have too much or too little of these. Now there are beings who cannot have too much of them, as perhaps the gods; there are others, again, to whom no particle of them is of use, those who are incurably wicked to whom all things are hurtful; others to whom they are useful to a certain degree: for this reason then the province of Justice is among *Men*.

We have next to speak of Equity and the Equitable, that is to say, of the relations of Equity to Justice and the Equitable to the Just; for when we look into the matter the two do not appear identical nor yet different in kind; and we sometimes commend the Equitable and the man who embodies it in his actions, so that by way of praise we commonly transfer the term also to other acts instead of the term good, thus showing that the more Equitable a thing is the better it is: at other times following a certain train of reasoning we arrive at a difficulty, in that the Equitable though distinct from the Just is yet praiseworthy; it seems to follow either that the Just is not good or the Equitable not Just, since they are by hypothesis different; or if both are good then they are identical.

This is a tolerably fair statement of the difficulty which on these grounds arises in respect of the Equitable; but, in fact, all these may be reconciled and really involve no contradiction: for the Equitable is Just, being also better than one form of Just, but is not better than the Just as though it were different from it in kind: Just and Equitable then are identical, and, both being good, the Equitable is the better of the two.

What causes the difficulty is this; the Equitable is Just, but not the Just which is in accordance with written law, being in fact a correction of that kind of Just. And the account of this is, that every law is necessarily universal while there are some things which it is not possible to speak of rightly in any universal or general statement. Where then there is a necessity for general statement, while a general statement cannot apply rightly to all cases, the law takes the generality of cases, being fully aware of the error thus involved; and rightly too notwithstanding, because the fault is not in the law, or in the framer of the law, but is inherent in the nature of the thing, because the matter of all action is necessarily such.

When then the law has spoken in general terms, and there arises a case of exception to the general rule, it is proper, in so far as the lawgiver omits the case and by reason of his universality of statement is wrong, to set right the omission by ruling it as the lawgiver himself would rule were he there present, and would have provided by law had he foreseen the case would arise. And so the Equitable is Just but better than one form of Just; I do not mean the abstract Just but the error which arises out of the universality of statement: and this is the nature of the Equitable, "a correction of Law, where Law is defective by reason of its universality."

This is the reason why not all things are according to law, because there are things about which it is simply impossible to lay down a law, and so we want special enactments for particular cases. For to speak generally, the rule of the undefined must be itself undefined also, just as the rule to measure Lesbian building is made of lead: for this rule shifts according to the form of each stone and the special enactment according to the facts of the case in question.

It is clear then what the Equitable is; namely that it is Just but better than one form of Just: and hence it appears too who the Equitable man is: he is one who has a tendency to choose and carry out these principles, and who is not apt to press the letter of the law on the worse side but content to waive his strict claims though backed by the law: and this moral state is Equity, being a species of Justice, not a different moral state from Justice.

The answer to the second of the two questions indicated above, "whether it is possible for a man to deal unjustly by himself," is obvious from what has been already stated.

In the first place, one class of Justs is those which are enforced by law in accordance with Virtue in the most extensive sense of the term: for instance, the law does not bid a man kill himself; and whatever it does not bid it forbids: well, whenever a man does hurt contrary to the law (unless by way of requital of hurt), voluntarily, *i.e.* knowing to whom he does it and wherewith, he acts Unjustly. Now he that from rage kills himself, voluntarily, does this in contravention of Right Reason, which the law does not permit. He therefore acts Unjustly: but towards whom? towards the Community, not towards himself (because he suffers with his own consent, and no man can be Unjustly dealt with with his own consent), and on this principle the Community punishes him; that is a certain infamy is attached to the suicide as to one who acts Unjustly towards the Community.

Next, a man cannot deal Unjustly by himself in the sense in which a man is Unjust who only does Unjust acts without being entirely bad (for the two things are different, because the Unjust man is in a way bad, as the coward is, not as though he were chargeable with badness in the full extent of the term, and so he does not act Unjustly in this sense), because if it were so then it would be possible for the same thing to have been taken away from and added to the same person: but this is really not possible, the Just and the Unjust always implying a plurality of persons.

Again, an Unjust action must be voluntary, done of deliberate purpose, and aggressive (for the man who hurts because he has first suffered and is merely requiting the same is not thought to act Unjustly), but here the man does to himself and suffers the same things at the same time.

Again, it would imply the possibility of being Unjustly dealt with with one's own consent.

And, besides all this, a man cannot act Unjustly without his act falling under some particular crime; now a man cannot seduce his own wife, commit a burglary on his own premises, or steal his own property.

After all, the general answer to the question is to allege what was settled respecting being Unjustly dealt with with one's own consent.

It is obvious, moreover, that being Unjustly dealt by and dealing Unjustly by others are both wrong; because the one is having less, the other having more, than the mean, and the case is parallel to that of the healthy in the healing art, and that of good condition in the art of training: but still the dealing Unjustly by others is the worst of the two, because this involves wickedness and is blameworthy; wickedness, I mean, either wholly, or nearly so (for not all voluntary wrong implies injustice), but the being Unjustly dealt by does not involve wickedness or injustice.

In itself then, the being Unjustly dealt by is the least bad, but accidentally it may be the greater evil of the two. However, scientific statement cannot take in such considerations; a pleurisy, for instance, is called a greater physical evil than a bruise: and yet this last may be the greater accidentally; it may chance that a bruise received in a fall may cause one to be captured by the enemy and slain.

Further: Just, in the way of metaphor and similitude, there may be I do not say between a man and himself exactly but between certain parts of his nature; but not Just of every kind, only such as belongs to the relation of master and slave, or to that of the head of a family. For all through this treatise the rational part of the Soul has been viewed as distinct from the irrational.

Now, taking these into consideration, there is thought to be a possibility of injustice towards one's self, because herein it is possible for men to suffer somewhat in contradiction of impulses really their own; and so it is thought that there is Just of a certain kind between these parts mutually, as between ruler and ruled.

Let this then be accepted as an account of the distinctions which we recognise respecting Justice and the rest of the moral virtues.

BOOK VI

HAVING stated in a former part of this treatise that men should choose the mean instead of either the excess or defect, and that the mean is according to the dictates of Right Reason; we will now proceed to explain this term.

For in all the habits which we have expressly mentioned, as likewise in all the others, there is, so to speak, a mark with his eye fixed on which the man who has Reason tightens or slacks his rope; and there is a certain limit of those mean states which we say are in accordance with Right Reason, and lie between excess on the one hand and defect on the other.

Now to speak thus is true enough but conveys no very definite meaning: as, in fact, in all other pursuits requiring attention and diligence on which skill and science are brought to bear; it is quite true of course to say that men are neither to labour nor relax too much or too little, but in moderation, and as Right Reason directs; yet if this were all a man had he would not be greatly the wiser; as, for instance, if in answer to the question, what are proper applications to the body, he were to be told, "Oh! of course, whatever the science of medicine, and in such manner as the physician, directs."

And so in respect of the mental states it is requisite not merely that this should be true which has been already stated, but further that it should be expressly laid down what Right Reason is, and what is the definition of it.

Now in our division of the Excellences of the Soul, we said there were two classes, the Moral and the Intellectual: the former we have already gone through; and we will now proceed to speak of the others, premising a few words respecting the Soul itself. It was stated before, you will remember, that the Soul consists of two parts, the Rational, and Irrational: we must now make a similar division of the Rational.

Let it be understood then that there are two parts of the Soul possessed of Reason; one whereby we realise those existences whose causes cannot be otherwise than they are, and one whereby we realise those which can be otherwise than they are (for there must be, answering to things generically different, generically different parts of the soul naturally adapted to each, since these parts of the soul possess their knowledge in virtue of a certain resemblance and appropriateness in themselves to the objects of which they are percipients); and let us name the former, "that which is apt to know," the latter, "that which is apt to calculate" (because deliberating and calculating are the same, and no one ever deliberates about things which cannot be otherwise than they are: and so the Calculative will be one part of the Rational faculty of the soul).

We must discover, then, which is the best state of each of these, because that will be the Excellence of each; and this again is relative to the work each has to do.

There are in the Soul three functions on which depend moral action and truth; Sense, Intellect, Appetition, whether vague Desire or definite Will. Now of these Sense is the originating cause of no moral action, as is seen from the fact that brutes have Sense but are in no way partakers of moral action.

[Intellect and Will are thus connected,] what in the Intellectual operation is Affirmation and Negation that in the Will is Pursuit and Avoidance. And so, since Moral Virtue is a State apt to exercise Moral Choice and Moral Choice is Will consequent on deliberation, the Reason must be true and the Will right, to constitute good Moral Choice, and what the Reason affirms the Will must pursue.

Now this Intellectual operation and this Truth is what bears upon Moral Action; of course truth and falsehood must be the good and the bad of that Intellectual Operation which is purely Speculative and concerned neither with action nor production, because this is manifestly the work of every Intellectual faculty, while of the faculty which is of a mixed Practical and Intellectual nature the work is that Truth which, as I have described above, corresponds to the right movement of the Will.

Now the starting-point of moral action is Moral Choice (I mean, what actually sets it in motion, not the final cause), and of Moral Choice, Appetition, and Reason directed to a certain result: and thus Moral Choice is neither independent of intellect, *i.e.* intellectual operation, nor of a certain moral state: for right or wrong action cannot exist independently of operation of the Intellect and moral character.

But operation of the Intellect by itself moves nothing, only when directed to a certain result, *i.e.* exercised in Moral Action (I say nothing of its being exercised in production, because this function is originated by the former: every one who makes makes with a view to somewhat further; and that which is or may be made is not an End in itself, but only relatively to somewhat else, and belonging to some one: whereas that which is or may be done is an End in itself, because acting well is an End in itself, and this is the object of the Will): and so Moral Choice is either Intellect put in a position of Will-ing, or Appetition subjected to the Intellectual Process. And such a Cause is Man.

But nothing which is done and past can be the object of Moral Choice; for instance, no man chooses to have sacked Troy; because, in fact, no one ever deliberates about what is past but only about that which is future and which may therefore be influenced, whereas what has been cannot not have been: and so Agathon is right in saying,

> "Of this alone is Deity bereft,
> To make undone whatever hath been done."

Thus then the Truth is the work of both the Intellectual Parts of the Soul; those states therefore are the Excellences of each in which each will best attain truth.

Commencing then from the point stated above we will now speak of these Excellences again. Let those faculties whereby the Soul attains truth in Affirmation or Negation, be assumed to be in number five: viz. Art, Knowledge, Practical Wisdom, Science, Intuition (Supposition and Opinion I do not include, because by these one may go wrong).

What Knowledge is is plain from the following considerations, if one is to speak accurately instead of being led away by resemblances. We all conceive that what we strictly speaking *know* cannot be otherwise than it is, because as to those things which can be otherwise than they are we are uncertain whether they are or are not the moment they cease to be within the sphere of our actual observation.

So then, whatever comes within the range of Knowledge is by necessity, and therefore eternal (because all things are so which exist necessarily), and all eternal things are without beginning and indestructible.

Again, all Knowledge is thought to be capable of being taught, and what comes within its range capable of being learned. And all teaching is based upon previous knowledge (a statement you will find in the Analytics also); for there are two ways of teaching, by Syllogism and by Induction. In fact, Induction is the source of universal propositions, and Syllogism reasons from these universals. Syllogism then may reason from principles which cannot be themselves proved Syllogistically; and therefore must be proved by Induction.

So Knowledge is "a state or mental faculty apt to demonstrate syllogistically," etc., as in the Analytics: because a man, strictly and properly speaking, *knows*, when he establishes his conclusion in a certain way and the principles are known to him: for if they are not better known to him then the conclusion such knowledge as he has will be merely accidental.

Let thus much be accepted as a definition of Knowledge.

Matter which may exist otherwise than it actually does in any given case (commonly called Contingent) is of two kinds, that which is the object of Making, and that which is the object of Doing; now Making and Doing are two different things (as we show in the exoteric treatise), and so that state of mind, conjoined with Reason, which is apt to Do, is distinct from that also conjoined with Reason, which is apt to Make: and for this reason they are not included one by the other, that is, Doing is not Making, nor Making Doing. Now as Architecture is an Art, and is the same as "a certain state of mind, conjoined with Reason, which is apt to Make," and as there is no Art which is not such a state, nor any such state which is not an Art, Art, in its strict and proper sense, must be "a state of mind, conjoined with true Reason, apt to Make."

Now all Art has to do with production, and contrivance, and seeing how any of those things may be produced which may either be or not be, and the origination of which rests with the maker and not with the thing made.

And, so neither things which exist or come into being necessarily, nor things in the way of nature, come under the province of Art, because these are self-originating. And since Making and Doing are distinct, Art must be concerned with the former and not the latter. And in a certain sense Art and Fortune are concerned with the same things, as Agathon says by the way,

"Art Fortune loves, and is of her beloved."

So Art, as has been stated, is "a certain state of mind, apt to Make, conjoined with true Reason;" its absence, on the contrary, is the same state conjoined with false Reason, and both are employed upon Contingent matter.

As for Practical Wisdom, we shall ascertain its nature by examining to what kind of persons we in common language ascribe it.

It is thought then to be the property of the Practically Wise man to be able to deliberate well respecting what is good and expedient for himself, not in any definite line, as what is conducive to health or strength, but what to living well. A proof of this is that we call men Wise in this or that, when they calculate well with a view to some good end in a case where there is no definite rule. And so, in a general way of speaking, the man who is good at deliberation will be Practically Wise. Now no man deliberates respecting things which cannot be otherwise than they are, nor such as lie not within the range of his own action: and so, since Knowledge requires strict demonstrative reasoning, of which Contingent matter does not admit (I say Contingent matter, because all matters of deliberation must be Contingent and deliberation cannot take place with respect to things which are Necessarily), Practical Wisdom cannot be Knowledge nor Art; nor the former, because what falls under the province of Doing must be Contingent; not the latter, because Doing and Making are different in kind.

It remains then that it must be "a state of mind true, conjoined with Reason, and apt to Do, having for its object those things which are good or bad for Man:" because of Making something beyond itself is always the object, but cannot be of Doing because the very well-doing is in itself an End.

For this reason we think Pericles and men of that stamp to be Practically Wise, because they can see what is good for themselves and for men in general, and we also think those to be such who are skilled in domestic management or civil government. In fact, this is the reason why we call the habit of perfected self-mastery by the name which in Greek it bears, etymologically signifying "that which preserves the Practical Wisdom:" for what it does preserve is the Notion I have mentioned, *i.e.* of one's own true interest.

For it is not every kind of Notion which the pleasant and the painful corrupt and pervert, as, for instance, that "the three angles of every rectilineal triangle are equal to two right angles," but only those bearing on moral action.

For the Principles of the matters of moral action are the final cause of them: now to the man who has been corrupted by reason of pleasure or pain the Principle immediately becomes obscured, nor does he see that it is his duty to choose and act in each instance with a view to this final cause and by reason of it: for viciousness has a tendency to destroy the moral Principle: and so Practical Wisdom must be "a state conjoined with reason, true, having human good for its object, and apt to do."

Then again Art admits of degrees of excellence, but Practical Wisdom does not: and in Art he who goes wrong purposely is preferable to him who does so unwittingly, but not so in respect of Practical Wisdom or the other Virtues. It plainly is then an Excellence of a certain kind, and not an Art.

Now as there are two parts of the Soul which have Reason, it must be the Excellence of the Opinionative [which we called before calculative or deliberative], because both Opinion and Practical Wisdom are exercised upon Contingent matter. And further, it is not simply a state conjoined with Reason, as is proved by the fact that such a state may be forgotten and so lost while Practical Wisdom cannot.

Now Knowledge is a conception concerning universals and Necessary matter, and there are of course certain First Principles in all trains of demonstrative reasoning (that is of all Knowledge because this is connected with reasoning): that faculty, then, which takes in the first principles of that which comes under the range of Knowledge, cannot be either Knowledge, or Art, or Practical Wisdom: not Knowledge, because what is the object of Knowledge must be derived from demonstrative reasoning; not either of the other two, because they are exercised upon Contingent matter only. Nor can it be Science which takes in these, because the Scientific Man must in some cases depend on demonstrative Reasoning.

It comes then to this: since the faculties whereby we always attain truth and are never deceived when dealing with matter Necessary or even Contingent are Knowledge, Practical Wisdom, Science, and Intuition, and the faculty which takes in First Principles cannot be any of the three first; the last, namely Intuition, must be it which performs this function.

Science is a term we use principally in two meanings: in the first place, in the Arts we ascribe it to those who carry their arts to the highest accuracy; Phidias, for instance, we call a Scientific or cunning sculptor; Polycleitus a Scientific or cunning statuary; meaning, in this instance, nothing else by Science than an excellence of art: in the other sense, we think some to be Scientific in a general way, not in any particular line or in any particular thing, just as Homer says of a man in his Margites; "Him the Gods made neither a digger of the ground, nor ploughman, nor in any other way Scientific."

So it is plain that Science must mean the most accurate of all Knowledge; but if so, then the Scientific man must not merely know the deductions from the First Principles but be in possession of truth respecting the First Principles. So that Science must be equivalent to

Intuition and Knowledge; it is, so to speak, Knowledge of the most precious objects, *with a head on.*

I say of the most precious things, because it is absurd to suppose πολιτικὴ, or Practical Wisdom, to be the highest, unless it can be shown that Man is the most excellent of all that exists in the Universe. Now if "healthy" and "good" are relative terms, differing when applied to men or to fish, but "white" and "straight" are the same always, men must allow that the Scientific is the same always, but the Practically Wise varies: for whatever provides all things well for itself, to this they would apply the term Practically Wise, and commit these matters to it; which is the reason, by the way, that they call some brutes Practically Wise, such that is as plainly have a faculty of forethought respecting their own subsistence.

And it is quite plain that Science and πολιτικὴ cannot be identical: because if men give the name of Science to that faculty which is employed upon what is expedient for themselves, there will be many instead of one, because there is not one and the same faculty employed on the good of all animals collectively, unless in the same sense as you may say there is one art of healing with respect to all living beings.

If it is urged that man is superior to all other animals, that makes no difference: for there are many other things more Godlike in their nature than Man, as, most obviously, the elements of which the Universe is composed.

It is plain then that Science is the union of Knowledge and Intuition, and has for its objects those things which are most precious in their nature. Accordingly, Anexagoras, Thales, and men of that stamp, people call Scientific, but not Practically wise because they see them ignorant of what concerns themselves; and they say that what they know is quite out of the common run certainly, and wonderful, and hard, and very fine no doubt, but still useless because they do not seek after what is good for them as men.

But Practical Wisdom is employed upon human matters, and such as are objects of deliberation (for we say, that to deliberate well is most peculiarly the work of the man who possesses this Wisdom), and no man deliberates about things which cannot be otherwise than they are, nor about any save those that have some definite End and this End good resulting from Moral Action; and the man to whom we should give the name of Good in Counsel, simply and without modification, is he who in the way of calculation has a capacity for attaining that of practical goods which is the best for Man.

Nor again does Practical Wisdom consist in a knowledge of general principles only, but it is necessary that one should know also the particular details, because it is apt to act, and action is concerned with details: for which reason sometimes men who have not much knowledge are more practical than others who have; among others, they who derive all they know from actual experience: suppose a man to know, for instance, that light meats are easy of digestion and wholesome, but not what kinds of meat are light, he will not produce a healthy state; that man will have a much better chance of doing so, who knows that the flesh of birds is light and wholesome. Since then Practical Wisdom is apt to act, one ought to have both kinds of knowledge, or, if only one, the knowledge of details rather than of Principles. So there will be in respect of Practical Wisdom the distinction of supreme and subordinate.

Further: πολιτικὴ and Practical Wisdom are the same mental state, but the point of view is not the same.

Of Practical Wisdom exerted upon a community that which I would call the Supreme is the faculty of Legislation; the subordinate, which is concerned with the details, generally has the common name πολιτικὴ, and its functions are Action and Deliberation (for the particular enactment is a matter of action, being the ultimate issue of this branch of Practical Wisdom, and therefore people commonly say, that these men alone are really engaged in government, because they alone act, filling the same place relatively to legislators, that workmen do to a master).

Again, that is thought to be Practical Wisdom in the most proper sense which has for its object the interest of the Individual: and this usually appropriates the common name: the others are called respectively Domestic Management, Legislation, Executive Government divided into two branches, Deliberative and Judicial. Now of course, knowledge for one's self is one kind of knowledge, but it admits of many shades of difference: and it is a common notion that the man who knows and busies himself about his own concerns merely is the man of Practical Wisdom, while they who extend their solicitude to society at large are considered meddlesome.

Euripides has thus embodied this sentiment; "How," says one of his Characters, "How foolish am I, who whereas I might have shared equally, idly numbered among the multitude of the army . . . for them that are busy and meddlesome [Jove hates]," because the generality of mankind seek their own good and hold that this is their proper business. It is then from this opinion that the notion has arisen that such men are the Practically-Wise. And yet it is just possible that the good of the individual cannot be secured independently of connection with a family or a community. And again, how a man should manage his own affairs is sometimes not quite plain, and must be made a matter of inquiry.

A corroboration of what I have said is the fact, that the young come to be geometricians, and mathematicians, and Scientific in such matters, but it is not thought that a young man can come to be possessed of Practical Wisdom: now the reason is, that this Wisdom has for its object particular facts, which come to be known from experience, which a young man has not because it is produced only by length of time.

By the way, a person might also inquire why a boy may be made a mathematician but not Scientific or a natural philosopher. Is not this the reason? that mathematics are taken in by the process of abstraction, but the principles of Science and natural philosophy must be gained by experiment; and the latter young men talk of but do not realise, while the nature of the former is plain and clear.

Again, in matter of practice, error attaches either to the general rule, in the process of deliberation, or to the particular fact: for instance, this would be a general rule, "All water of a certain gravity is bad;" the particular fact, "this water is of that gravity."

And that Practical Wisdom is not knowledge is plain, for it has to do with the ultimate issue, as has been said, because every object of action is of this nature.

To Intuition it is opposed, for this takes in those principles which cannot be proved by reasoning, while Practical Wisdom is concerned with the ultimate particular fact which cannot be realised by Knowledge but by Sense; I do not mean one of the five senses, but the same by which we take in the mathematical fact, that no rectilineal figure can be contained by less than three lines, i.e. that a triangle is the ultimate figure, because here also is a stopping point.

This however is Sense rather than Practical Wisdom, which is of another kind.

Now the acts of inquiring and deliberating differ, though deliberating is a kind of inquiring. We ought to ascertain about Good Counsel likewise what it is, whether a kind of Knowledge, or Opinion, or Happy Conjecture, or some other kind of faculty. Knowledge it obviously is not, because men do not inquire about what they know, and Good Counsel is a kind of deliberation, and the man who is deliberating is inquiring and calculating.

Neither is it Happy Conjecture; because this is independent of reasoning, and a rapid operation; but men deliberate a long time, and it is a common saying that one should execute speedily what has been re-solved upon in deliberation, but deliberate slowly.

Quick perception of causes again is a different faculty from good counsel, for it is a species of Happy Conjecture. Nor is Good Counsel Opinion of any kind.

Well then, since he who deliberates ill goes wrong, and he who deliberates well does so rightly, it is clear that Good Counsel is rightness of some kind, but not of Knowledge nor of Opinion: for Knowledge cannot be called right because it cannot be wrong, and Rightness of Opinion is Truth: and again, all which is the object of opinion is definitely marked out.

Still, however, Good Counsel is not independent of Reason. Does it remain then that it is a rightness of Intellectual Operation simply, because this does not amount to an assertion; and the objection to Opinion was that it is not a process of inquiry but already a definite assertion; whereas whosoever deliberates, whether well or ill, is engaged in inquiry and calculation.

Well, Good Counsel is a Rightness of deliberation, and so the first question must regard the nature and objects of deliberation. Now remember Rightness is an equivocal term; we plainly do not mean Rightness of any kind whatever; the ἀκρατὴς, for instance, or the bad man, will obtain by his calculation what he sets before him as an object, and so he may be said to have deliberated *rightly* in one sense, but will have attained a great evil. Whereas to have deliberated well is thought to be a good, because God Counsel is Rightness of deliberation of such a nature as is apt to attain good.

But even this again you may get by false reasoning, and hit upon the right effect though not through right means, your middle term being fallacious: and so neither will this be yet Good Counsel in consequence of which you get what you ought but not through proper means.

Again, one man may hit on a thing after long deliberation, another quickly. And so that before described will not be yet Good Counsel, but the Rightness must be with reference to what is expedient; and you must have a proper end in view, pursue it in a right manner and right time.

Once more. One may deliberate well either generally or towards some particular End. Good counsel in the general then is that which goes right towards that which is the End in a general way of consideration; in particular, that which does so towards some particular End.

Since then deliberating well is a quality of men possessed of

Practical Wisdom, Good Counsel must be "Rightness in respect of what conduces to a given End, of which Practical Wisdom is the true conception."

There is too the faculty of Judiciousness, and also its absence, in virtue of which we call men Judicious or the contrary.

Now Judiciousness is neither entirely identical with Knowledge or Opinion (for then all would have been Judicious), nor is it any one specific science, as medical science whose object matter is things wholesome; or geometry whose object matter is magnitude: for it has not for its object things which always exist and are immutable, nor of those things which come into being just any which may chance; but those in respect of which a man might doubt and deliberate.

And so it has the same object matter as Practical Wisdom; yet the two faculties are not identical, because Practical Wisdom has the capacity for commanding and taking the initiative, for its End is "what one should do or not do:" but Judiciousness is only apt to decide upon suggestions (though we do in Greek put "well" on to the faculty and its concrete noun, these really mean exactly the same as the plain words), and Judiciousness is neither the having Practical Wisdom, nor attaining it: but just as learning is termed συνιέναι when a man uses his knowledge, so judiciousness consists in employing the Opinionative faculty in judging concerning those things which come within the province of Practical Wisdom, when another enunciates them; and not judging merely, but judging well (for εὐ and καλῶς mean exactly the same thing). And the Greek name of this faculty is derived from the use of the term συνιέναι in learning: μανθάνειν and συνιέναι being often used as synonymous.

The faculty called γνώμη, in right of which we call men εὐγνώμονες, or say they have γνώμη, is "the right judgment of the equitable man." A proof of which is that we most commonly say that the equitable man has a tendency to make allowance, and the making allowance in certain cases is equitable. And συγγνώμη (the word denoting allowance) is right γνώμη having a capacity of making equitable decisions. By "right" I mean that which attains the True.

Now all these mental states tend to the same object, as indeed common language leads us to expect: I mean, we speak of γνώμη, Judiciousness, Practical Wisdom, and Practical Intuition, attributing the possession of γνώμη and Practical Intuition to the same Individuals whom we denominate Practically-Wise and Judicious: because all these faculties are employed upon the extremes, i.e. on particular details; and in right of his aptitude for deciding on the matters

which come within the province of the Practically-Wise, a man is
Judicious and possessed of good γνώμη; *i.e.* he is disposed to make allowance, for considerations of equity are entertained by all good men
alike in transactions with their fellows.

And all matters of Moral Action belong to the class of particulars,
otherwise called extremes: for the man of Practical Wisdom must know
them, and Judiciousness and γνώμη are concerned with matters of
Moral Actions, which are extremes.

Intuition, moreover, takes in the extremes at both ends: I mean, the
first and last terms must be taken in not by reasoning but by Intuition
[so that Intuition comes to be of two kinds], and that which belongs to
strict demonstrative reasonings takes in immutable, *i.e.* Necessary, first
terms; while that which is employed in practical matters takes in the extreme, the Contingent, and the minor Premiss: for the minor Premisses
are the source of the Final Cause, Universals being made up out of
Particulars. To take in these, of course, we must have Sense, *i.e.* in
other words Practical Intuition.

And for this reason these are thought to be simply gifts of nature; and
whereas no man is thought to be Scientific by nature, men are thought
to have γνώμη, and Judiciousness, and Practical Intuition: a proof of
which is that we think these faculties are a consequence even of particular ages, and this given age has Practical Intuition and γνώμη, we
say, as if under the notion that nature is the cause. And thus Intuition
is both the beginning and end, because the proofs are based upon the
one kind of extremes and concern the other.

And so one should attend to the undemonstrable dicta and opinions
of the skilful, the old and the Practically-Wise, no less than to those
which are based on strict reasoning, because they see aright, having
gained their power of moral vision from experience.

Well, we have now stated the nature and objects of Practical
Wisdom and Science respectively, and that they belong each to a different part of the Soul. But I can conceive a person questioning their
utility. "Science," he would say, "concerns itself with none of the
causes of human happiness (for it has nothing to do with producing
anything): Practical Wisdom has this recommendation, I grant, but
where is the need of it, since its province is those things which are just
and honourable, and good for man, and these are the things which the
good man as such does; but we are not a bit the more apt to do them
because we know them, since the Moral Virtues are Habits; just as we
are not more apt to be healthy or in good condition from mere knowledge of what relates to these (I mean, of course, things so called not

from their producing health, etc., but from their evidencing it in a particular subject), for we are not more apt to be healthy and in good condition merely from knowing the art of medicine or training.

"If it be urged that *knowing what is* good does not by itself make a Practically-Wise man but *becoming* good; still this Wisdom will be no use either to those that are good, and so have it already, or to those who have it not; because it will make no difference to them whether they have it themselves or put themselves under the guidance of others who have; and we might be contented to be in respect of this as in respect of health: for though we wish to be healthy still we do not set about learning the art of healing.

"Furthermore, it would seem to be strange that, though lower in the scale than Science, it is to be its master; which it is, because whatever produces results takes the rule and directs in each matter."

This then is what we are to talk about, for these are the only points now raised.

Now first we say that being respectively Excellences of different parts of the Soul they must be choice-worthy, even on the supposition that they neither of them produce results.

In the next place we say that they *do* produce results; that Science makes Happiness, not as the medical art but as healthiness makes health: because, being a part of Virtue in its most extensive sense, it makes a man happy by being possessed and by working.

Next, Man's work *as Man* is accomplished by virtue of Practical Wisdom and Moral Virtue, the latter giving the right aim and direction, the former the right means to its attainment; but of the fourth part of the Soul, the mere nutritive principle, there is no such Excellence, because nothing is in its power to do or leave undone.

As to our not being more apt to do what is noble and just by reason of possessing Practical Wisdom, we must begin a little higher up, taking this for our starting-point. As we say that men may do things in themselves just and yet not be just men; for instance, when men do what the laws require of them, either against their will, or by reason of ignorance or something else, at all events not for the sake of the things themselves; and yet they do what they ought and all that the good man should do; so it seems that to be a good man one must do each act in a particular frame of mind, I mean from Moral Choice and for the sake of the things themselves which are done. Now it is Virtue which makes the Moral Choice right, but whatever is naturally required to carry out that Choice comes under the province not of Virtue but of a different faculty. We must halt, as it were, awhile, and speak more clearly on these points.

There is then a certain faculty, commonly named Cleverness, of such a nature as to be able to do and attain whatever conduces to *any* given purpose: now if that purpose be a good one the faculty is praiseworthy; if otherwise, it goes by a name which, denoting strictly the ability, implies the willingess to do *anything*; we accordingly call the Practically-Wise Clever, and also those who can and will do anything.

Now Practical Wisdom is not identical with Cleverness, nor is it without this power of adapting means to ends: but this Eye of the Soul (as we may call it) does not attain its proper state without goodness, as we have said before and as is quite plain, because the syllogisms into which Moral Action may be analysed have for their Major Premiss, "since —— is the End and the Chief Good" (fill up the blank with just anything you please, for we merely want to exhibit the Form, so that anything will do), but *how* this blank should be filled is seen only by the good man: because Vice distorts the moral vision and causes men to be deceived in respect of practical principles.

It is clear, therefore, that a man cannot be a Practically-Wise, without being a good, man.

We must inquire again also about Virtue: for it may be divided into Natural Virtue and Matured, which two bear to each other a relation similar to that which Practical Wisdom bears to Cleverness, one not of identity but resemblance. I speak of Natural Virtue, because men hold that each of the moral dispositions attach to us all somehow by nature: we have dispositions towards justice, self-mastery and courage, for instance, immediately from our birth: but still we seek Goodness in its highest sense as something distinct from these, and that these dispositions should attach to us in a somewhat different fashion. Children and brutes have these natural states, but then they are plainly hurtful unless combined with an intellectual element: at least thus much is matter of actual experience and observation, that as a strong body destitute of sight must, if set in motion, fall violently because it has not sight, so it is also in the case we are considering: but if it can get the intellectual element it then excels in acting. Just so the Natural State of Virtue, being like this strong body, will then be Virtue in the highest sense when it too is combined with the intellectual element.

So that, as in the case of the Opinionative faculty, there are two forms, Cleverness and Practical Wisdom; so also in the case of the Moral there are two, Natural Virtue and Matured; and of these the latter cannot be formed without Practical Wisdom.

This leads some to say that all the Virtues are merely intellectual Practical Wisdom, and Socrates was partly right in his inquiry and partly wrong: wrong in that he thought all the Virtues were merely intellectual Practical Wisdom, right in saying they were not independent of that faculty.

A proof of which is that now all, in defining Virtue, and on the "state" [mentioning also to what standard it has reference, namely that] "which is accordant with Right Reason:" now "right" means in accordance with Practical Wisdom. So then all seem to have an instinctive notion that that state which is in accordance with Practical Wisdom is Virtue; however, we must make a slight change in their statement, because that state is Virtue, not merely which is in accordance with but which implies the possession of Right Reason; which, upon such matters, is Practical Wisdom. The difference between us and Socrates is this: he thought the Virtues were reasoning processes (*i.e.* that they were all instances of Knowledge in its strict sense), but we say they imply the possession of Reason.

From what has been said then it is clear that one cannot be, strictly speaking, good without Practical Wisdom nor Practically-Wise without moral goodness.

And by the distinction between Natural and Matured Virtue one can meet the reasoning by which it might be argued "that the Virtues are separable because the same man is not by nature most inclined to all at once so that he will have acquired this one before he has that other:" we would reply that this is possible with respect to the Natural Virtues but not with respect to those in right of which a man is denominated simply good: because they will all belong to him together with the one faculty of Practical Wisdom.

It is plain too that even had it not been apt to act we should have needed it, because it is the Excellence of a part of the Soul; and that the moral choice cannot be right independently of Practical Wisdom and Moral Goodness; because this gives the right End, that causes the doing these things which conduce to the End.

Then again, it is not Master of Science (*i.e.* of the superior part of the Soul), just as neither is the healing art Master of health; for it does not make use of it, but looks how it may come to be: so it commands for the sake of it but does not command it.

The objection is, in fact, about as valid as if a man should say πολιτικὴ governs the gods because it gives orders about all things in the communty.

APPENDIX

On ἐπιστήμη, from I. Post. Analyt. chap. i. and ii.

(Such parts only are translated as throw light on the *Ethics*.)

ALL teaching, and all intellectual learning, proceeds on the basis of previous knowledge, as will appear on an examination of all. The Mathematical Sciences, and every other system, draw their conclusions in this method. So too of reasonings, whether by syllogism, or induction: for both teach through what is previously known, the former assuming the premisses as from wise men, the latter proving universals from the evidentness of the particulars. In like manner too rhetoricians persuade, either through examples (which amounts to induction), or through enthymemes (which amounts to syllogism).

Well, we suppose that we *know* things (in the strict and proper sense of the word) when we suppose ourselves to know the cause by reason of which the thing is to be the cause of it; and that this cannot be otherwise. It is plain that the idea intended to be conveyed by the term *knowing* is something of this kind; because they who do not really know suppose themselves thus related to the matter in hand and they who do know really are: so that of whatsoever there is properly speaking Knowledge this cannot be otherwise than it is. Whether or no there is another way of knowing we will say afterwards, but we do say that we know through demonstration; by which I mean a syllogism apt to produce Knowledge, *i.e.* in right of which, through having it, we know.

If Knowledge then is such as we have described it, the Knowledge produced by demonstrative reasoning must be drawn from premisses *true*, and *first*, and *incapable of syllogistic proof*, and *better known*, and *prior in order of time*, and *causes of the conclusion*; for so the principles will be akin to the conclusion demonstrated.

(Syllogism, of course, there may be without such premisses, but it will not be demonstration because it will not produce knowledge.)

True, they must be; because it is impossible to know that which is not.

First, that is indemonstrable; because, if demonstrable, he cannot be said to *know* them who has no demonstration of them: for knowing such things as are demonstrable is the same as having demonstration of them.

Causes they must be, and *better known*, and *prior* in time; *causes*, because we then know when we are acquainted with the cause; and *prior*, if causes; and *known beforehand*, not merely comprehended in idea but known to exist. (The terms prior, and better known, bear two senses: for *prior by nature* and *prior relatively to ourselves*, are not the same; nor *better known by nature*, and *better known to us*. I mean, by *prior*, and *better known relatively to ourselves*, such things as are nearer to sensation, but abstractedly so such as are further. Those are furthest which are most universal, those nearest which are particulars; and these are mutually opposed.)

And by *first*, I mean *principles akin to the conclusion*, for principle means the same as first. And the principle or first step in demonstration is a proposition incapable of syllogistic proof, *i.e.* one to which there is none prior. Now of such syllogistic principles I call that a θέσις which you cannot demonstrate, and which is unnecessary with a view to learning something else. That which is necessary in order to learn something else is an Axiom.

Further, since one is to believe and know the thing by having a syllogism of the kind called demonstration, and what constitutes it to be such is the nature of the premisses, it is necessary not merely to *know before*, but to *know better than the conclusion*, either all or at least some of, the principles; because that which is the cause of a quality inhering in something else always inheres itself more: as the cause of our loving is itself more lovable. So, since the principles are the cause of our knowing and believing, we know and believe them more, because by reason of them we know also the conclusion following.

Further: the man who is to have the Knowledge which comes through demonstration must not merely know and believe his principles better than he does his conclusion, but he must believe nothing more firmly than the contradictories of those principles out of which the contrary fallacy may be constructed: since he who *knows*, is to be simply and absolutely infallible.

BOOK VII

NEXT we must take a different point to start from, and observe that of what is to be avoided in respect of moral character there are three forms; Vice, Imperfect Self-Control, and Brutishness. Of the two former it is plain what the contraries are, for we call the one Virtue, the other Self-Control; and as answering to Brutishness it will be most suitable to assign Superhuman, *i.e.* heroical and godlike Virtue, as, in Homer, Priam says of Hector "that he was very excellent, nor was he like the offspring of mortal man, but of a god:" and so, if, as is commonly said, men are raised to the position of gods by reason of very high excellence in Virtue, the state opposed to the Brutish will plainly be of this nature: because as brutes are not virtuous or vicious so neither are gods; but the state of these is something more precious than Virtue, of the former something different in kind from Vice.

And as, on the one hand, it is a rare thing for a man to be godlike (a term the Lacedæmonians are accustomed to use when they admire a man exceedingly; σεῖος ἀνὴρ they call him), so the brutish man is rare; the character is found most among barbarians, and some cases of it are caused by disease or maiming; also such men as exceed in vice all ordinary measures we therefore designate by this opprobrious term. Well, we must in a subsequent place make some mention of this disposition, and Vice has been spoken of before: for the present we must speak of Imperfect Self-Control and its kindred faults of Softness and Luxury, on the one hand, and of Self-Control and Endurance on the other; since we are to conceive of them, not as being the same states exactly as Virtue and Vice respectively, nor again as differing in kind.

And we should adopt the same course as before, *i.e.* state the phænomena, and, after raising and discussing difficulties which suggest themselves, then exhibit, if possible, all the opinions afloat respecting these affections of the moral character; or, if not all, the greater part and the most important: for we may consider we have illustrated the matter sufficiently when the difficulties have been solved, and such theories as are most approved are left as a residuum.

The chief points may be thus enumerated. It is thought,

I. That Self-Control and Endurance belong to the class of things good and praiseworthy, while Imperfect Self-Control and Softness belong to that of things low and blameworthy.

II. That the man of Self-Control is identical with the man who is apt to abide by his resolution, and the man of Imperfect Self-Control with him who is apt to depart from his resolution.

III. That the man of Imperfect Self-Control does things at the instigation of his passions, knowing them to be wrong, while the man of Self-Control, knowing his lusts to be wrong, refuses, by the influence of reason, to follow their suggestions.

IV. That the man of Perfected Self-Mastery unites the qualities of Self-Control and Endurance, and some say that every one who unites these is a man of Perfect Self-Mastery, others do not.

V. Some confound the two characters of the man who has *no* Self-Control, and the man of *Imperfect* Self-Control, while others distinguish between them.

VI. It is sometimes said that the man of Practical Wisdom cannot be a man of Imperfect Self-Control, sometimes that men who are Practically Wise and Clever are of Imperfect Self-Control.

VII. Again, men are said to be of Imperfect Self-Control, not simply but with the addition of the thing wherein, as in respect of anger, of honour, and gain.

These then are pretty well the common statements.

Now a man may raise a question as to the nature of the right conception in violation of which a man fails of Self-Control.

That he can so fail when *knowing* in the strict sense what is right some say is impossible: for it is a strange thing, as Socrates thought, that while Knowledge is present in his mind something else should master him and drag him about like a slave. Socrates in fact contended generally against the theory, maintaining there is no such state as that of Imperfect Self-Control, for that no one acts contrary to what is best conceiving it to be best but by reason of ignorance what is best.

With all due respect to Socrates, his account of the matter is at variance with plain facts, and we must inquire with respect to the affection, if it be caused by ignorance what is the nature of the ignorance: for that the man so failing does not suppose his acts to be right before he is under the influence of passion is quite plain.

There are people who partly agree with Socrates and partly not: that nothing can be stronger than Knowledge they agree, but that no man acts in contravention of his conviction of what is better they do not agree; and so they say that it is not Knowledge, but only Opinion, which the man in question has and yet yields to the instigation of his pleasures.

But then, if it is Opinion and not Knowledge, that is if the opposing conception be not strong but only mild (as in the case of real doubt), the not abiding by it in the face of strong lusts would be excusable: but wickedness is not excusable, nor is anything which deserves blame.

Well then, is it Practical Wisdom which in this case offers opposition: for that is the strongest principle? The supposition is absurd, for we shall have the same man uniting Practical Wisdom and Imperfect Self-Control, and surely no single person would maintain that it is consistent with the character of Practical Wisdom to do voluntarily what is very wrong; and besides we have shown before that the very mark of a man of this character is aptitude to act, as distinguished from mere knowledge of what is right; because he is a man conversant with particular details, and possessed of all the other virtues.

Again, if the having strong and bad lusts is necessary to the idea of the man of Self-Control, this character cannot be identical with the man of Perfected Self-Mastery, because the having strong desires or bad ones does not enter into the idea of this latter character: and yet the man of Self-Control must have such: for suppose them good; then the moral state which should hinder a man from following their suggestions must be bad, and so Self-Control would not be in all cases good: suppose them on the other hand to be weak and not wrong, it would be nothing grand; nor anything great, supposing them to be wrong and weak.

Again, if Self-Control makes a man apt to abide by all opinions without exception, it may be bad, as suppose the case of a false opinion: and if Imperfect Self-Control makes a man apt to depart from all without exception, we shall have cases where it will be good; take that of Neoptolemus in the Philoctetes of Sophocles, for instance: he is to be praised for not abiding by what he was persuaded to by Ulysses, because he was pained at being guilty of falsehood.

Or again, false sophistical reasoning presents a difficulty: for because men wish to prove paradoxes that they may be counted clever when they succeed, the reasoning that has been used becomes a difficulty: for the intellect is fettered; a man being unwilling to abide by the conclusion because it does not please his judgment, but unable to advance because he cannot disentangle the web of sophistical reasoning.

Or again, it is conceivable on this supposition that folly joined with Imperfect Self-Control may turn out, in a given case, goodness: for by reason of his imperfection of self-control a man acts in a way which contradicts his notions; now his notion is that what is really good is bad and ought not to be done; and so he will eventually do what is good and not what is bad.

Again, on the same supposition, the man who acting on conviction pursues and chooses things because they are pleasant must be thought a better man than he who does so not by reason of a quasi-rational conviction but of Imperfect Self-Control: because he is more open to cure by reason of the possibility of his receiving a contrary conviction. But to the man of Imperfect Self-Control would apply the proverb, "when water chokes, what should a man drink then?" for had he never been convinced at all in respect of what he does, then by a conviction in a contrary direction he might have stopped in his course; but now though he has had convictions he notwithstanding acts against them.

Again, if any and every thing is the object-matter of Imperfect and Perfect Self-Control, who is the man of Imperfect Self-Control simply? because no one unites all cases of it, and we commonly say that some men are so simply, not adding any particular thing in which they are so.

Well, the difficulties raised are pretty near such as I have described them, and of these theories we must remove some and leave others as established; because the solving of a difficulty is a positive act of establishing something as true.

Now we must examine first whether men of Imperfect Self-Control act with a knowledge of what is right or not: next, if with such knowledge, in what sense; and next what are we to assume is the object-matter of the man of Imperfect Self-Control, and of the man of Self-Control; I mean, whether pleasure and pain of all kinds or certain definite ones; and as to Self-Control and Endurance, whether these are designations of the same character or different. And in like manner we must go into all questions which are connected with the present.

But the real starting point of the inquiry is, whether the two characters of Self-Control and Imperfect Self-Control are distinguished by their object-matter, or their respective relations to it. I mean, whether the man of Imperfect Self-Control is such simply by virtue of having such and such object-matter; or not, but by virtue of his being related to it in such and such a way, or by virtue of both: next, whether Self-Control and Imperfect Self-Control are unlimited in their object-matter: because he who is designated without any addition a man of

Imperfect Self-Control is not unlimited in his object-matter, but has exactly the same as the man who has lost all Self-Control: nor is he so designated because of his relation to this object-matter merely (for then his character would be identical with that just mentioned, loss of all Self-Control), but because of his relation to it being such and such. For the man who has lost all Self-Control is led on with deliberate moral choice, holding that it is his line to pursue pleasure as it rises: while the man of Imperfect Self-Control does not think that he ought to pursue it, but does pursue it all the same.

Now as to the notion that it is True Opinion and not Knowledge in contravention of which men fail in Self-Control, it makes no difference to the point in question, because some of those who hold Opinions have no doubt about them but suppose themselves to have accurate Knowledge; if then it is urged that men holding opinions will be more likely than men who have Knowledge to act in contravention of their conceptions, as having but a moderate belief in them; we reply, Knowledge will not differ in this respect from Opinion: because some men believe their own Opinions no less firmly than others do their positive Knowledge: Heraclitus is a case in point.

Rather the following is the account of it: the term *knowing* has two senses; both the man who does not use his Knowledge, and he who does, are said to *know*: there will be a difference between a man's acting wrongly, who though possessed of Knowledge does not call it into operation, and his doing so who has it and actually exercises it: the latter is a strange case, but the mere having, if not exercising, presents no anomaly.

Again, as there are two kinds of propositions affecting action, universal and particular, there is no reason why a man may not act against his Knowledge, having both propositions in his mind, using the universal but not the particular, for the particulars are the objects of moral action.

There is a difference also in universal propositions; a universal proposition may relate partly to a man's self and partly to the thing in question: take the following for instance; "dry food is good for every man," this may have the two minor premisses, "this is a man," and "so and so is dry food;" but whether a given substance is so and so a man either has not the Knowledge or does not exert it. According to these different senses there will be an immense difference, so that for a man to *know* in the one sense, and yet act wrongly, would be nothing strange, but in any of the other senses it would be a matter for wonder.

Again, men may have Knowledge in a way different from any of those which have been now stated: for we constantly see a man's state so differing by having and not using Knowledge, that he has it in a sense and also has not; when a man is asleep, for instance, or mad, or drunk: well, men under the actual operation of passion are in exactly similar conditions; for anger, lust, and some other such-like things, manifestly make changes even in the body, and in some they even cause madness; it is plain then that we must say the men of Imperfect Self-Control are in a state similar to these.

And their saying what embodies Knowledge is no proof of their actually then exercising it, because they who are under the operation of these passions repeat demonstrations; or verses of Empedocles, just as children, when first learning, string words together, but as yet know nothing of their meaning, because they must grow into it, and this is a process requiring time: so that we must suppose these men who fail in Self-Control to say these moral sayings just as actors do.

Furthermore, a man may look at the account of the phænomenon in the following way, from an examination of the actual working of the mind: All action may be analysed into a syllogism, in which the one premiss is an universal maxim and the other concerns particulars of which Sense [moral or physical, as the case may be] is cognisant: now when one results from these two, it follows necessarily that, as far as theory goes the mind must assert the conclusion, and in practical propositions the man must act accordingly.

For instance, let the universal be, "All that is sweet should be tasted," the particular, "This is sweet;" it follows necessarily that he who is able and is not hindered should not only draw, but put in practice, the conclusion "This is to be tasted." When then there is in the mind one universal proposition forbidding to taste, and the other "All that is sweet is pleasant" with its minor "This is sweet" (which is the one that really works), and desire happens to be in the man, the first universal bids him avoid this but the desire leads him on to taste; for it has the power of moving the various organs: and so it results that he fails in Self-Control, in a certain sense under the influence of Reason and Opinion not contrary in itself to Reason but only accidentally so; because it is the desire that is contrary to Right Reason, but not the Opinion: and so for this reason brutes are not accounted of Imperfect Self-Control, because they have no power of conceiving universals but only of receiving and retaining particular impressions.

As to the manner in which the ignorance is removed and the man of Imperfect Self-Control recovers his Knowledge, the account is the same as with respect to him who is drunk or asleep, and is not peculiar to this affection, so physiologists are the right people to apply to. But whereas the minor premiss of every practical syllogism is an opinion on matter cognisable by Sense and determines the actions; he who is under the influence of passion either has not this, or so has it that his having does not amount to *knowing* but merely saying, as a man when drunk might repeat Empedocles' verses; and because the minor term is neither universal, nor is thought to have the power of producing Knowledge in like manner as the universal term: and so the result which Socrates was seeking comes out, that is to say, the affection does not take place in the presence of that which is thought to be specially and properly Knowledge, nor is this dragged about by reason of the affection, but in the presence of that Knowledge which is conveyed by Sense.

Let this account then be accepted of the question respecting the failure in Self-Control, whether it is with Knowledge or not; and, if with knowledge, with what kind of knowledge such failure is possible.

The next question to be discussed is whether there is a character to be designated by the term "of Imperfect Self-Control" simply, or whether all who are so are to be accounted such, in respect of some particular thing; and, if there is such a character, what is his object-matter.

Now that pleasures and pains are the object-matter of men of Self-Control and of Endurance, and also of men of Imperfect Self-Control and Softness, is plain.

Further, things which produce pleasure are either necessary, or objects of choice in themselves but yet admitting of excess. All bodily things which produce pleasure are necessary; and I call such those which relate to food and other grosser appetites, in short such bodily things as we assumed were the Object-matter of absence of Self-Control and of Perfected Self-Mastery.

The other class of objects are not necessary, but objects of choice in themselves: I mean, for instance, victory, honour, wealth, and such-like good or pleasant things. And those who are excessive in their liking for such things contrary to the principle of Right Reason which is in their own breasts we do not designate men of Imperfect Self-Control simply, but with the addition of the thing wherein, as in respect of money, or gain, or honour, or anger, and not simply; because we consider them as different characters and only having that title in right of a kind of resemblance (as when we add to a man's name "conqueror in the Olympic games" the account of him as Man differs but little from the account of him as the Man who conquered in the Olympic games, but still it is different). And a proof of the real difference between these so designated with an addition and those simply so called is this, that Imperfect Self-Control is blamed, not as an error merely but also as being a vice, either wholly or partially; but none of these other cases is so blamed.

But of those who have for their object-matter the bodily enjoyments, which we say are also the object-matter of the man of Perfected Self-Mastery and the man who has lost all Self-Control, he that pursues excessive pleasures and too much avoids things which are painful (as hunger and thirst, heat and cold, and everything connected with touch and taste), not from moral choice but in spite of his moral choice and intellectual conviction, is termed "a man of Imperfect Self-Control," not with the addition of any particular object-matter as we do in respect of want of control of anger but simply.

And a proof that the term is thus applied is that the kindred term "Soft" is used in respect of these enjoyments but not in respect of any of those others. And for this reason we put into the same rank the man of Imperfect Self-Control, the man who has lost it entirely, the man who has it, and the man of Perfected Self-Mastery; but not any of those other characters, because the former have for their object-matter the same pleasures and pains: but though they have the same object-matter, they are not related to it in the same way, but two of them act upon moral choice, two without it. And so we should say that man is more entirely given up to his passions who pursues excessive pleasures, and avoids moderate pains, being either not at all, or at least but little, urged by desire, than the man who does so because his desire is very strong: because we think what would the former be likely to do if he had the additional stimulus of youthful lust and violent pain consequent on the want of those pleasures which we have denominated necessary?

Well then, since of desires and pleasures there are some which are in kind honourable and good (because things pleasant are divisible, as we said before, into such as are naturally objects of choice, such as are naturally objects of avoidance, and such as are in themselves indifferent, money, gain, honour, victory, for instance); in respect of all such and those that are indifferent, men are blamed not merely for being affected by or desiring or liking them, but for exceeding in any way in these feelings.

And so they are blamed, whosoever in spite of Reason are mastered by, that is pursue, any object, though in its nature noble and good; they, for instance, who are more earnest than they should be respecting honour, or their children or parents; not but what these are good objects and men are praised for being earnest about them: but still they admit of excess; for instance, if any one, as Niobe did, should fight even against the gods, or feel towards his father as Satyrus, who got therefrom the nickname of φιλοπάτωρ, because he was thought to be very foolish.

Now depravity there is none in regard of these things, for the reason assigned above, that each of them in itself is a thing naturally choice-worthy, yet the excesses in respect of them are wrong and matter for blame: and similarly there is no Imperfect Self-Control in respect of these things; that being not merely a thing that should be avoided but blameworthy.

But because of the resemblance of the affection to the Imperfection of Self-Control the term is used with the addition in each case of the particular object-matter, just as men call a man a bad physician, or bad actor, whom they would not think of calling simply bad. As then in these cases we do not apply the term simply because each of the states is not a vice, but only like a vice in the way of analogy, so it is plain that in respect of Imperfect Self-Control and Self-Control we must limit the names to those states which have the same object-matter as Perfected Self-Mastery and utter loss of Self-Control, and that we do apply it to the case of anger only in the way of resemblance: for which reason, with an addition, we designate a man of Imperfect Self-Control in respect of anger, as of honour or of gain.

As there are some things naturally pleasant, and of these two kinds; those, namely, which are pleasant generally, and those which are so rel-atively to particular kinds of animals and men; so there are others which are not naturally pleasant but which come to be so in conse-quence either of maimings, or custom, or depraved natural tastes: and one may observe moral states similar to those we have been speaking of, having respectively these classes of things for their object-matter.

I mean the Brutish, as in the case of the female who, they say, would rip up women with child and eat the fœtus; or the tastes which are found among the savage tribes bordering on the Pontus, some liking raw flesh, and some being cannibals, and some lending one another their children to make feasts of; or what is said of Phalaris. These are instances of Brutish states, caused in some by disease or madness; take, for instance, the man who sacrificed and ate his mother, or him who devoured the liver of his fellow-servant. Instances again of those caused by disease or by custom, would be, plucking out of hair, or eating one's nails, or eating coals and earth. . . . Now wherever nature is really the cause no one would think of calling men of Imperfect Self-Control, . . . nor, in like manner, such as are in a diseased state through custom.

Obviously the having any of these inclinations is something foreign to what is denominated Vice, just as Brutishness is: and when a man has them his mastering them is not properly Self-Control, nor his being mastered by them Imperfection of Self-Control in the proper sense, but only in the way of resemblance; just as we may say a man of ungovernable wrath fails of Self-Control in respect of anger but not simply fails of Self-Control. For all excessive folly, cowardice, absence of Self-Control, or irritability, are either Brutish or morbid. The man, for instance, who is naturally afraid of all things, even if a mouse should stir, is cowardly after a Brutish sort; there was a man again who, by reason of disease, was afraid of a cat: and of the fools, they who are naturally destitute of Reason and live only by Sense are Brutish, as are some tribes of the far-off barbarians, while others who are so by reason of diseases, epileptic or frantic, are in morbid states.

So then, of these inclinations, a man may sometimes merely have one without yielding to it: I mean, suppose that Phalaris had restrained his unnatural desire to eat a child: or he may both have and yield to it. As then Vice when such as belongs to human nature is called Vice simply, while the other is so called with the addition of "brutish" or "morbid," but not simply Vice, so manifestly there is Brutish and Morbid Imperfection of Self-Control, but that alone is entitled to the name without any qualification which is of the nature of utter absence of Self-Control, as it is found in Man.

It is plain then that the object-matter of Imperfect Self-Control and Self-Control is restricted to the same as that of utter absence of Self-Control and that of Perfected Self-Mastery, and that the rest is the object-matter of a different species so named metaphorically and not simply: we will now examine the position, "that Imperfect Self-Control in respect of Anger is less disgraceful than that in respect of Lusts."

In the first place, it seems that Anger does in a way listen to Reason but mishears it; as quick servants who run out before they have heard the whole of what is said and then mistake the order; dogs, again, bark at the slightest stir, before they have seen whether it be friend or foe; just so Anger, by reason of its natural heat and quickness, listening to Reason, but without having heard the command of Reason, rushes to its revenge. That is to say, Reason or some impression on the mind shows there is insolence or contempt in the offender, and then Anger, reasoning as it were that one ought to fight against what is such, fires up immediately: whereas Lust, if Reason or Sense, as the case may be, merely says a thing is sweet, rushes to the enjoyment of it: and so Anger follows Reason in a manner, but Lust does not and is therefore more disgraceful: because he that cannot control his anger yields in a manner to Reason, but the other to his Lust and not to Reason at all.

Again, a man is more excusable for following such desires as are natural, just as he is for following such Lusts as are common to all and to that degree in which they are common. Now Anger and irritability are more natural than Lusts when in excess and for objects not necessary. (This was the ground of the defence the man made who beat his father. "My father," he said, "used to beat his, and his father his again, and this little fellow here," pointing to his child, "will beat me when he is grown a man: it runs in the family." And the father, as he was being dragged along, bid his son leave off beating him at the door, because he had himself been used to drag his father so far and no farther.)

Again, characters are less unjust in proportion as they involve less insidiousness. Now the Angry man is not insidious, nor is Anger, but quite open: but Lust is: as they say of Venus,

> "Cyprus-born Goddess, *weaver of deceits*."

Or Homer of the girdle called the Cestus,

> "Persuasiveness *cheating* e'en the subtlest mind."

And so since this kind of Imperfect Self-Control is more unjust, it is also more disgraceful than that in respect of Anger, and is simply Imperfect Self-Control, and Vice in a certain sense.

Again, no man feels pain in being insolent, but every one who acts through Anger does act with pain; and he who acts insolently does it with pleasure. If then those things are most unjust with which we have most right to be angry, then Imperfect Self-Control, arising from Lust, is more so than that arising from Anger: because in Anger there is no insolence.

Well then, it is clear that Imperfect Self-Control in respect of Lusts is more disgraceful than that in respect of Anger and that the object-matter of Self-Control, and the Imperfection of it, are bodily Lusts and pleasures; but of these last we must take into account the differences; for, as was said at the commencement, some are proper to the human race and natural both in kind and degree, others Brutish, and others caused by maimings and diseases.

Now the first of these only are the object-matter of Perfected Self-

Mastery and utter absence of Self-Control; and therefore we never attribute either of these states to Brutes (except metaphorically, and whenever any one kind of animal differs entirely from another in insolence, mischievousness, or voracity), because they have not moral choice or process of deliberation, but are quite different from that kind of creature just as are madmen from other men.

Brutishness is not so low in the scale as Vice, yet it is to be regarded with more fear: because it is not that the highest principle has been corrupted, as in the human creature, but the subject has it not at all.

It is much the same, therefore, as if one should compare an inanimate with an animate being, which were the worse: for the badness of that which has no principle of origination is always less harmful; now Intellect is a principle of origination. A similar case would be the comparing injustice and an unjust man together: for in different ways each is the worst: a bad man would produce ten thousand times as much harm as a bad brute.

Now with respect to the pleasures and pains which come to a man through Touch and Taste, and the desiring or avoiding such (which we determined before to constitute the object-matter of the states of utter absence of Self-Control and Perfected Self-Mastery), one may be so disposed as to yield to temptations to which most men would be superior, or to be superior to those to which most men would yield: in respect of pleasures, these characters will be respectively the man of Imperfect Self-Control, and the man of Self-Control; and, in respect of pains, the man of Softness and the man of Endurance: but the moral state of most men is something between the two, even though they lean somewhat to the worse characters.

Again, since of the pleasures indicated some are necessary and some are not, others are so to a certain degree but not the excess or defect of them, and similarly also of Lusts and pains, the man who pursues the excess of pleasant things, or such as are in themselves excess, or from moral choice, for their own sake, and not for anything else which is to result from them, is a man utterly void of Self-Control: for he must be incapable of remorse, and so incurable, because he that has not remorse is incurable. (He that has too little love of pleasure is the opposite character, and the man of Perfected Self-Mastery the mean character.) He is of a similar character who avoids the bodily pains, not because he *cannot*, but because he *chooses not to*, withstand them.

But of the characters who go wrong without *choosing* so to do, the one is led on by reason of pleasure, the other because he avoids the pain it would cost him to deny his lust; and so they are different the one

from the other. Now every one would pronounce a man worse for
doing something base without any impulse of desire, or with a very
slight one, than for doing the same from the impulse of a very strong
desire; for striking a man when not angry than if he did so in wrath: because one naturally says, "What would he have done had he been
under the influence of passion?" (and on this ground, by the bye, the
man utterly void of Self-Control is worse than he who has it imper-
fectly). However, of the two characters which have been mentioned [as
included in that of utter absence of Self-Control], the one is rather
Softness, the other properly the man of no Self-Control.

Furthermore, to the character of Imperfect Self-Control is opposed
that of Self-Control, and to that of Softness that of Endurance: because
Endurance consists in continued resistance but Self-Control in actual
mastery, and continued resistance and actual mastery are as different as
not being conquered is from conquering; and so Self-Control is more
choiceworthy than Endurance.

Again, he who fails when exposed to those temptations against which
the common run of men hold out, and are well able to do so, is Soft
and Luxurious (Luxury being a kind of Softness): the kind of man, I
mean, to let his robe drag in the dirt to avoid the trouble of lifting it,
and who, aping the sick man, does not however suppose himself
wretched though he is like a wretched man. So it is too with respect to
Self-Control and the Imperfection of it: if a man yields to pleasures or
pains which are violent and excessive it is no matter for wonder, but
rather for allowance if he made what resistance he could (instances
are, Philoctetes in Theodectes' drama when wounded by the viper; or
Cercyon in the Alope of Carcinus, or men who in trying to suppress
laughter burst into a loud continuous fit of it, as happened, you remember, to Xenophantus), but it is a matter for wonder when a man
yields to and cannot contend against those pleasures or pains which the
common herd are able to resist; always supposing his failure not to be
owing to natural constitution or disease, I mean, as the Scythian kings
are constitutionally Soft, or the natural difference between the sexes.

Again, the man who is a slave to amusement is commonly thought
to be destitute of Self-Control, but he really is Soft; because amusement is an act of relaxing, being an act of resting, and the character in
question is one of those who exceed due bounds in respect of this.

Moreover of Imperfect Self-Control there are two forms, Pre-
cipitancy and Weakness: those who have it in the latter form though
they have made resolutions do not abide by them by reason of passion;
the others are led by passion because they have never formed any reso-

lutions at all: while there are some who, like those who by tickling themselves beforehand get rid of ticklishness, having felt and seen beforehand the approach of temptation, and roused up themselves and their resolution, yield not to passion; whether the temptation be somewhat pleasant or somewhat painful. The Precipitate form of Imperfect Self-Control they are most liable to who are constitutionally of a sharp or melancholy temperament: because the one by reason of the swiftness, the other by reason of the violence, of their passions, do not wait for Reason, because they are disposed to follow whatever notion is impressed upon their minds.

Again, the man utterly destitute of Self-Control, as was observed before, is not given to remorse: for it is part of his character that he abides by his moral choice: but the man of Imperfect Self-Control is almost made up of remorse: and so the case is not as we determined it before, but the former is incurable and the latter may be cured: for depravity is like chronic diseases, dropsy and consumption for instance, but Imperfect Self-Control is like acute disorders: the former being a continuous evil, the latter not so. And, in fact, Imperfect Self-Control and Confirmed Vice are different in kind: the latter being imperceptible to its victim, the former not so.

But, of the different forms of Imperfect Self-Control, those are better who are carried off their feet by a sudden access of temptation than they who have Reason but do not abide by it; these last being overcome by passion less in degree, and not wholly without premeditation as are the others: for the man of Imperfect Self-Control is like those who are soon intoxicated and by little wine and less than the common run of men.

Well then, that Imperfection of Self-Control is not Confirmed Viciousness is plain: and yet perhaps it is such in a way, because in one sense it is contrary to moral choice and in another the result of it: at all events, in respect of the actions, the case is much like what Demodocus said of the Miletians. "The people of Miletus are not fools, but they do just the kind of things that fools do;" and so they of Imperfect Self-Control are not unjust, but they do unjust acts.

But to resume. Since the man of Imperfect Self-Control is of such a character as to follow bodily pleasures in excess and in defiance of Right Reason, without acting on any deliberate conviction, whereas the man utterly destitute of Self-Control does act upon a conviction which rests on his natural inclination to follow after these pleasures; the former may be easily persuaded to a different course, but the latter not: for Virtue and Vice respectively preserve and corrupt the moral principle;

now the motive is the principle or starting point in moral actions, just as axioms and postulates are in mathematics: and neither in morals nor mathematics is it Reason which is apt to teach the principle; but Excellence, either natural or acquired by custom, in holding right notions with respect to the principle. He who does this in morals is the man of Perfected Self-Mastery, and the contrary character is the man utterly destitute of Self-Control.

Again, there is a character liable to be taken off his feet in defiance of Right Reason because of passion; whom passion so far masters as to prevent his acting in accordance with Right Reason, but not so far as to make him be convinced that it is his proper line to follow after such pleasures without limit: this character is the man of Imperfect Self-Control, better than he who is utterly destitute of it, and not a bad man simply and without qualification: because in him the highest and best part, *i.e.* principle, is preserved: and there is another character opposed to him who is apt to abide by his resolutions, and not to depart from them; at all events, not at the instigation of passion.

It is evident then from all this, that Self-Control is a good state and the Imperfection of it a bad one.

Next comes the question, whether a man is a man of Self-Control for abiding by his conclusions and moral choice be they of what kind they may, or only by the right one; or again, a man of Imperfect Self-Control for not abiding by his conclusions and moral choice be they of whatever kind; or, to put the case we did before, is he such for not abiding by false conclusions and wrong moral choice?

Is not this the truth, that *incidentally* it is by conclusions and moral choice of any kind that the one character abides and the other does not, but *per se* true conclusions and right moral choice: to explain what is meant by incidentally, and *per se*; suppose a man chooses or pursues this thing for the sake of that, he is said to pursue and choose that *per se*, but this only incidentally. For the term *per se* we use commonly the word "simply," and so, in a way, it is opinion of any kind soever by which the two characters respectively abide or not, but he is "simply" entitled to the designations who abides or not by the true opinion.

There are also people, who have a trick of abiding by their own opinions, who are commonly called Positive, as they who are hard to be persuaded, and whose convictions are not easily changed: now these people bear some resemblance to the character of Self-Control, just as the prodigal to the liberal or the rash man to the brave, but they are different in many points. The man of Self-Control does not change by reason of passion and lust, yet when occasion so requires he will be easy of persuasion: but the Positive man changes not at the call of Reason, though many of this class take up certain desires and are led by their pleasures. Among the class of Positive are the Opinionated, the Ignorant, and the Bearish: the first, from the motives of pleasure and pain: I mean, they have the pleasurable feeling of a kind of victory in not having their convictions changed, and they are pained when their decrees, so to speak, are reversed; so that, in fact, they rather resemble the man of Imperfect Self-Control than the man of Self-Control.

Again, there are some who depart from their resolutions not by reason of any Imperfection of Self-Control; take, for instance, Neoptolemus in the Philoctetes of Sophocles. Here certainly pleasure was the motive of his departure from his resolution, but then it was one of a noble sort: for to be truthful was noble in his eyes and he had been persuaded by Ulysses to lie.

So it is not every one who acts from the motive of pleasure who is utterly destitute of Self-Control or base or of Imperfect Self-Control, only he who acts from the impulse of a base pleasure.

Moreover as there is a character who takes less pleasure than he ought in bodily enjoyments, and he also fails to abide by the conclusion of his Reason, the man of Self-Control is the mean between him and the man of Imperfect Self-Control: that is to say, the latter fails to abide by them because of somewhat too much, the former because of somewhat too little; while the man of Self-Control abides by them, and never changes by reason of anything else than such conclusions.

Now of course since Self-Control is good both the contrary States must be bad, as indeed they plainly are: but because the one of them is seen in few persons, and but rarely in them, Self-Control comes to be viewed as if opposed only to the Imperfection of it, just as Perfected Self-Mastery is thought to be opposed only to utter want of Self-Control.

Again, as many terms are used in the way of similitude, so people have come to talk of the Self-Control of the man of Perfected Self-Mastery in the way of similitude: for the man of Self-Control and the man of Perfected Self-Mastery have this in common, that they do nothing against Right Reason on the impulse of bodily pleasures, but then the former has bad desires, the latter not; and the latter is so constituted as not even to feel pleasure contrary to his Reason, the former feels but does not yield to it.

Like again are the man of Imperfect Self-Control and he who is utterly destitute of it, though in reality distinct: both follow bodily pleasures, but the latter under a notion that it is the proper line for him to take, the former without any such notion.

And it is not possible for the same man to be at once a man of Practical Wisdom and of Imperfect Self-Control: because the character of Practical Wisdom includes, as we showed before, goodness of moral character. And again, it is not knowledge merely, but aptitude for action, which constitutes Practical Wisdom: and of this aptitude the man of Imperfect Self-Control is destitute. But there is no reason why the Clever man should not be of Imperfect Self-Control: and the reason why some men are occasionally thought to be men of Practical Wisdom, and yet of Imperfect Self-Control, is this, that Cleverness differs from Practical Wisdom in the way I stated in a former book, and is very near it so far as the intellectual element is concerned but differs in respect of the moral choice.

Nor is the man of Imperfect Self-Control like the man who both has and calls into exercise his knowledge, but like the man who, having it, is overpowered by sleep or wine. Again, he acts voluntarily (because he knows, in a certain sense, what he does and the result of it), but he is not a confirmed bad man, for his moral choice is good, so he is at all events only half bad. Nor is he unjust, because he does not act with deliberate intent: for of the two chief forms of the character, the one is not apt to abide by his deliberate resolutions, and the other, the man of constitutional strength of passion, is not apt to deliberate at all.

So in fact the man of Imperfect Self-Control is like a community which makes all proper enactments, and has admirable laws, only does not act on them, verifying the scoff of Anaxandrides,

"That State did will it, which cares nought for laws;"

whereas the bad man is like one which acts upon its laws, but then unfortunately they are bad ones.

Imperfection of Self-Control and Self-Control, after all, are above the average state of men; because he of the latter character is more true to his Reason, and the former less so, than is in the power of most men.

Again, of the two forms of Imperfect Self-Control that is more easily cured which they have who are constitutionally of strong passions, than that of those who form resolutions and break them; and they that are so through habituation than they that are so naturally; since of course custom is easier to change than nature, because the very resemblance of custom to nature is what constitutes the difficulty of changing it; as Evenus says,

"Practice, I say, my friend, doth long endure,
And at the last is even very nature."

We have now said then what Self-Control is, what Imperfection of Self-Control, what Endurance, and what Softness, and how these states are mutually related.

To consider the subject of Pleasure and Pain falls within the province of the Social-Science Philosopher, since he it is who has to fix the Master-End which is to guide us in dominating any object absolutely evil or good.

But we may say more: an inquiry into their nature is absolutely necessary. First, because we maintained that Moral Virtue and Moral Vice are both concerned with Pains and Pleasures: next, because the greater part of mankind assert that Happiness must include Pleasure (which by the way accounts for the word they use, μακάριος; χαίρειν being the root of that word).

Now some hold that no one Pleasure is good, either in itself or as a matter of result, because God and Pleasure are not identical. Others that some Pleasures are good but the greater number bad. There is yet a third view; granting that every Pleasure is good, still the Chief Good cannot possibly be Pleasure.

In support of the first opinion (that Pleasure is utterly not-good) it is urged that:

1. Every Pleasure is a sensible process towards a complete state; but no such process is akin to the end to be attained: e.g. no process of building to the completed house.

2. The man of Perfected Self-Mastery avoids Pleasures.

3. The man of Practical Wisdom aims at avoiding Pain, not at attaining Pleasure.

4. Pleasures are an impediment to thought, and the more so the more keenly they are felt. An obvious instance will readily occur.

5. Pleasure cannot be referred to any Art: and yet every good is the result of some Art.

6. Children and brutes pursue Pleasures.

In support of the second (that not all Pleasures are good), That there are some base and matter of reproach, and some even hurtful: because some things that are pleasant produce disease.

In support of the third (that Pleasure is not the Chief Good), That it is not an End but a process towards creating an End.

This is, I think, a fair account of current views on the matter.

But that the reasons alleged do not prove it either to be not-good or the Chief Good is plain from the following considerations.

First. Good being either absolute or relative, of course the natures and states embodying it will be so too; therefore also the movements and the processes of creation. So, of those which are thought to be bad some will be bad absolutely, but relatively not bad, perhaps even choice-worthy; some not even choice-worthy relatively to any particular person, only at certain times or for a short time but not in themselves choice-worthy.

Others again are not even Pleasures at all though they produce that impression on the mind: all such I mean as imply pain and whose purpose is cure; those of sick people, for instance.

Next, since Good may be either an active working or a state, those [κινήσεις or γενέσεις] which tend to place us in our natural state are pleasant incidentally because of that tendency: but the active working is really in the desires excited in the remaining (sound) part of our state or nature: for there are Pleasures which have no connection with pain or desire: the acts of contemplative intellect, for instance, in which case there is no deficiency in the nature or state of him who performs the acts.

A proof of this is that the same pleasant thing does not produce the sensation of Pleasure when the natural state is being filled up or completed as when it is already in its normal condition: in this latter case what give the sensation are things pleasant *per se*, in the former even those things which are contrary. I mean, you find people taking pleasure in sharp or bitter things of which no one is naturally or in itself pleasant; of course not therefore the Pleasures arising from them, because it is obvious that as is the classification of pleasant things such must be that of the Pleasures arising from them.

Next, it does not follow that there must be something else better than any given pleasure because (as some say) the End must be better than the process which creates it. For it is not true that all Pleasures are processes or even attended by any process, but (some are) active workings or even Ends: in fact they result not from our coming to be something but from our using our powers. Again, it is not true that the End is, in every case, distinct from the process: it is true only in the case of such processes as conduce to the perfecting of the natural state.

For which reason it is wrong to say that Pleasure is "a sensible process of production." For "process etc." should be substituted "active working of the natural stage," for "sensible" "unimpeded." The reason of its being thought to be a "process etc." is that it is good in the highest sense: people confusing "active working" and "process," whereas they really are distinct.

Next, as to the argument that there are bad pleasures because some things which are pleasant are also hurtful to health, it is the same as saying that some healthful things are bad for "business." In this sense, of course, both may be said to be bad, but then this does not make them out to be bad *simpliciter*: the exercise of the pure Intellect sometimes hurts a man's health: but what hinders Practical Wisdom or any state whatever is, not the Pleasure peculiar to, but some Pleasure foreign to it: the Pleasures arising from the exercise of the pure Intellect or from learning only promote each.

Next. "No Pleasure is the work of any Art." What else would you expect? No active working is the work of any Art, only the faculty of so working. Still the perfumer's Art or the cook's are thought to belong to Pleasure.

Next. "The man of Perfected Self-Mastery avoids Pleasures." "The man of Practical Wisdom aims at escaping Pain rather than at attaining Pleasure."

"Children and brutes pursue Pleasures."

One answer will do for all.

We have already said in what sense all Pleasures are good *per se* and in what sense not all are good: it is the latter class that brutes and children pursue, such as are accompanied by desire and pain, that is the bodily Pleasures (which answer to this description) and the excesses of them: in short, those in respect of which the man utterly destitute of Self-Control is thus utterly destitute. And it is the absence of the pain arising from these Pleasures that the man of Practical Wisdom aims at. It follows that these Pleasures are what the man of Perfected Self-Mastery avoids: for obviously he has Pleasures peculiarly his own.

Then again, it is allowed that Pain is an evil and a thing to be avoided partly as bad *per se*, partly as being a hindrance in some particular way. Now the contrary of that which is to be avoided, *qua* it is to be avoided, *i.e.* evil, is good. Pleasure then must be *a* good.

The attempted answer of Speusippus, "that Pleasure may be opposed and yet not contrary to Pain, just as the greater portion of any magnitude is contrary to the less but only opposed to the exact half," will not hold: for he cannot say that Pleasure is identical with evil of any kind.

Again. Granting that some Pleasures are low, there is no reason why some particular Pleasure may not be very good, just as some particular Science may be although there are some which are low.

Perhaps it even follows, since each state may have active working unimpeded, whether the active workings of all be Happiness or that of some one of them, that this active working, if it be unimpeded, must be choiceworthy: now Pleasure is exactly this. So that the Chief Good may be Pleasure of some kind, though most Pleasures be (let us assume) low *per se*.

And for this reason all men think the happy life is pleasant, and interweave Pleasure with Happiness. Reasonably enough: because Happiness is perfect, but no impeded active working is perfect; and therefore the happy man needs as an addition the goods of the body and the goods external and fortune that in these points he may not be fettered. As for those who say that he who is being tortured on the wheel, or falls into great misfortunes is happy provided only he be good, they talk nonsense, whether they mean to do so or not. On the other hand, because fortune is needed as an addition, some hold good fortune to be identical with Happiness: which it is not, for even this in excess is a hindrance, and perhaps then has no right to be called good fortune since it is good only in so far as it contributes to Happiness.

The fact that all animals, brute and human alike, pursue Pleasure, is some presumption of its being in a sense the Chief Good;

("There must be something in what most folks say,") only as one and the same nature or state neither is nor is thought to be the best, so neither do all pursue the same Pleasure, Pleasure nevertheless all do. Nay further, what they pursue is, perhaps, not what they think nor what they would say they pursue, but really one and the same: for in all there is some instinct above themselves. But the bodily Pleasures have received the name exclusively, because theirs is the most frequent form and that which is universally partaken of; and so, because to many these alone are known they believe them to be the only ones which exist.

It is plain too that, unless Pleasure and its active working be good, it will not be true that the happy man's life embodies Pleasure: for why will he want it on the supposition that it is not good and that he can live even with Pain? because, assuming that Pleasure is not good, then Pain is neither evil nor good, and so why should he avoid it?

Besides, the life of the good man is not more pleasurable than any other unless it be granted that his active workings are so too.

Some inquiry into the bodily Pleasures is also necessary for those who say that some Pleasures, to be sure, are highly choice-worthy (the good ones to wit), but not the bodily Pleasures; that is, those which are the object-matter of the man utterly destitute of Self-Control.

If so, we ask, why are the contrary Pains bad? they cannot be (on their assumption) because the contrary of bad is good.

May we not say that the necessary bodily Pleasures are good in the sense in which that which is not-bad is good? or that they are good only up to a certain point? because such states or movements as cannot have too much of the better cannot have too much of Pleasure, but those which can of the former can also of the latter. Now the bodily Pleasures do admit of excess: in fact the low bad man is such because he pursues the excess of them instead of those which are necessary (meat, drink, and the objects of other animal appetites do give pleasure to all, but not in right manner or degree to all). But his relation to Pain is exactly the contrary: it is not excessive Pain, but Pain at all, that he avoids [which makes him to be in this way too a bad low man], because only in the case of him who pursues excessive Pleasure is Pain contrary to excessive Pleasure.

It is not enough however merely to state the truth, we should also show how the false view arises; because this strengthens conviction. I mean, when we have given a probable reason why that impresses people as true which really is not true, it gives them a stronger conviction of the truth. And so we must now explain why the bodily Pleasures appear to people to be more choiceworthy than any others.

The first obvious reason is, that bodily Pleasure drives out Pain; and because Pain is felt in excess men pursue Pleasure in excess, *i.e.* generally bodily Pleasure, under the notion of its being a remedy for that Pain. These remedies, moreover, come to be violent ones; which is the very reason they are pursued, since the impression they produce on the mind is owing to their being looked at side by side with their contrary.

And, as has been said before, there are the two following reasons why bodily Pleasure is thought to be not-good.

1. Some Pleasures of this class are actings of a low nature, whether congenital as in brutes, or acquired by custom as in low bad men.

2. Others are in the nature of cures, cures that is of some deficiency; now of course it is better to have [the healthy state] originally than that it should accrue afterwards.

But some Pleasures result when natural states are being perfected: these therefore are good as a matter of result.

Again, the very fact of their being violent causes them to be pursued by such as can relish no others: such men in fact create violent thirsts for themselves (if harmless ones then we find no fault, if harmful then it is bad and low) because they have no other things to take pleasure in, and the neutral state is distasteful to some people constitutionally; for toil of some kind is inseparable from life, as physiologists testify, telling us that the acts of seeing or hearing are painful, only that we are used to the pain and do not find it out.

Similarly in youth the constant growth produces a state much like that of vinous intoxication, and youth is pleasant. Again, men of the melancholic temperament constantly need some remedial process (because the body, from its temperament, is constantly being worried), and they are in a chronic state of violent desire. But Pleasure drives out Pain; not only such Pleasure as is directly contrary to Pain but even any Pleasure provided it be strong: and this is how men come to be utterly destitute of Self-Mastery, i.e. low and bad.

But those Pleasures which are unconnected with Pains do not admit of excess: i.e. such as belong to objects which are naturally pleasant and not merely as a matter of result: by the latter class I mean such as are remedial, and the reason why these are thought to be pleasant is that the cure results from the action in some way of that part of the constitution which remains sound. By "pleasant naturally" I mean such as put into action a nature which is pleasant.

The reason why no one and the same thing is invariably pleasant is that our nature is, not simple, but complex, involving something different from itself (so far as we are corruptible beings). Suppose then that one part of this nature be doing something, this something is, to the other part, unnatural: but, if there be an equilibrium of the two natures, then whatever is being done is indifferent. It is obvious that if there be any whose nature is simple and not complex, to such a being the same course of acting will always be the most pleasurable.

For this reason it is that the Divinity feels Pleasure which is always one, i.e. simple: not motion merely but also motionlessness acts, and Pleasure resides rather in the absence than in the presence of motion.

The reason why the Poet's dictum "change is of all things most pleasant" is true, is "a baseness in our blood;" for as the bad man is easily changeable, bad must be also the nature that craves change, i.e. it is neither simple nor good.

We have now said our say about Self-Control and its opposite; and about Pleasure and Pain. What each is, and how the one set is good the other bad. We have yet to speak of Friendship.

BOOK VIII

NEXT would seem properly to follow a dissertation on Friendship: because, in the first place, it is either itself a virtue or connected with virtue; and next it is a thing most necessary for life, since no one would choose to live without friends though he should have all the other good things in the world: and, in fact, men who are rich or possessed of authority and influence are thought to have special need of friends: for where is the use of such prosperity if there be taken away the doing of kindnesses of which friends are the most usual and most commendable objects? Or how can it be kept or preserved without friends? because the greater it is so much the more slippery and hazardous: in poverty moreover and all other adversities men think friends to be their only refuge.

Furthermore, Friendship helps the young to keep from error: the old, in respect of attention and such deficiencies in action as their weakness makes them liable to; and those who are in their prime, in respect of noble deeds ("They *two* together going," Homer says, you may remember), because they are thus more able to devise plans and carry them out.

Again, it seems to be implanted in us by Nature: as, for instance, in the parent towards the offspring and the offspring towards the parent (not merely in the human species, but likewise in birds and most animals), and in those of the same tribe towards one another, and specially in men of the same nation; for which reason we commend those men who love their fellows: and one may see in the course of travel how close of kin and how friendly man is to man.

Furthermore, Friendship seems to be the bond of Social Communities, and legislators seem to be more anxious to secure it than Justice even. I mean, Unanimity is somewhat like to Friendship, and this they certainly aim at and specially drive out faction as being inimical.

Again, where people are in Friendship Justice is not required; but, on the other hand, though they are just they need Friendship in addition, and that principle which is most truly just is thought to partake of the nature of Friendship.

Lastly, not only is it a thing necessary but honourable likewise: since we praise those who are fond of friends, and the having numerous friends is thought a matter of credit to a man; some go so far as to hold, that "good man" and "friend" are terms synonymous.

Yet the disputed points respecting it are not few: some men lay down that it is a kind of resemblance, and that men who are like one another are friends: whence come the common sayings, "Like will to like," "Birds of a feather," and so on. Others, on the contrary, say, that all such come under the maxim, "Two of a trade never agree."

Again, some men push their inquiries on these points higher and reason physically: as Euripides, who says,

> "The earth by drought consumed doth love the rain,
> And the great heaven, overcharged with rain,
> Doth love to fall in showers upon the earth."

Heraclitus, again, maintains, that "contrariety is expedient, and that the best agreement arises from things differing, and that all things come into being in the way of the principle of antagonism."

Empedocles, among others, in direct opposition to these, affirms, that "like aims at like."

These physical questions we will take leave to omit, inasmuch as they are foreign to the present inquiry; and we will examine such as are proper to man and concern moral characters and feelings: as, for instance, "Does Friendship arise among all without distinction, or is it impossible for bad men to be friends?" and, "Is there but one species of Friendship, or several?" for they who ground the opinion that there is but one on the fact that Friendship admits of degrees hold that upon insufficient proof; because things which are different in species admit likewise of degrees (on this point we have spoken before).

Our view will soon be cleared on these points when we have ascertained what is properly the object-matter of Friendship: for it is thought that not everything indiscriminately, but some peculiar matter alone, is the object of this affection; that is to say, what is good, or pleasurable, or useful. Now it would seem that that is useful through which accrues any good or pleasure, and so the objects of Friendship, as absolute Ends, are the good and the pleasurable.

A question here arises; whether it is good absolutely or that which is good to the individuals, for which men feel Friendship (these two being sometimes distinct): and similarly in respect of the pleasurable. It seems then that each individual feels it towards that which is good to himself, and that abstractedly it is the real good which is the object of Friendship, and to each individual that which is good to each. It comes then to this; that each individual feels Friendship not for what *is* but for that which *conveys to his mind the impression of being* good to himself. But this will make no real difference, because that which is truly the object of Friendship will also convey this impression to the mind.

There are then three causes from which men feel Friendship: but the term is not applied to the case of fondness for things inanimate because there is no requital of the affection nor desire for the good of those objects: it certainly savours of the ridiculous to say that a man fond of wine wishes well to it: the only sense in which it is true being that he wishes it to be kept safe and sound for his own use and benefit. But to the friend they say one should wish all good for his sake. And when men do thus wish good to another (he not reciprocating the feeling), people call them Kindly; because Friendship they describe as being "Kindliness between persons who reciprocate it." But must they not add that the feeling must be mutually known? for many men are kindly disposed towards those whom they have never seen but whom they conceive to be amiable or useful: and this notion amounts to the same thing as a real feeling between them.

Well, these are plainly Kindly-disposed towards one another: but how can one call them friends while their mutual feelings are unknown to one another? to complete the idea of Friendship, then, it is requisite that they have kindly feelings towards one another, and wish one another good from one of the aforementioned causes, and that these kindly feelings should be mutually known.

As the motives to Friendship differ in kind so do the respective feelings and Friendships. The species then of Friendship are three, in number equal to the objects of it, since in the line of each there may be "mutual affection mutually known."

Now they who have Friendship for one another desire one another's good according to the motive of their Friendship; accordingly they whose motive is utility have no Friendship for one another really, but only in so far as some good arises to them from one another.

And they whose motive is pleasure are in like case: I mean, they have Friendship for men of easy pleasantry, not because they are of a given character but because they are pleasant to themselves. So then they whose motive to Friendship is utility love their friends for what is good to themselves; they whose motive is pleasure do so for what is pleasurable to themselves; that is to say, not in so far as the friend beloved *is* but in so far as he is useful or pleasurable. These Friendships then are a matter of result: since the object is not beloved in that he is the man he is but in that he furnishes advantage or pleasure as the case may be.

Such Friendships are of course very liable to dissolution if the parties do not continue alike: I mean, that the others cease to have any friendship for them when they are no longer pleasurable or useful. Now it is the nature of utility not to be permanent but constantly varying: so, of course, when the motive which made them friends is vanished, the Friendship likewise dissolves; since it existed only relatively to those circumstances.

Friendship of this kind is thought to exist principally among the old (because men at that time of life pursue not what is pleasurable but what is profitable); and in such, of men in their prime and of the young, as are given to the pursuit of profit. They that are such have no intimate intercourse with one another; for sometimes they are not even pleasurable to one another: nor, in fact, do they desire such intercourse unless their friends are profitable to them, because they are pleasurable only in so far as they have hopes of advantage. With these Friendships is commonly ranked that of hospitality.

But the Friendship of the young is thought to be based on the motive of pleasure: because they live at the beck and call of passion and generally pursue what is pleasurable to themselves and the object of the present moment: and as their age changes so likewise do their pleasures.

This is the reason why they form and dissolve Friendships rapidly: since the Friendship changes with the pleasurable object and such pleasure changes quickly.

The young are also much given up to Love; this passion being, in great measure, a matter of impulse and based on pleasure: for which cause they conceive Friendships and quickly drop them, changing often in the same day: but these wish for society and intimate intercourse with their friends, since they thus attain the object of their Friendship.

That then is perfect Friendship which subsists between those who are good and whose similarity consists in their goodness: for these men wish one another's good in similar ways; in so far as they are good (and good they are in themselves); and those are specially friends who wish good to their friends for their sakes, because they feel thus towards them on their own account and not as a mere matter of result; so the

Friendship between these men continues to subsist so long as they are good; and goodness, we know, has in it a principle of permanence.

Moreover, each party is good abstractedly and also relatively to his friend, for all good men are not only abstractedly good but also useful to one another. Such friends are also mutually pleasurable because all good men are so abstractedly, and also relatively to one another, inasmuch as to each individual those actions are pleasurable which correspond to his nature, and all such as are like them. Now when men are good these will be always the same, or at least similar.

Friendship then under these circumstances is permanent, as we should reasonably expect, since it combines in itself all the requisite qualifications of friends. I mean, that Friendship of whatever kind is based upon good or pleasure (either abstractedly or relatively to the person entertaining the sentiment of Friendship), and results from a similarity of some sort; and to this kind belong all the aforementioned requisites in the parties themselves, because in this the parties are similar, and so on: moreover, in it there is the abstractedly good and the abstractedly pleasant, and as these are specially the object-matter of Friendship so the feeling and the state of Friendship is found most intense and most excellent in men thus qualified.

Rare it is probable Friendships of this kind will be, because men of this kind are rare. Besides, all requisite qualifications being presupposed, there is further required time and intimacy: for, as the proverb says, men cannot know one another "till they have eaten the requisite quantity of salt together;" nor can they in fact admit one another to intimacy, much less be friends, till each has appeared to the other and been proved to be a fit object of Friendship. They who speedily commence an interchange of friendly actions may be said to wish to be friends, but they are not so unless they are also proper objects of Friendship and mutually known to be such: that is to say, a desire for Friendship may arise quickly but not Friendship itself.

Well, this Friendship is perfect both in respect of the time and in all other points; and exactly the same and similar results accrue to each party from the other; which ought to be the case between friends.

The friendship based upon the pleasurable is, so to say, a copy of this, since the good are sources of pleasure to one another: and that based on utility likewise, the good being also useful to one another. Between men thus connected Friendships are most permanent when the same result accrues to both from one another, pleasure, for instance; and not merely so but from the same source, as in the case of two men of easy pleasantry; and not as it is in that of a lover and the object of his affection, these not deriving their pleasure from the same causes, but the former from seeing the latter and the latter from receiving the attentions of the former: and when the bloom of youth fades the Friendship sometimes ceases also, because then the lover derives no pleasure from seeing and the object of his affection ceases to receive the attentions which were paid before: in many cases, however, people so connected continue friends, if being of similar tempers they have come from custom to like one another's disposition.

Where people do not interchange pleasure but profit in matters of Love, the Friendship is both less intense in degree and also less permanent: in fact, they who are friends because of advantage commonly part when the advantage ceases; for, in reality, they never were friends of one another but of the advantage.

So then it appears that from motives of pleasure or profit bad men may be friends to one another, or good men to bad men, or men of neutral character to one of any character whatever: but disinterestedly, for the sake of one another, plainly the good alone can be friends; because bad men have no pleasure even in themselves unless in so far as some advantage arises.

And further, the Friendship of the good is alone superior to calumny; it not being easy for men to believe a third person respecting one whom they have long tried and proved: there is between good men mutual confidence, and the feeling that one's friend would never have done one wrong, and all other such things as are expected in Friendship really worthy the name; but in the other kinds there is nothing to prevent all such suspicions.

I call them Friendships, because since men commonly give the name of friends to those who are connected from motives of profit (which is justified by political language, for alliances between states are thought to be contracted with a view to advantage), and to those who are attached to one another by the motive of pleasure (as children are), we may perhaps also be allowed to call such persons friends, and say there are several species of Friendship; primarily and specially that of the good, in that they are good, and the rest only in the way of resemblance: I mean, people connected otherwise are friends in that way in which there arises to them somewhat good and some mutual resemblance (because, we must remember the pleasurable is good to those who are fond of it).

These secondary Friendships, however, do not combine very well; that is to say, the same persons do not become friends by reason of advantage and by reason of the pleasurable, for these matters of result are not often combined. And Friendship having been divided into these kinds, bad men will be friends by reason of pleasure or profit, this being their point of resemblance; while the good are friends for one another's sake, that is, in so far as they are good.

These last may be termed abstractedly and simply friends, the former as a matter of result and termed friends from their resemblance to these last.

Further; just as in respect of the different virtues some men are termed good in respect of a certain inward state, others in respect of acts of working, so is it in respect of Friendship: I mean, they who live together take pleasure in, and impart good to, one another: but they who are asleep or are locally separated do not perform acts, but only are in such a state as to act in a friendly way if they acted at all: distance has in itself no direct effect upon Friendship, but only prevents the acting it out: yet, if the absence be protracted, it is thought to cause a forgetfulness even of the Friendship: and hence it has been said, "many and many a Friendship doth want of intercourse destroy."

Accordingly, neither the old nor the morose appear to be calculated for Friendship, because the pleasurableness in them is small, and no one can spend his days in company with that which is positively painful or even not pleasurable; since to avoid the painful and aim at the pleasurable is one of the most obvious tendencies of human nature. They who get on with one another very fairly, but are not in habits of intimacy, are rather like people having kindly feelings towards one another than friends; nothing being so characteristic of friends as the living with one another, because the necessitous desire assistance, and the happy companionship, they being the last persons in the world for solitary existence: but people cannot spend their time together unless they are mutually pleasurable and take pleasure in the same objects, a quality which is thought to appertain to the Friendship of companionship.

The connection then subsisting between the good is Friendship *par excellence*, as has already been frequently said: since that which is abstractedly good or pleasant is thought to be an object of Friendship and choiceworthy, and to each individual whatever is such to him; and the good man to the good man for both these reasons.

(Now the entertaining the sentiment is like a feeling, but Friendship itself like a state: because the former may have for its object even things inanimate, but requital of Friendship is attended with moral choice which proceeds from a moral state: and again, men wish good to the objects of their Friendship for their sakes, not in the way of a mere feeling but of moral state.)

And the good, in loving their friend, love their own good (inasmuch as the good man, when brought into that relation, becomes a good to him with whom he is so connected), so that either party loves his own good, and repays his friend equally both in wishing well and in the pleasurable: for equality is said to be a tie of Friendship. Well, these points belong most to the Friendship between good men.

But between morose or elderly men Friendship is less apt to arise, because they are somewhat awkward-tempered, and take less pleasure in intercourse and society; these being thought to be specially friendly and productive of Friendship: and so young men become friends quickly, old men not so (because people do not become friends with any, unless they take pleasure in them); and in like manner neither do the morose. Yet men of these classes entertain kindly feelings towards one another: they wish good to one another and render mutual assistance in respect of their needs, but they are not quite friends, because they neither spend their time together nor take pleasure in one another, which circumstances are thought specially to belong to Friendship.

To be a friend to many people, in the way of the perfect Friendship, is not possible; just as you cannot be in love with many at once: it is, so to speak, a state of excess which naturally has but one object; and besides, it is not an easy thing for one man to be very much pleased with many people at the same time, nor perhaps to find many really good. Again, a man needs experience, and to be in habits of close intimacy, which is very difficult.

But it *is* possible to please many on the score of advantage and pleasure: because there are many men of the kind, and the services may be rendered in a very short time.

Of the two imperfect kinds that which most resembles the perfect is the Friendship based upon pleasure, in which the same results accrue from both and they take pleasure in one another or in the same objects; such as are the Friendships of the young, because a generous spirit is most found in these. The Friendship because of advantage is the connecting link of shopkeepers.

Then again, the very happy have no need of persons who are profitable, but of pleasant ones they have because they wish to have people to live intimately with; and what is painful they bear for a short time indeed, but continuously no one could support it, nay, not even the Chief Good itself, if it were painful to him individually: and so they look out for pleasant friends: perhaps they ought to require such to be good also; and good moreover to themselves individually, because then they will have all the proper requisites of Friendship.

Men in power are often seen to make use of several distinct friends: for some are useful to them and others pleasurable, but the two are not often united: because they do not, in fact, seek such as shall combine pleasantness and goodness, nor such as shall be useful for honourable purposes: but with a view to attain what is pleasant they look out for men of easy-pleasantry; and again, for men who are clever at executing any business put into their hands: and these qualifications are not commonly found united in the same man.

It has been already stated that the good man unites the qualities of pleasantness and úsefulness: but then such an one will not be a friend to a superior unless he be also his superior in goodness: for if this be not the case, he cannot, being surpassed in one point, make things equal by a proportionate degree of Friendship. And characters who unite superiority of station and goodness are not common.

Now all the kinds of Friendship which have been already mentioned exist in a state of equality, inasmuch as either the same results accrue to both and they wish the same things to one another, or else they barter one thing against another; pleasure, for instance, against profit: it has been said already that Friendships of this latter kind are less intense in degree and less permanent.

And it is their resemblance or dissimilarity to the same thing which makes them to be thought to be and not to be Friendships: they show like Friendships in right of their likeness to that which is based on virtue (the one kind having the pleasurable, the other the profitable, both of which belong also to the other); and again, they do not show like Friendships by reason of their unlikeness to that true kind; which unlikeness consists herein, that while that is above calumny and so permanent these quickly change and differ in many other points.

But there is another form of Friendship, that, namely, in which the one party is superior to the other; as between father and son, elder and younger, husband and wife, ruler and ruled. These also differ one from another: I mean, the Friendship between parents and children is not the same as between ruler and the ruled, nor has the father the same towards the son as the son towards the father, nor the husband towards the wife as she towards him; because the work, and therefore the excellence, of each of these is different, and different therefore are the causes of their feeling Friendship; distinct and different therefore are their feelings and states of Friendship.

And the same results do not accrue to each from the other, nor in fact ought they to be looked for: but, when children render to their parents what they ought to the authors of their being, and parents to their sons what they ought to their offspring, the Friendship between such parties will be permanent and equitable.

Further; the feeling of Friendship should be in a due proportion in all Friendships which are between superior and inferior; I mean, the better man, or the more profitable, and so forth, should be the object of a stronger feeling than he himself entertains, because when the feeling of Friendship comes to be after a certain rate then equality in a certain sense is produced, which is thought to be a requisite in Friendship.

(It must be remembered, however, that the equal is not in the same case as regards Justice and Friendship: for in strict Justice the exactly proportioned equal ranks first, and the actual numerically equal ranks second, while in Friendship this is exactly reversed.)

And that equality is thus requisite is plainly shown by the occurrence of a great difference of goodness or badness, or prosperity, or something else: for in this case, people are not any longer friends, nay they do not even feel that they ought to be. The clearest illustration is perhaps the case of the gods, because they are most superior in all good things. It is obvious too, in the case of kings, for they who are greatly their inferiors do not feel entitled to be friends to them; nor do people very insignificant to be friends to those of very high excellence or wisdom. Of course, in such cases it is out of the question to attempt to define up to what point they may continue friends: for you may remove many points of agreement and the Friendship last nevertheless; but when one of the parties is very far separated (as a god from men), it cannot continue any longer.

This has given room for a doubt, whether friends do really wish to their friends the very highest goods, as that they may be gods: because, in case the wish were accomplished, they would no longer have them for friends; nor in fact would they have the good things they had, because friends are good things. If then it has been rightly said that a friend wishes to his friend good things for that friend's sake, it must be understood that he is to remain such as he now is: that is to say, he will wish the greatest good to him of which as man he is capable: yet perhaps not all, because each man desires good for himself most of all.

It is thought that desire for honour makes the mass of men wish rather to be the objects of the feeling of Friendship than to entertain it themselves (and for this reason they are fond of flatterers, a flatterer being a friend inferior or at least pretending to be such and rather to entertain towards another the feeling of Friendship than to be himself the object of it), since the former is thought to be nearly the same as being honoured, which the mass of men desire. And yet men seem to choose honour, not for its own sake, but incidentally: I mean, the common run of men delight to be honoured by those in power because of the hope it raises; that is, they think they shall get from them anything they may happen to be in want of, so they delight in honour as an earnest of future benefit. They again who grasp at honour at the hands of the good and those who are really acquainted with their merits desire to confirm their own opinion about themselves: so they take pleasure in the conviction that they are good, which is based on the sentence of those who assert it. But in being the objects of Friendship men delight for its own sake, and so this may be judged to be higher than being honoured and Friendship to be in itself choiceworthy. Friendship, moreover, is thought to consist in feeling, rather than being the object of, the sentiment of Friendship, which is proved by the delight mothers have in the feeling: some there are who give their children to be adopted and brought up by others, and knowing them bear this feeling towards them never seeking to have it returned, if both are not possible; but seeming to be content with seeing them well off and bearing this feeling themselves towards them, even though they, by reason of ignorance, never render to them any filial regard or love.

Since then Friendship stands rather in the entertaining, than in being the object of, the sentiment, and they are praised who are fond of their friends, it seems that entertaining the sentiment is the Excellence of friends; and so, in whomsoever this exists in due proportion these are stable friends and their Friendship is permanent. And in this way may they who are unequal best be friends, because they may thus be made equal.

Equality, then, and similarity are a tie to Friendship, and specially the similarity of goodness, because good men, being stable in themselves, are also stable as regards others, and neither ask degrading services nor render them, but, so to say, rather prevent them: for it is the part of the good neither to do wrong themselves nor to allow their friends in so doing.

The bad, on the contrary, have no principle of stability: in fact, they do not even continue like themselves: only they come to be friends for a short time from taking delight in one another's wickedness. Those connected by motives of profit, or pleasure, hold together somewhat longer: so long, that is to say, as they can give pleasure or profit mutually.

The Friendship based on motives of profit is thought to be most of all formed out of contrary elements: the poor man, for instance, is thus a friend of the rich, and the ignorant of the man of information; that is to say, a man desiring that of which he is, as it happens, in want, gives something else in exchange for it. To this same class we may refer the lover and beloved, the beautiful and the ill-favoured. For this reason lovers sometimes show in a ridiculous light by claiming to be the objects of as intense a feeling as they themselves entertain: of course if they are equally fit objects of Friendship they are perhaps entitled to claim this, but if they have nothing of the kind it is ridiculous.

Perhaps, moreover, the contrary does not aim at its contrary for its own sake but incidentally: the mean is really what is grasped at; it being good for the dry, for instance, not to become wet but to attain the mean, and so of the hot, etc.

However, let us drop these question, because they are in fact somewhat foreign to our purpose.

It seems too, as was stated at the commencement, that Friendship and Justice have the same object-matter, and subsist between the same persons: I mean that in every Communion there is thought to be some principle of Justice and also some Friendship: men address as friends, for instance, those who are their comrades by sea, or in war, and in like manner also those who are brought into Communion with them in other ways: and the Friendship, because also the Justice, is co-extensive with the Communion. This justifies the common proverb, "the goods of friends are common," since Friendship rests upon Communion.

Now brothers and intimate companions have all in common, but other people have their property separate, and some have more in common and others less, because the Friendships likewise differ in degree. So too do the various principles of Justice involved, not being the same between parents and children as between brothers, nor between companions as between fellow-citizens merely, and so on of all the other conceivable Friendships. Different also are the principles of Injustice as regards these different grades, and the acts become intensified by being done to friends; for instance, it is worse to rob your companion than one who is merely a fellow-citizen; to refuse help to a brother than to a stranger; and to strike your father than any one else. So then the Justice naturally increases with the degree of Friendship, as being between the same parties and of equal extent.

All cases of Communion are parts, so to say, of the great Social one, since in them men associate with a view to some advantage and to procure some of those things which are needful for life; and the great Social Communion is thought originally to have been associated and to continue for the sake of some advantage: this being the point at which legislators aim, affirming that to be just which is generally expedient.

All the other cases of Communion aim at advantage in particular points; the crew of a vessel at that which is to result from the voyage which is undertaken with a view to making money, or some such object; comrades in war at that which is to result from the war, grasping either at wealth or victory, or it may be a political position; and those of the same tribe, or Demus, in like manner.

Some of them are thought to be formed for pleasure's sake, those, for instance, of bacchanals or club-fellows, which are with a view to Sacrifice or merely company. But all these seem to be ranged under the great Social one, inasmuch as the aim of this is, not merely the expediency of the moment but, for life and at all times; with a view to which the members of the institute sacrifices and their attendant assemblies, to render honour to the gods and procure for themselves respite from toil combined with pleasure. For it appears that sacrifices and religious assemblies in old times were made as a kind of first-fruits after the ingathering of the crops, because at such seasons they had most leisure.

So then it appears that all the instances of Communion are parts of the great Social one: and corresponding Friendships will follow upon such Communions.

Of Political Constitutions there are three kinds; and equal in number are the deflections from them, being, so to say, corruptions of them.

The former are Kingship, Aristocracy, and that which recognises the principle of wealth, which it seems appropriate to call Timocracy (I give to it the name of a political constitution because people commonly do so). Of these the best is Monarchy, and Timocracy the worst.

From Monarchy the deflection is Despotism; both being Monarchies but widely differing from each other; for the Despot looks to his own advantage, but the King to that of his subjects: for he is in fact no King who is not thoroughly independent and superior to the rest in all good things, and he that is this has no further wants: he will not then have to look to his own advantage but to that of his subjects, for he that is not in such a position is a mere King elected by lot for the nonce.

But Despotism is on a contrary footing to this Kingship, because the Despot pursues his own good: and in the case of this its inferiority is most evident, and what is worse is contrary to what is best. The Transition to Despotism is made from Kingship, Despotism being a corrupt form of Monarchy, that is to say, the bad King comes to be a Despot.

From Aristocracy to Oligarchy the transition is made by the fault of the Rulers in distributing the public property contrary to right proportion; and giving either all that is good, or the greatest share, to themselves; and the offices to the same persons always, making wealth their idol; thus a few bear rule and they bad men in the place of the best.

From Timocracy the transition is to Democracy, they being contiguous: for it is the nature of Timocracy to be in the hands of a multitude, and all in the same grade of property are equal. Democracy is the least vicious of all, since herein the form of the constitution undergoes least change.

Well, these are generally the changes to which the various Constitutions are liable, being the least in degree and the easiest to make.

Likenesses, and, as it were, models of them, one may find even in Domestic life: for instance, the Communion between a Father and his Sons presents the figure of Kingship, because the children are the Father's care: and hence Homer names Jupiter Father because Kingship is intended to be a paternal rule. Among the Persians, however, the Father's rule is Despotic, for they treat their Sons as slaves. (The relation of Master to Slaves is of the nature of Despotism because the point regarded herein is the Master's interest): this now strikes me to be as it ought, but the Persian custom to be mistaken; because for different persons there should be different rules.

Between Husband and Wife the relation takes the form of Aristocracy, because he rules by right and in such points only as the Husband should, and gives to the Wife all that befits her to have. Where the Husband lords it in everything he changes the relation into an Oligarchy; because he does it contrary to right and not as being the better of the two. In some instances the Wives take the reins of government, being heiresses: here the rule is carried on not in right of goodness but by reason of wealth and power, as it is in Oligarchies.

Timocracy finds its type in the relation of Brothers: they being equal except as to such differences as age introduces: for which reason, if they are very different in age, the Friendship comes to be no longer a fraternal one: while Democracy is represented specially by families which have no head (all being there equal), or in which the proper head is weak and so every member does that which is right in his own eyes.

Attendant then on each form of Political Constitution there plainly is Friendship exactly co-extensive with the principle of Justice; that between a King and his Subjects being in the relation of a superiority of benefit, inasmuch as he benefits his subjects; it being assumed that he is a good king and takes care of their welfare as a shepherd tends his flock; whence Homer (to quote him again) calls Agamemnon, "shepherd of the people." And of this same kind is the Paternal Friendship, only that it exceeds the former in the greatness of the benefits done; because the father is the author of being (which is esteemed the greatest benefit) and of maintenance and education (these things are also, by the way, ascribed to ancestors generally): and by the law of nature the father has the right of rule over his sons, ancestors over their descendants, and the king over his subjects.

These friendships are also between superiors and inferiors, for which reason parents are not merely loved but also honoured. The principle of Justice also between these parties is not exactly the same but according to proportion, because so also is the Friendship.

Now between Husband and Wife there is the same Friendship as in Aristocracy: for the relation is determined by relative excellence, and the better person has the greater good, and each has what befits: so too also is the principle of Justice between them.

The Fraternal Friendship is like that of Companions, because brothers are equal and much of an age, and such persons have generally like feelings and like dispositions. Like to this also is the Friendship of a Timocracy, because the citizens are intended to be equal and equitable: rule, therefore, passes from hand to hand, and is distributed on equal terms: so too is the Friendship accordingly.

In the deflections from the constitutional forms, just as the principle of Justice is but small so is the Friendship also: and least of all in the most perverted form: in Despotism there is little or no Friendship. For generally wherever the ruler and the ruled have nothing in common there is no Friendship because there is no Justice; but the case is as between an artisan and his tool, or between soul and body, and master and slave; all these are benefited by those who use them, but towards things inanimate there is neither Friendship nor Justice: nor even towards a horse or an ox, or a slave *qua* slave, because there is nothing in common: a slave as such is an animate tool, a tool an inanimate slave. *Qua* slave, then, there is no Friendship towards him, only *qua* man: for it is thought that there is some principle of Justice between every man, and every other who can share in law and be a party to an agreement; and so somewhat of Friendship, in so far as he is man. So in Despotisms the Friendships and the principle of Justice are inconsiderable in extent, but in Democracies they are most considerable because they who are equal have much in common.

Now of course all Friendship is based upon Communion, as has been already stated: but one would be inclined to separate off from the rest the Friendship of Kindred, and that of Companions: whereas those of men of the same city, or tribe, or crew, and all such, are more peculiarly, it would seem, based upon Communion, inasmuch as they plainly exist in right of some agreement expressed or implied: among these one may rank also the Friendship of Hospitality.

The Friendship of Kindred is likewise of many kinds, and appears in all its varieties to depend on the Parental: parents, I mean, love their children as being a part of themselves, children love their parents as being themselves somewhat derived from them. But parents know their offspring more than these know that they are from the parents, and the source is more closely bound to that which is produced than that which is produced is to that which formed it: of course, whatever is derived from one's self is proper to that from which it is so derived (as, for instance, a tooth or a hair, or any other thing whatever to him that has it): but the source to it is in no degree proper, or in an inferior degree at least.

Then again the greater length of time comes in: the parents love their offspring from the first moment of their being, but their offspring them only after a lapse of time when they have attained intelligence or instinct. These considerations serve also to show why mothers have greater strength of affection than fathers.

Now parents love their children as themselves (since what is derived from themselves becomes a kind of other Self by the fact of separation), but children their parents as being sprung from them. And brothers love one another from being sprung from the same; that is, their sameness with the common stock creates a sameness with one another; whence come the phrases, "same blood," "root," and so on. In fact they are the same, in a sense, even in the separate distinct individuals.

Then again the being brought up together, and the nearness of age, are a great help towards Friendship, for a man likes one of his own age and persons who are used to one another are companions, which accounts for the resemblance between the Friendship of Brothers and that of Companions.

And cousins and all other relatives derive their bond of union from these, that is to say, from their community of origin: and the strength of this bond varies according to their respective distances from the common ancestor.

Further: the Friendship felt by children towards parents, and by men towards the gods, is as towards something good and above them; because these have conferred the greatest possible benefits, in that they are the causes of their being and being nourished, and of their having been educated after they were brought into being.

And Friendship of this kind has also the pleasurable and the profitable more than that between persons unconnected by blood, in proportion as their life is also more shared in common. Then again in the Fraternal Friendship there is all that there is in that of Companions, and more in the good, and generally in those who are alike; in proportion as they are more closely tied and from their very birth have a feeling of affection for one another to begin with, and as they are more like in disposition who spring from the same stock and have grown up together and been educated alike: and besides this they have the greatest opportunities in respect of time for proving one another, and can therefore depend most securely upon the trial. The elements of Friendship between other consanguinities will be of course proportionably similar.

Between Husband and Wife there is thought to be Friendship by a law of nature: man being by nature disposed to pair, more than to associate in Communities: in proportion as the family is prior in order of time and more absolutely necessary than the Community. And procreation is more common to him with other animals; all the other animals have Communion thus far, but human creatures cohabit not merely for the sake of procreation but also with a view to life in general: because in this connection the works are immediately divided, and some belong to the man, others to the woman: thus they help one the other, putting what is peculiar to each into the common stock.

And for these reasons this Friendship is thought to combine the profitable and the pleasurable: it will be also based upon virtue if they are good people; because each has goodness, and they may take delight in this quality in each other. Children too are thought to be a tie: accordingly the childless sooner separate, for the children are a good common to both and anything in common is a bond of union.

The question how a man is to live with his wife, or (more generally) one friend with another, appears to be no other than this, how it is just that they should: because plainly there is not the same principle of Justice between a friend and friend, as between strangers, or companions, or mere chance fellow-travellers.

There are then, as was stated at the commencement of this book, three kinds of Friendship, and in each there may be friends on a footing of equality and friends in the relation of superior and inferior; we find, I mean, that people who are alike in goodness, become friends, and better with worse, and so also pleasant people; again, because of advantage people are friends, either balancing exactly their mutual profitableness or differing from one another herein. Well then, those who are equal should in right of this equality be equalised also by the degree of their Friendship and the other points, and those who are on a footing of inequality by rendering Friendship in proportion to the superiority of the other party.

Fault-finding and blame arises, either solely or most naturally, in Friendship of which utility is the motive: for they who are friends by reason of goodness, are eager to do kindnesses to one another because this is a natural result of goodness and Friendship; and when men are vying with each other for this End there can be no fault-finding nor contention: since no one is annoyed at one who entertains for him the sentiment of Friendship and does kindnesses to him, but if of a refined mind he requites him with kind actions. And suppose that one of the two exceeds the other, yet as he is attaining his object he will not find fault with his friend, for good is the object of each party.

Neither can there well be quarrels between men who are friends for pleasure's sake: because supposing them to delight in living together then both attain their desire; or if not, a man would be put in a ridiculous light who should find fault with another for not pleasing him, since it is in his power to forbear intercourse with him. But the Friendship because of advantage is very liable to fault-finding; because, as the parties use one another with a view to advantage, the requirements are continually enlarging, and they think they have less than of right belongs to them, and find fault because though justly entitled they do not get as much as they want: while they who do the kindnesses, can never come up to the requirements of those to whom they are being done.

It seems also, that as the Just is of two kinds, the unwritten and the legal, so Friendship because of advantage is of two kinds, what may be called the Moral, and the Legal: and the most fruitful source of complaints is that parties contract obligations and discharge them not in the same line of Friendship. The Legal is upon specified conditions, either purely tradesmanlike from hand to hand or somewhat more gentlemanly as regards time but still by agreement of *quid pro quo*.

In this Legal kind the obligation is clear and admits of no dispute, the friendly element is the delay in requiring its discharge: and for this reason in some countries no actions can be maintained at Law for the recovery of such debts, it being held that they who have dealt on the footing of credit must be content to abide the issue.

That which may be termed the Moral kind is not upon specified conditions, but a man gives as to his friend and so on: but still he expects to receive an equivalent, or even more, as though he had not given but lent: he also will find fault, because he does not get the obligation discharged in the same way as it was contracted.

Now this results from the fact, that all men, or the generality at least, *wish* what is honourable, but, when tested, *choose* what is profitable; and the doing kindnesses disinterestedly is honourable while receiving benefits is profitable. In such cases one should, if able, make a return proportionate to the good received, and do so willingly, because one ought not to make a disinterested friend of a man against his inclination: one should act, I say, as having made a mistake originally in receiving kindness from one from whom one ought not to have received it, he being not a friend nor doing the act disinterestedly; one should therefore discharge one's self of the obligation as having received a kindness on specified terms: and if able a man would engage to repay the kindness, while if he were unable even the doer of it would not expect it of him: so that if he is able he ought to repay it. But one ought at the first to ascertain from whom one is receiving kindness, and on what understanding, that on that same understanding one may accept it or not.

A question admitting of dispute is whether one is to measure a kindness by the good done to the receiver of it, and make this the standard by which to requite, or by the kind intention of the doer?

For they who have received kindnesses frequently plead in depreciation that they have received from their benefactors such things as were small for them to give, or such as they themselves could have got from others: while the doers of the kindnesses affirm that they gave the best they had, and what could not have been got from others, and under danger, or in such-like straits.

May we not say, that as utility is the motive of the Friendship the advantage conferred on the receiver must be the standard? because he it is who requests the kindness and the other services him in his need on the understanding that he is to get an equivalent: the assistance rendered is then exactly proportionate to the advantage which the receiver has obtained, and he should therefore repay as much as he gained by it, or even more, this being more creditable.

In Friendships based on goodness, the question, of course, is never raised, but herein the motive of the doer seems to be the proper standard, since virtue and moral character depend principally on motive.

Quarrels arise also in those Friendships in which the parties are unequal because each party thinks himself entitled to the greater share, and of course, when this happens, the Friendship is broken up.

The man who is better than the other thinks that having the greater share pertains to him of right, for that more is always awarded to the good man: and similarly the man who is more profitable to another than that other to him: "one who is useless," they say, "ought not to share equally, for it comes to a tax, and not a Friendship, unless the fruits of the Friendship are reaped in proportion to the works done:" their notion being, that as in a money partnership they who contribute more receive more so should it be in Friendship likewise.

On the other hand, the needy man and the less virtuous advance the opposite claim: they urge that "it is the very business of a good friend to help those who are in need, else what is the use of having a good or powerful friend if one is not to reap the advantage of all?"

Now each seems to advance a right claim and to be entitled to get more out of the connection than the other, only *not more of the same thing*: but the superior man should receive more respect, the needy man more profit: respect being the reward of goodness and beneficence, profit being the aid of need.

This is plainly the principle acted upon in Political Communities: he receives no honour who gives no good to the common stock: for the property of the Public is given to him who does good to the Public, and honour is the property of the Public; it is not possible both to make money out of the Public and receive honour likewise; because no one will put up with the less in every respect: so to him who suffers loss as regards money they award honour, but money to him who can be paid by gifts: since, as has been stated before, the observing due proportion equalises and preserves Friendship.

Like rules then should be observed in the intercourse of friends who are unequal; and to him who advantages another in respect of money, or goodness, that other should repay honour, making requital according to his power; because Friendship requires what is possible, not what is strictly due, this being not possible in all cases, as in the honours paid to the gods and to parents: no man could ever make the due return in these cases, and so he is thought to be a good man who pays respect according to his ability.

For this reason it may be judged never to be allowable for a son to disown his father, whereas a father may his son: because he that owes is bound to pay; now a son can never, by anything he has done, fully requite the benefits first conferred on him by his father, and so is always a debtor. But they to whom anything is owed may cast off their debtors: therefore the father may his son. But at the same time it must perhaps be admitted, that it seems no father ever *would* sever himself utterly from a son, except in a case of exceeding depravity: because, independently of the natural Friendship, it is like human nature not to put away from one's self the assistance which a son might render. But to the son, if depraved, assisting his father is a thing to be avoided, or at least one which he will not be very anxious to do; most men being willing enough to receive kindness, but averse to doing it as unprofitable.

Let thus much suffice on these points.

BOOK IX

WELL, in all the Friendships the parties to which are dissimilar it is the proportionate which equalises and preserves the Friendship, as has been already stated: I mean, in the Social Friendship the cobbler, for instance, gets an equivalent for his shoes after a certain rate; and the weaver, and all others in like manner. Now in this case a common measure has been provided in money, and to this accordingly all things are referred and by this are measured: but in the Friendship of Love the complaint is sometimes from the lover that, though he loves exceedingly, his love is not requited; he having perhaps all the time nothing that can be the object of Friendship: again, oftentimes from the object of love that he who as a suitor promised any and every thing now performs nothing. These cases occur because the Friendship of the lover for the beloved object is based upon pleasure, that of the other for him upon utility, and in one of the parties the requisite quality is not found: for, as these are respectively the grounds of the Friendship, the Friendship comes to be broken up because the motives to it cease to exist: the parties loved not one another but qualities in one another which are not permanent, and so neither are the Friendships: whereas the Friendship based upon the moral character of the parties, being independent and disinterested, is permanent, as we have already stated.

Quarrels arise also when the parties realise different results and not those which they desire; for the not attaining one's special object is all one, in this case, with getting nothing at all: as in the well-known case where a man made promises to a musician, rising in proportion to the excellence of his music; but when, the next morning, the musician claimed the performance of his promises, he said that he had given him pleasure for pleasure: of course, if each party had intended this, it would have been all right: but if the one desires amusement and the other gain, and the one gets his object but the other not, the dealing cannot be fair: because a man fixes his mind upon what he happens to want, and will give so and so for that specific thing.

159

The question then arises, who is to fix the rate? the man who first gives, or the man who first takes? because, *prima facie*, the man who first gives seems to leave the rate to be fixed by the other party. This, they say, was in fact the practice of Protagoras: when he taught a man anything he would bid the learner estimate the worth of the knowledge gained by his own private opinion; and then he used to take so much from him. In such cases some people adopt the rule,

"With specified reward a friend should be content."

They are certainly fairly found fault with who take the money in advance and then do nothing of what they said they would do, their promises having been so far beyond their ability; for such men do not perform what they agreed. The Sophists, however, are perhaps obliged to take this course, because no one would give a sixpence for their knowledge. These then, I say, are fairly found fault with, because they do not what they have already taken money for doing.

In cases where no stipulation as to the respective services is made they who disinterestedly do the first service will not raise the question (as we have said before), because it is the nature of Friendship, based on mutual goodness to be free from such quarrels: the requital is to be made with reference to the intention of the other, the intention being characteristic of the true friend and of goodness.

And it would seem the same rule should be laid down for those who are connected with one another as teachers and learners of philosophy; for here the value of the commodity cannot be measured by money, and, in fact, an exactly equivalent price cannot be set upon it, but perhaps it is sufficient to do what one can, as in the case of the gods or one's parents.

But where the original giving is not upon these terms, but avowedly for some return, the most proper course is perhaps for the requital to be such as *both* shall allow to be proportionate; and, where this cannot be, then for the receiver to fix the value would seem to be not only necessary but also fair: because when the first giver gets that which is equivalent to the advantage received by the other, or to what he would have given to secure the pleasure he has had, then he has the value from him: for not only is this seen to be the course adopted in matters of buying and selling but also in some places the law does not allow of actions upon voluntary dealings; on the principle that when one man has trusted another he must be content to have the obligation discharged in the same spirit as he originally contracted it: that is to say, it is thought fairer for the trusted, than for the trusting, party, to fix the value. For, in general, those who have and those who wish to get things do not set the same value on them: what is their own, and what they give in each case, appears to them worth a great deal: but yet the return is made according to the estimate of those who have received first: it should perhaps be added that the receiver should estimate what he has received, not by the value he sets upon it now that he has it, but by that which he set upon it before he obtained it.

Questions also arise upon such points as the following: Whether one's father has an unlimited claim on one's services and obedience, or whether the sick man is to obey his physician? or, in an election of a general, the warlike qualities of the candidates should be alone regarded?

In like manner whether one should do a service rather to one's friend or to a good man? whether one should rather requite a benefactor or give to one's companion, supposing that both are not within one's power?

Is not the true answer that it is no easy task to determine all such questions accurately, inasmuch as they involve numerous differences of all kinds, in respect of amount and what is honourable and what is necessary? It is obvious, of course, that no one person can unite in himself all claims. Again, the requital of benefits is, in general, a higher duty than doing unsolicited kindnesses to one's companion; in other words, the discharging of a debt is more obligatory upon one than the duty of giving to a companion. And yet this rule may admit of exceptions; for instance, which is the higher duty? for one who has been ransomed out of the hands of robbers to ransom in return his ransomer, be he who he may, or to repay him on his demand though he has not been taken by robbers, or to ransom his own father? for it would seem that a man ought to ransom his father even in preference to himself.

Well then, as has been said already, as a general rule the debt should be discharged, but if in a particular case the giving greatly preponderates as being either honourable or necessary, we must be swayed by these considerations: I mean, in some cases the requital of the obligation previously existing may not be equal; suppose, for instance, that the original benefactor has conferred a kindness on a good man, knowing him to be such, whereas this said good man has to repay it believing him to be a scoundrel.

And again, in certain cases no obligation lies on a man to lend to one who has lent to him; suppose, for instance, that a bad man lent to him, as being a good man, under the notion that he should get repaid, whereas the said good man has no hope of repayment from him being a bad man. Either then the case is really as we have supposed it and then the claim is not equal, or it is not so but supposed to be; and still in so acting people are not to be thought to act wrongly. In short, as has been oftentimes stated before, all statements regarding feelings and actions can be definite only in proportion as their object-matter is so; it is of course quite obvious that all people have not the same claim upon one, nor are the claims of one's father unlimited; just as Jupiter does not claim all kinds of sacrifice without distinction: and since the claims of parents, brothers, companions, and benefactors, are all different, we must give to each what belongs to and befits each.

And this is seen to be the course commonly pursued: to marriages men commonly invite their relatives, because these are from a common stock and therefore all the actions in any way pertaining thereto are common also: and to funerals men think that relatives ought to assemble in preference to other people, for the same reason.

And it would seem that in respect of maintenance it is our duty to assist our parents in preference to all others, as being their debtors, and because it is more honourable to succour in these respects the authors of our existence than ourselves. Honour likewise we ought to pay to our parents just as to the gods, but then, not all kinds of honour: not the same, for instance, to a father as to a mother: nor again to a father the honour due to a scientific man or to a general but that which is a father's due, and in like manner to a mother that which is a mother's.

To all our elders also the honour befitting their age, by rising up in their presence, turning out of the way for them, and all similar marks of respect: to our companions again, or brothers, frankness and free participation in all we have. And to those of the same family, or tribe, or city, with ourselves, and all similarly connected with us, we should constantly try to render their due, and to discriminate what belongs to each in respect of nearness of connection, or goodness, or intimacy: of course in the case of those of the same class the discrimination is easier; in that of those who are in different classes it is a matter of more trouble. This, however, should not be a reason for giving up the attempt, but we must observe the distinctions so far as it is practicable to do so.

A question is also raised as to the propriety of dissolving or not dissolving those Friendships the parties to which do not remain what they were when the connection was formed.

Now surely in respect of those whose motive to Friendship is utility or pleasure there can be nothing wrong in breaking up the connection when they no longer have those qualities: because they were friends [not of one another, but] of those qualities: and, these having failed, it is only reasonable to expect that they should cease to entertain the sentiment.

But a man has reason to find fault if the other party, being really attached to him because of advantage or pleasure, pretended to be so because of his moral character: in fact, as we said at the commencement, the most common source of quarrels between friends is their not being friends on the same grounds as they suppose themselves to be.

Now when a man has been deceived in having supposed himself to excite the sentiment of Friendship by reason of his moral character, the other party doing nothing to indicate this, he has but himself to blame: but when he has been deceived by the pretence of the other he has a right to find fault with the man who has so deceived him, aye even more than with utterers of false coin, in proportion to the greater preciousness of that which is the object-matter of the villainy.

But suppose a man takes up another as being a good man, who turns out, and is found by him, to be a scoundrel, is he bound still to entertain Friendship for him? or may we not say at once it is impossible? since it is not everything which is the object-matter of Friendship, but only that which is good; and so there is no obligation to be a bad man's friend, nor, in fact, ought one to be such: for one ought not to be a lover of evil, nor to be assimilated to what is base; which would be implied, because we have said before, like is friendly to like.

Are we then to break with him instantly? not in all cases; only where our friends are incurably depraved; when there is a chance of amendment we are bound to aid in repairing the moral character of our friends even more than their substance, in proportion as it is better and more closely related to Friendship. Still he who should break off the connection is not to be judged to act wrongly, for he never was a friend to such a character as the other now is, and therefore, since the man is changed and he cannot reduce him to his original state, he backs out of the connection.

To put another case: suppose that one party remains what he was when the Friendship was formed, while the other becomes morally improved and widely different from his friend in goodness; is the improved character to treat the other as a friend?

May we not say it is impossible? The case of course is clearest where there is a great difference, as in the Friendships of boys: for suppose that of two boyish friends the one still continues a boy in mind and the other becomes a man of the highest character, how can they be friends? since they neither are pleased with the same objects nor like and dislike the same things: for these points will not belong to them as regards one another, and without them it was assumed they cannot be friends because they cannot live in intimacy: and of the case of those who cannot do so we have spoken before.

Well then, is the improved party to bear himself towards his former friend in no way differently to what he would have done had the connection never existed?

Surely he ought to bear in mind the intimacy of past times, and just as we think ourselves bound to do favours for our friends in preference to strangers, so to those who have been friends and are so no longer we should allow somewhat on the score of previous Friendship, whenever the cause of severance is not excessive depravity on their part.

Now the friendly feelings which are exhibited towards our friends, and by which Friendships are characterised, seem to have sprung out of those which we entertain towards ourselves.

I mean, people define a friend to be "one who intends and does what is good (or what he believes to be good) to another for that other's sake;" or "one who wishes his friend to be and to live for that friend's own sake" (which is the feeling of mothers towards their children, and of friends who have come into collision). Others again, "one who lives with another and chooses the same objects," or "one who sympathises with his friend in his sorrows and in his joys" (this too is especially the case with mothers).

Well, by some one of these marks people generally characterise Friendship: and each of these the good man has towards himself, and all others have them in so far as they suppose themselves to be good. (For, as has been said before, goodness, that is the good man, seems to be a measure to every one else.)

For he is at unity in himself, and with every part of his soul he desires the same objects; and he wishes for himself both what is, and what he believes to be, good; and he does it (it being characteristic of the good man to work at what is good); and for the sake of himself, inasmuch as he does it for the sake of his Intellectual Principle which is generally thought to be a man's Self. Again, he wishes himself, and specially this Principle whereby he is an intelligent being, to live and be preserved in life, because existence is a good to him that is a good man.

But it is to himself that each individual wishes what is good, and no man, conceiving the possibility of his becoming other than he now is, chooses that that New Self should have all things indiscriminately: a god, for instance, has at the present moment the Chief Good, but he has it in right of being whatever he actually now is: and the Intelligent Principle must be judged to be each man's Self, or at least eminently so [though other Principles help, of course, to constitute him the man he is].

Furthermore, the good man wishes to continue to live with himself; for he can do it with pleasure, in that his memories of past actions are full of delight and his anticipations of the future are good and such are pleasurable. Then, again, he has good store of matter for his Intellect to contemplate, and he most especially sympathises with his Self in its griefs and joys, because the objects which give him pain and pleasure are at all times the same, not one thing to-day and a different one to-morrow: because he is not given to repentance, if one may so speak. It is then because each of these feelings are entertained by the good man towards his own Self and a friend feels towards a friend as towards himself (a friend being in fact another Self), that Friendship is thought to be some one of these things and they are accounted friends in whom they are found. Whether or no there can really be Friendship between a man and his Self is a question we will not at present entertain: there may be thought to be Friendship, in so far as there are two or more of the aforesaid requisites, and because the highest degree of Friendship, in the usual acceptation of that term, resembles the feeling entertained by a man towards himself.

But it may be urged that the aforesaid requisites are to all appearance found in the common run of men, though they are men of a low stamp.

May it not be answered, that they share in them only in so far as they please themselves, and conceive themselves to be good? for certainly, they are not either really, or even apparently, found in any one of those who are very depraved and villainous; we may almost say not even in those who are bad men at all: for they are at variance with themselves and lust after different things from those which in cool reason they wish for, just as men who fail of Self-Control: I mean, they choose things which, though hurtful, are pleasurable, in preference to those which in their own minds they believe to be good: others again, from cowardice and indolence, decline to do what still they are convinced is best for them: while they who from their depravity have actually done many dreadful actions hate and avoid life, and accordingly kill themselves: and the wicked seek others in whose company to spend their time, but fly from themselves because they have many unpleasant subjects of memory, and can only look forward to others like them when in solitude but drown their remorse in the company of others: and as they

have nothing to raise the sentiment of Friendship so they never feel it
towards themselves.

Neither, in fact, can they who are of this character sympathise with
their Selves in their joys and sorrows, because their soul is, as it were,
rent by faction, and the one principle, by reason of the depravity in
them, is grieved at abstaining from certain things, while the other and
better principle is pleased thereat; and the one drags them this way and
the other that way, as though actually tearing them asunder. And
though it is impossible actually to have at the same time the sensations
of pain and pleasure; yet after a little time the man is sorry for having
been pleased, and he could wish that those objects had not given him
pleasure; for the wicked are full of remorse.

It is plain then that the wicked man cannot be in the position of a
friend even towards himself, because he has in himself nothing which
can excite the sentiment of Friendship. If then to be thus is exceedingly
wretched it is a man's duty to flee from wickedness with all his might
and to strive to be good, because thus may he be friends with himself
and may come to be a friend to another.

Kindly Feeling, though resembling Friendship, is not identical with
it, because it may exist in reference to those whom we do not know and
without the object of it being aware of its existence, which Friendship
cannot. (This, by the way, has also been said before.) And further, it is
not even Affection because it does not imply intensity nor yearning,
which are both consequences of Affection. Again, Affection requires intimacy but Kindly Feeling may arise quite suddenly, as happens sometimes in respect of men against whom people are matched in any way,
I mean they come to be kindly disposed to them and sympathise in
their wishes, but still they would not join them in any action, because,
as we said, they conceive this feeling of kindness suddenly and so have
but a superficial liking.

What it does seem to be is the starting point of a Friendship; just as
pleasure, received through the sight, is the commencement of Love:
for no one falls in love without being first pleased with the personal appearance of the beloved object; and yet he who takes pleasure in it does
not therefore necessarily love, but when he wearies for the object in its
absence and desires its presence. Exactly in the same way men cannot
be friends without having passed through the stage of Kindly Feeling,
and yet they who are in that stage do not necessarily advance to
Friendship: they merely have an inert wish for the good of those toward
whom they entertain the feeling, but would not join them in any action, nor put themselves out of the way for them. So that, in a

metaphorical way of speaking, one might say that it is dormant Friendship, and when it has endured for a space and ripened into intimacy comes to be real Friendship; but not that whose object is advantage or pleasure, because such motives cannot produce even Kindly Feeling.

I mean, he who has received a kindness requires it by Kindly Feeling towards his benefactor, and is right in so doing: but he who wishes another to be prosperous, because he has hope of advantage through his instrumentality, does not seem to be kindly disposed to that person but rather to himself; just as neither is he his friend if he pays court to him for any interested purpose.

Kindly Feeling always arises by reason of goodness and a certain amiability, when one man gives another the notion of being a fine fellow, or brave man, etc., as we said was the case sometimes with those matched against one another.

Unity of Sentiment is also plainly connected with Friendship, and therefore is not the same as Unity of Opinion, because this might exist even between people unacquainted with one another.

Nor do men usually say people are united in sentiment merely because they agree in opinion on *any* point, as, for instance, on points of astronomical science (Unity of Sentiment herein not having any connection with Friendship), but they say that Communities have Unity of Sentiment when they agree respecting points of expediency and take the same line and carry out what has been determined in common consultation.

Thus we see that Unity of Sentiment has for its object matters of action, and such of these as are of importance, and of mutual, or, in the case of single States, common, interest: when, for instance, all agree in the choice of magistrates, or forming alliance with the Lacedæmonians, or appointing Pittacus ruler (that is to say, supposing he himself was willing). But when each wishes himself to be in power (as the brothers in the Phœnissæ), they quarrel and form parties: for, plainly, Unity of Sentiment does not merely imply that each entertains the same idea be it what it may, but that they do so in respect of the same object, as when both the populace and the sensible men of a State desire that the best men should be in office, because then all attain their object.

Thus Unity of Sentiment is plainly a social Friendship, as it is also said to be: since it has for its object-matter things expedient and relating to life.

And this Unity exists among the good: for they have it towards themselves and towards one another, being, if I may be allowed the expression, in the same position: I mean, the wishes of such men are steady and do not ebb and flow like the Euripus, and they wish what is just and expedient and aim at these things in common.

The bad, on the contrary, can as little have Unity of Sentiment as they can be real friends, except to a very slight extent, desiring as they do unfair advantage in things profitable while they shirk labour and service for the common good: and while each man wishes for these things for himself he is jealous of and hinders his neighbour: and as they do not watch over the common good it is lost. The result is that they quarrel while they are for keeping one another to work but are not willing to perform their just share.

Benefactors are commonly held to have more Friendship for the objects of their kindness than these for them: and the fact is made a subject of discussion and inquiry, as being contrary to reasonable expectation.

The account of the matter which satisfies most persons is that the one are debtors and the others creditors: and therefore that, as in the case of actual loans the debtors wish their creditors out of the way while the creditors are anxious for the preservation of their debtors, so those who have done kindnesses desire the continued existence of the people they have done them to, under the notion of getting a return of their good offices, while these are not particularly anxious about requital.

Epicharmus, I suspect, would very probably say that they who give this solution judge from their own baseness; yet it certainly is like human nature, for the generality of men have short memories on these points, and aim rather at receiving than conferring benefits.

But the real cause, it would seem, rests upon nature, and the case is not parallel to that of creditors; because in this there is no affection to the persons, but merely a wish for their preservation with a view to the return: whereas, in point of fact, they who have done kindnesses feel friendship and love for those to whom they have done them, even though they neither are, nor can by possibility hereafter be, in a position to serve their benefactors.

And this is the case also with artisans; every one, I mean, feels more affection for his own work than that work possibly could for him if it were animate. It is perhaps specially the case with poets: for these entertain very great affection for their poems, loving them as their own children. It is to this kind of thing I should be inclined to compare the case of benefactors: for the object of their kindness is their own work, and so they love this more than this loves its creator.

And the account of this is that existence is to all a thing choiceworthy and an object of affection; now we exist by acts of working, that is, by living and acting; he then that has created a given work exists, it may be said, by his act of working: therefore he loves his work because he loves existence. And this is natural, for the work produced displays in act what existed before potentially.

Then again, the benefactor has a sense of honour in right of his action, so that he may well take pleasure in him in whom this resides; but to him who has received the benefit there is nothing honourable in respect of his benefactor, only something advantageous which is both less pleasant and less the object of Friendship.

Again, pleasure is derived from the actual working out of a present action, from the anticipation of a future one, and from the recollection of a past one: but the highest pleasure and special object of affection is that which attends on the actual working. Now the benefactor's work abides (for the honourable is enduring), but the advantage of him who has received the kindness passes away.

Again, there is pleasure in recollecting honourable actions, but in recollecting advantageous ones there is none at all or much less (by the way though, the contrary is true of the expectation of advantage).

Further, the entertaining the feeling of Friendship is like acting on another; but being the object of the feeling is like being acted upon.

So then, entertaining the sentiment of Friendship, and all feelings connected with it, attend on those who, in the given case of a benefaction, are the superior party.

Once more: all people value most what has cost them much labour in the production; for instance, people who have themselves made their money are fonder of it than those who have inherited it: and receiving kindness is, it seems, unlaborious, but doing it is laborious. And this is the reason why the female parents are most fond of their offspring; for their part in producing them is attended with most labour, and they know more certainly that they are theirs. This feeling would seem also to belong to benefactors.

A question is also raised as to whether it is right to love one's Self best, or some one else: because men find fault with those who love themselves best, and call them in a disparaging way lovers of Self; and the bad man is thought to do everything he does for his own sake merely, and the more so the more depraved he is; accordingly men reproach him with never doing anything unselfish: whereas the good man acts from a sense of honour (and the more so the better man he is), and for his friend's sake, and is careless of his own interest.

But with these theories facts are at variance, and not unnaturally: for it is commonly said also that a man is to love most him who is most his friend, and he is most a friend who wishes good to him to whom he wishes it for that man's sake even though no one knows. Now these conditions, and in fact all the rest by which a friend is characterised, belong specially to each individual in respect of his Self: for we have said before that all the friendly feelings are derived to others from those which have Self primarily for their object. And all the current proverbs support this view; for instance, "one soul," "the goods of friends are common," "equality is a tie of Friendship," "the knee is nearer than the shin." For all these things exist specially with reference to a man's own Self: he is specially a friend to himself and so he is bound to love himself the most.

It is with good reason questioned which of the two parties one should follow, both having plausibility on their side. Perhaps then, in respect of theories of this kind, the proper course is to distinguish and define how far each is true, and in what way. If we could ascertain the sense in which each uses the term "Self-loving," this point might be cleared up.

Well now, they who use it disparagingly give the name to those who, in respect of wealth, and honours, and pleasures of the body, give to themselves the larger share: because the mass of mankind grasp after these and are earnest about them as being the best things; which is the reason why they are matters of contention. They who are covetous in regard to these gratify their lusts and passions in general, that is to say the irrational part of their soul: now the mass of mankind are so disposed, for which reason the appellation has taken its rise from that mass which is low and bad. Of course they are justly reproached who are Self-loving in this sense.

And that the generality of men are accustomed to apply the term to denominate those who do give such things to themselves is quite plain: suppose, for instance, that a man were anxious to do, more than other men, acts of justice, or self-mastery, or any other virtuous acts, and, in general, were to secure to himself that which is abstractedly noble and honourable, no one would call him Self-loving, nor blame him.

Yet might such an one be judged to be more truly Self-loving: certainly he gives to himself the things which are most noble and most good, and gratifies that Principle of his nature which is most rightfully authoritative, and obeys it in everything: and just as that which possesses the highest authority is thought to constitute a Community or any other system, so also in the case of Man: and so he is most truly Self-loving who loves and gratifies this Principle.

Again, men are said to have, or to fail of having, self-control according as the Intellect controls or not, it being plainly implied thereby that this Principle constitutes each individual; and people are thought to have done of themselves, and voluntarily, those things specially which are done with Reason.

It is plain, therefore, that this Principle does, either entirely or specially, constitute the individual man, and that the good man specially loves this. For this reason then he must be specially Self-loving, in a kind other than that which is reproached, and as far superior to it as living in accordance with Reason is to living at the beck and call of passion, and aiming at the truly noble to aiming at apparent advantage.

Now all approve and commend those who are eminently earnest about honourable actions, and if all would vie with one another in respect of the καλὸν, and be intent upon doing what is most truly noble and honourable, society at large would have all that is proper while each individual in particular would have the greatest of goods, Virtue being assumed to be such.

And so the good man ought to be Self-loving: because by doing what is noble he will have advantage himself and will do good to others: but the bad man ought not to be, because he will harm himself and his neighbours by following low and evil passions. In the case of the bad man, what he ought to do and what he does are at variance, but the good man does what he ought to do, because all Intellect chooses what is best for itself and the good man puts himself under the direction of Intellect.

Of the good man it is true likewise that he does many things for the sake of his friends and his country, even to the extent of dying for them, if need be: for money and honours, and, in short, all the good things which others fight for, he will throw away while eager to secure to himself the καλὸν: he will prefer a brief and great joy to a tame and enduring one, and to live nobly for one year rather than ordinarily for many, and one great and noble action to many trifling ones. And this is perhaps that which befalls men who die for their country and friends; they choose great glory for themselves: and they will lavish their own money that their friends may receive more, for hereby the friend gets the money but the man himself the καλὸν; so, in fact, he gives to himself the greater good. It is the same with honours and offices; all these things he will give up to his friend, because this reflects honour and praise on himself: and so with good reason is he esteemed a fine character since he chooses the honourable before all things else. It is possible also to give up the opportunities of action to a friend; and to have caused a friend's doing a thing may be more noble than having done it one's self.

In short, in all praiseworthy things the good man does plainly give to himself a larger share of the honourable. In this sense it is right to be Self-loving, in the vulgar acceptation of the term it is not.

A question is raised also respecting the Happy man, whether he will want Friends, or no?

Some say that they who are blessed and independent have no need of Friends, for they already have all that is good, and so, as being independent, want nothing further: whereas the notion of a friend's office is to be as it were a second Self and procure for a man what he cannot get by himself: hence the saying,

"When Fortune gives us good, what need we Friends?"

On the other hand, it looks absurd, while we are assigning to the Happy man all other good things, not to give him Friends, which are, after all, thought to be the greatest of external goods.

Again, if it is more characteristic of a friend to confer than to receive kindnesses, and if to be beneficent belongs to the good man and to the character of virtue, and if it is more noble to confer kindnesses on friends than strangers, the good man will need objects for his benefactions. And out of this last consideration springs a question whether the need of Friends be greater in prosperity or adversity, since the unfortunate man wants people to do him kindnesses and they who are fortunate want objects for their kind acts.

Again, it is perhaps absurd to make our Happy man a solitary, because no man would choose the possession of all goods in the world on the condition of solitariness, man being a social animal and formed by nature for living with others: of course the Happy man has this qualification since he has all those things which are good by nature: and it is obvious that the society of friends and good men must be preferable to that of strangers and ordinary people, and we conclude, therefore, that the Happy man does need Friends.

But then, what do they mean whom we quoted first, and how are they right? Is it not that the mass of mankind mean by Friends those who are useful? and of course the Happy man will not need such because he has all good things already; neither will he need such as are Friends with a view to the pleasurable, or at least only to a slight extent;

because his life, being already pleasurable, does not want pleasure imported from without; and so, since the Happy man does not need Friends of these kinds, he is thought not to need any at all.

But it may be, this is not true: for it was stated originally, that Happiness is a kind of Working; now Working plainly is something that must come into being, not be already there like a mere piece of property.

If then the being happy consists in living and working, and the good man's working is in itself excellent and pleasurable (as we said at the commencement of the treatise), and if what is our own reckons among things pleasurable, and if we can view our neighbours better than ourselves and their actions better than we can our own, then the actions of their Friends who are good men are pleasurable to the good; inasmuch as they have both the requisites which are naturally pleasant. So the man in the highest state of happiness will need Friends of this kind, since he desires to contemplate good actions, and actions of his own, which those of his friend, being a good man, are.

Again, common opinion requires that the Happy man live with pleasure to himself: now life is burthensome to a man in solitude, for it is not easy to work continuously by one's self, but in company with, and in regard to others, it is easier, and therefore the working, being pleasurable in itself, will be more continuous (a thing which should be in respect of the Happy man); for the good man, in that he is good, takes pleasure in the actions which accord with Virtue and is annoyed at those which spring from Vice, just as a musical man is pleased with beautiful music and annoyed by bad. And besides, as Theognis says, Virtue itself may be improved by practice, from living with the good.

And, upon the following considerations more purely metaphysical, it will probably appear that the good friend is naturally choiceworthy to the good man. We have said before, that whatever is naturally good is also in itself good and pleasant to the good man; now the fact of living, so far as animals are concerned, is characterised generally by the power of sentience, in man it is characterised by that of sentience, or of rationality (the faculty of course being referred to the actual operation of the faculty, certainly the main point is the actual operation of it); so that living seems mainly to consist in the act of sentience or exerting rationality: now the fact of living is in itself one of the things that are good and pleasant (for it is a definite totality, and whatever is such belongs to the nature of good), but what is naturally good is good to the good man: for which reason it seems to be pleasant to all. (Of course one must not suppose a life which is depraved and corrupted, nor one spent in pain, for that which is such is indefinite as are its inherent qualities: however, what is to be said of pain will be clearer in what is to follow.)

If then the fact of living is in itself good and pleasant (and this appears from the fact that all desire it, and specially those who are good and in high happiness; their course of life being most choiceworthy and their existence most choiceworthy likewise), then also he that sees perceives that he sees: and he that hears perceives that he hears; and he that walks perceives that he walks; and in all the other instances in like manner there is a faculty which reflects upon and perceives the fact that we are working, so that we can perceive that we perceive and intellectually know that we intellectually know: but to perceive that we perceive or that we intellectually know is to perceive that we exist, since existence was defined to be perceiving or intellectually knowing. Now to perceive that one lives is a thing pleasant in itself, life being a thing naturally good, and the perceiving of the presence in ourselves of things naturally good being pleasant.

Therefore the fact of living is choiceworthy, and to the good specially so since existence is good and pleasant to them: for they receive pleasure from the internal consciousness of that which in itself is good.

But the good man is to his friend as to himself, friend being but a name for a second Self; therefore as his own existence is choiceworthy to each so too, or similarly at least, is his friend's existence. But the ground of one's own existence being choiceworthy is the perceiving of one's self being good, any such perception being in itself pleasant. Therefore one ought to be thoroughly conscious of one's friend's existence, which will result from living with him, that is sharing in his words and thoughts: for this is the meaning of the term as applied to the human species, not mere feeding together as in the case of brutes.

If then to the man in a high state of happiness existence is in itself choiceworthy, being naturally good and pleasant, and so too a friend's existence, then the friend also must be among things choiceworthy. But whatever is choiceworthy to a man he should have or else he will be in this point deficient. The man therefore who is to come up to our notion "Happy" will need good Friends.

Are we then to make our friends as numerous as possible? or, as in respect of acquaintance it is thought to have been well said "have not thou many acquaintances yet be not without;" so too in respect of Friendship may we adopt the precept, and say that a man should not be without friends, nor again have exceeding many friends?

Now as for friends who are intended for use, the maxim I have quoted will, it seems, fit in exceedingly well, because to requite the services of many is a matter of labour, and a whole life would not be long enough to do this for them. So that, if more numerous than what will suffice for one's own life, they become officious, and are hindrances in respect of living well: and so we do not want them. And again, of those who are to be for pleasure a few are quite enough, just like sweetening in our food.

But of the good are we to make as many as ever we can, or is there any measure of the number of friends, as there is of the number to constitute a Political Community? I mean, you cannot make one out of ten men, and if you increase the number to one hundred thousand it is not any longer a Community. However, the number is not perhaps some one definite number but any between certain extreme limits.

Well, of friends likewise there is a limited number, which perhaps may be laid down to be the greatest number with whom it would be possible to keep up intimacy; this being thought to be one of the greatest marks of Friendship, and it being quite obvious that it is not possible to be intimate with many, in other words, to part one's self among many. And besides it must be remembered that they also are to be friends to one another if they are all to live together: but it is a matter of difficulty to find this in many men at once.

It comes likewise to be difficult to bring home to one's self the joys and sorrows of many: because in all probability one would have to sympathise at the same time with the joys of this one and the sorrows of that other.

Perhaps then it is well not to endeavour to have very many friends but so many as are enough for intimacy: because, in fact, it would seem not to be possible to be very much a friend to many at the same time: and, for the same reason, not to be in love with many objects at the same time: love being a kind of excessive Friendship which implies but one object: and all strong emotions must be limited in the number towards whom they are felt.

And if we look to facts this seems to be so: for not many at a time become friends in the way of companionship, all the famous Friendships of the kind are between *two* persons: whereas they who have many friends, and meet everybody on the footing of intimacy, seem to be friends really to no one except in the way of general society; I mean the characters denominated as over-complaisant.

To be sure, in the way merely of society, a man may be a friend to many without being necessarily over-complaisant, but being truly good: but one cannot be a friend to many because of their virtue, and for the persons' own sake; in fact, it is a matter for contentment to find even a few such.

Again: are friends most needed in prosperity or in adversity? they are required, we know, in both states, because the unfortunate need help and the prosperous want people to live with and to do kindnesses to: for they have a desire to act kindly to some one.

To have friends is more necessary in adversity, and therefore in this case useful ones are wanted; and to have them in prosperity is more ho- nourable, and this is why the prosperous want good men for friends, it being preferable to confer benefits on, and to live with, these. For the very presence of friends is pleasant even in adversity: since men when grieved are comforted by the sympathy of their friends.

And from this, by the way, the question might be raised, whether it is that they do in a manner take part of the weight of calamities, or only that their presence, being pleasurable, and the consciousness of their sympathy, make the pain of the sufferer less.

However, we will not further discuss whether these which have been suggested or some other causes produce the relief, at least the effect we speak of is a matter of plain fact.

But their presence has probably a mixed effect: I mean, not only is the very seeing friends pleasant, especially to one in misfortune, and ac- tual help towards lessening the grief is afforded (the natural tendency of a friend, if he is gifted with tact, being to comfort by look and word, because he is well acquainted with the sufferer's temper and disposition and therefore knows what things give him pleasure and pain), but also the perceiving a friend to be grieved at his misfortunes causes the suf- ferer pain, because every one avoids being cause of pain to his friends. And for this reason they who are of a manly nature are cautious not to implicate their friends in their pain; and unless a man is exceedingly callous to the pain of others he cannot bear the pain which is thus caused to his friends: in short, he does not admit men to wail with him, not being given to wail at all: women, it is true, and men who resem- ble women, like to have others to groan with them, and love such as friends and sympathisers. But it is plain that it is our duty in all things to imitate the highest character.

On the other hand, the advantages of friends in our prosperity are the pleasurable intercourse and the consciousness that they are pleased at our good fortune.

It would seem, therefore, that we ought to call in friends readily on occasion of good fortune, because it is noble to be ready to do good to others: but on occasion of bad fortune, we should do so with reluctance; for we should as little as possible make others share in our ills; on which principle goes the saying, "I am unfortunate, let that suffice." The most proper occasion for calling them in is when with small trouble or annoyance to themselves they can be of very great use to the person who needs them.

But, on the contrary, it is fitting perhaps to go to one's friends in their misfortunes unasked and with alacrity (because kindness is the friend's office and specially towards those who are in need and who do not demand it as a right, this being more creditable and more pleasant to both); and on occasion of their good fortune to go readily, if we can forward it in any way (because men need their friends for this likewise), but to be backward in sharing it, any great eagerness to receive advantage not being creditable.

One should perhaps be cautious not to present the appearance of sullenness in declining the sympathy or help of friends, for this happens occasionally.

It appears then that the presence of friends is, under all circumstances, choiceworthy.

May we not say then that, as seeing the beloved object is most prized by lovers and they choose this sense rather than any of the others because Love

> "Is engendered in the eyes,
>   With gazing fed,"

in like manner intimacy is to friends most choiceworthy, Friendship being communion? Again, as a man is to himself so is he to his friend; now with respect to himself the perception of his own existence is choiceworthy, therefore is it also in respect of his friend.

And besides, their Friendship is acted out in intimacy, and so with good reason they desire this. And whatever in each man's opinion constitutes existence, or whatsoever it is for the sake of which they choose life, herein they wish their friends to join with them; and so some men drink together, others gamble, others join in gymnastic exercises or hunting, others study philosophy together: in each case spending their days together in that which they like best of all things in life, for since they wish to be intimate with their friends they do and partake in those things whereby they think to attain this object.

Therefore the Friendship of the wicked comes to be depraved; for, being unstable, they share in what is bad and become depraved in being made like to one another: but the Friendship of the good is good, growing with their intercourse; they improve also, as it seems, by repeated acts, and by mutual correction, for they receive impress from one another in the points which give them pleasure; whence says the poet,

"Thou from the good, good things shalt surely learn."

Here then we will terminate our discourse of Friendship. The next thing is to go into the subject of Pleasure.

BOOK X

NEXT, it would seem, follows a discussion respecting Pleasure, for it is thought to be most closely bound up with our kind: and so men train the young, guiding them on their course by the rudders of Pleasure and Pain. And to like and dislike what one ought is judged to be most important for the formation of good moral character: because these feelings extend all one's life through, giving a bias towards and exerting an influence on the side of Virtue and Happiness, since men choose what is pleasant and avoid what is painful.

Subjects such as these then, it would seem, we ought by no means to pass by, and specially since they involve much difference of opinion. There are those who call Pleasure the Chief Good; there are others who on the contrary maintain that it is exceedingly bad; some perhaps from a real conviction that such is the case, others from a notion that it is better, in reference to our life and conduct, to show up Pleasure as bad, even if it is not so really; arguing that, as the mass of men have a bias towards it and are the slaves of their pleasures, it is right to draw them to the contrary, for that so they may possibly arrive at the mean.

I confess I suspect the soundness of this policy; in matters respecting men's feelings and actions theories are less convincing than facts: whenever, therefore, they are found conflicting with actual experience, they not only are despised but involve the truth in their fall: he, for instance, who deprecates Pleasure, if once seen to aim at it, gets the credit of backsliding to it as being universally such as he said it was, the mass of men being incapable of nice distinctions.

Real accounts, therefore, of such matters seem to be most expedient, not with a view to knowledge merely but to life and conduct: for they are believed as being in harmony with facts, and so they prevail with the wise to live in accordance with them.

But of such considerations enough: let us now proceed to the current maxims respecting Pleasure.

Now Eudoxus thought Pleasure to be the Chief Good because he saw all, rational and irrational alike, aiming at it: and he argued that, since in all what was the object of choice must be good and what most so the best, the fact of all being drawn to the same thing proved this thing to be the best for all: "For each," he said, "finds what is good for itself just as it does its proper nourishment, and so that which is good for all, and the object of the aim of all, is their Chief Good."

(And his theories were received, not so much for their own sake, as because of his excellent moral character; for he was thought to be eminently possessed of perfect self-mastery, and therefore it was not thought that he said these things because he was a lover of Pleasure but that he really was so convinced.)

And he thought his position was not less proved by the argument from the contrary: that is, since Pain was in itself an object of avoidance to all the contrary must be in like manner an object of choice.

Again he urged that that is most choiceworthy which we choose, not by reason of, or with a view to, anything further; and that Pleasure is confessedly of this kind because no one ever goes on to ask to what purpose he is pleased, feeling that Pleasure is in itself choiceworthy.

Again, that when added to any other good it makes it more choiceworthy; as, for instance, to actions of justice, or perfected self-mastery; and good can only be increased by itself.

However, this argument at least seems to prove only that it belongs to the class of goods, and not that it does so more than anything else: for every good is more choiceworthy in combination with some other than when taken quite alone. In fact, it is by just such an argument that Plato proves that Pleasure is not the Chief Good: "For," says he, "the life of Pleasure is more choiceworthy in combination with Practical Wisdom than apart from it; but, if the compound be better, then simple Pleasure cannot be the Chief Good; because the very Chief Good cannot by any addition become more choiceworthy than it is already:" and it is obvious that nothing else can be the Chief Good, which by combination with any of the things in themselves good comes to be more choiceworthy.

What is there then of such a nature? (meaning, of course, whereof we can partake; because that which we are in search of must be such).

As for those who object that "what all aim at is not necessarily good," I confess I cannot see much in what they say, because what all *think* we say *is*. And he who would cut away this ground from under us will not bring forward things more dependable: because if the argument had rested on the desires of irrational creatures there might have been something in what he says, but, since the rational also desire Pleasure, how can his objection be allowed any weight? and it may be that, even in the lower animals, there is some natural good principle above themselves which aims at the good peculiar to them.

Nor does that seem to be sound which is urged respecting the argument from the contrary: I mean, some people say "it does not follow that Pleasure must be good because Pain is evil, since evil may be opposed to evil, and both evil and good to what is indifferent:" now what they say is right enough in itself but does not hold in the present instance. If both Pleasure and Pain were bad both would have been objects of avoidance; or if neither then neither would have been, at all events they must have fared alike: but now men do plainly avoid the one as bad and choose the other as good, and so there is a complete opposition.

Nor again is Pleasure therefore excluded from being a good because it does not belong to the class of qualities: the acts of virtue are not qualities, neither is Happiness [yet surely both are goods].

Again, they say the Chief Good is limited but Pleasure unlimited, in that it admits of degrees.

Now if they judge this from the act of feeling Pleasure then the same thing will apply to justice and all the other virtues, in respect of which clearly it is said that men are more or less of such and such characters (according to the different virtues), they are more just or more brave, or one may practise justice and self-mastery more or less.

If, on the other hand, they judge in respect of the Pleasures themselves then it may be they miss the true cause, namely, that some are unmixed and others mixed: for just as health, being in itself limited, admits of degrees, why should not Pleasure do so and yet be limited? in the former case we account for it by the fact that there is not the same adjustment of parts in all men, nor one and the same always in the same individual: but health, though relaxed, remains up to a certain point, and differs in degrees; and of course the same may be the case with Pleasure.

Again, assuming the Chief Good to be perfect and all Movements and Generations imperfect, they try to show that Pleasure is a Movement and a Generation.

Yet they do not seem warranted in saying even that it is a Movement: for to every Movement are thought to belong swiftness and slowness, and if not in itself, as to that of the universe, yet relatively: but to Pleasure neither of these belongs: for though one may have got quickly into the state of Pleasure, as into that of anger, one cannot be in the state quickly, nor relatively to the state of any other person; but we can walk or grow, and so on, quickly or slowly.

Of course it is possible to change into the state of Pleasure quickly or slowly, but to act in the state (by which, I mean have the perception of Pleasure) quickly, is not possible.

And how can it be a Generation? because, according to notions generally held, not *any*thing is generated from *any*thing, but a thing resolves itself into that out of which it was generated: whereas of that of which Pleasure is a Generation Pain is a Destruction.

Again, they say that Pain is a lack of something suitable to nature and Pleasure a supply of it.

But these are affections of the body: now if Pleasure really is a supplying of somewhat suitable to nature, that must feel the Pleasure in which the supply takes place, therefore the body of course: yet this is not thought to be so: neither then is Pleasure a supplying, only a person of course will be pleased when a supply takes place just as he will be pained when he is cut.

This notion would seem to have arisen out of the Pains and Pleasures connected with natural nourishment; because, when people have felt a lack and so have had Pain first, they, of course, are pleased with the supply of their lack.

But this is not the case with all Pleasures: those attendant on mathematical studies, for instance, are unconnected with any Pain; and of such as attend on the senses those which arise through the sense of Smell; and again, many sounds, and sights, and memories, and hopes: now of what can these be Generations? because there has been here no lack of anything to be afterwards supplied.

And to those who bring forward disgraceful Pleasures we may reply that these are not really pleasant things; for it does not follow because they are pleasant to the ill-disposed that we are to admit that they are pleasant except to them; just as we should not say that those things are really wholesome, or sweet, or bitter, which are so to the sick, or those objects really white which give that impression to people labouring under ophthalmia.

Or we might say thus, that the Pleasures are choiceworthy but not as derived from these sources: just as wealth is, but not as the price of treason; or health, but not on the terms of eating anything however loathsome.

Or again, may we not say that Pleasures differ in kind? those derived from honourable objects, for instance, are different from those arising from disgraceful ones; and it is not possible to experience the Pleasure of the just man without being just, or of the musical man without being musical; and so on of others.

The distinction commonly drawn between the friend and the flatterer would seem to show clearly either that Pleasure is not a good, or that there are different kinds of Pleasure: for the former is thought to have good as the object of his intercourse, the latter Pleasure only; and this last is reproached, but the former men praise as having different objects in his intercourse.

Again, no one would choose to live with a child's intellect all his life through, though receiving the highest possible Pleasure from such objects as children receive it from; or to take Pleasure in doing any of the most disgraceful things, though sure never to be pained.

There are many things also about which we should be diligent even though they brought no Pleasure; as seeing, remembering, knowing, possessing the various Excellences; and the fact that Pleasures do follow on these naturally makes no difference, because we should certainly choose them even though no Pleasure resulted from them.

It seems then to be plain that Pleasure is not the Chief Good, nor is every kind of it choiceworthy: and that there are some choiceworthy in themselves, differing in kind, *i.e.* in the sources from which they are derived. Let this then suffice by way of an account of the current maxims respecting Pleasure and Pain.

Now what it is, and how characterised, will be more plain if we take up the subject afresh.

An act of Sight is thought to be complete at any moment; that is to say, it lacks nothing the accession of which subsequently will complete its whole nature.

Well, Pleasure resembles this: because it is a whole, as one may say; and one could not at any moment of time take a Pleasure whose whole nature would be completed by its lasting for a longer time. And for this reason it is not a Movement: for all Movement takes place in time of certain duration and has a certain End to accomplish; for instance, the Movement of house-building is then only complete when the builder has produced what he intended, that is, either in the whole time [necessary to complete the whole design], or in a given portion. But all the subordinate Movements are incomplete in the parts of the time, and are different in kind from the whole movement and from one another (I mean, for instance, that the fitting the stones together is a Movement different from that of fluting the column, and both again from the construction of the Temple as a whole: but this last is complete as lacking nothing to the result proposed; whereas that of the basement, or of the triglyph, is incomplete, because each is a Movement of a part merely).

As I said then, they differ in kind, and you cannot at any time you choose find a Movement complete in its whole nature, but, if at all, in the whole time requisite.

And so it is with the Movement of walking and all others: for, if motion be a Movement from one place to another place, then of it too there are different kinds, flying, walking, leaping, and such-like. And not only so, but there are different kinds even in walking: the where-from and where-to are not the same in the whole Course as in a portion of it; nor in one portion as in another; nor is crossing this line the same as crossing that: because a man is not merely crossing a line but a line in a given place, and this is in a different place from that.

Of Movement I have discoursed exactly in another treatise. I will now therefore only say that it seems not to be complete at any given moment; and that most movements are incomplete and specifically different, since the whence and whither constitute different species.

But of Pleasure the whole nature is complete at any given moment: it is plain then that Pleasure and Movement must be different from one another, and that Pleasure belongs to the class of things whole and complete. And this might appear also from the impossibility of moving except in a definite time, whereas there is none with respect to the sensation of Pleasure, for what exists at the very present moment is a kind of "whole."

From these considerations then it is plain that people are not warranted in saying that Pleasure is a Movement or a Generation: because these terms are not applicable to all things, only to such as are divisible and not "wholes:" I mean that of an act of Sight there is no Generation, nor is there of a point, nor of a monad, nor is any one of these a Movement or a Generation: neither then of Pleasure is there Movement or Generation, because it is, as one may say, "a whole."

Now since every Percipient Faculty works upon the Object answering to it, and perfectly the Faculty in a good state upon the most excellent of the Objects within its range (for Perfect Working is thought to be much what I have described; and we will not raise any question about saying "the Faculty" works, instead of, "that subject wherein the Faculty resides"), in each case the best Working is that of the Faculty in its best state upon the best of the Objects answering to it. And this will be, further, most perfect and most pleasant: for Pleasure is attendant upon every Percipient Faculty, and in like manner on every intellectual operation and speculation; and that is most pleasant which is most perfect, and that most perfect which is the Working of the best Faculty upon the most excellent of the Objects within its range.

And Pleasure perfects the Working. But Pleasure does not perfect it in the same way as the Faculty and Object of Perception do, being good; just as health and the physician are not in similar senses causes of a healthy state.

And that Pleasure does arise upon the exercise of every Percipient Faculty is evident, for we commonly say that sights and sounds are pleasant; it is plain also that this is especially the case when the Faculty is most excellent and works upon a similar Object: and when both the Object and Faculty of Perception are such, Pleasure will always exist, supposing of course an agent and a patient.

Furthermore, Pleasure perfects the act of Working not in the way of an inherent state but as a supervening finish, such as is bloom in people at their prime. Therefore so long as the Object of intellectual or sensitive Perception is such as it should be and also the Faculty which discerns or realises the Object, there will be Pleasure in the Working: because when that which has the capacity of being acted on and that which is apt to act are alike and similarly related, the same result follows naturally.

How is it then that no one feels Pleasure continuously? is it not that he wearies, because all human faculties are incapable of unintermitting exertion; and so, of course, Pleasure does not arise either, because that follows upon the act of Working. But there are some things which please when new, but afterwards not in the like way, for exactly the same reason: that at first the mind is roused and works on these Objects with its powers at full tension; just as they who are gazing stedfastly at anything; but afterwards the act of Working is not of the kind it was at first, but careless, and so the Pleasure too is dulled.

Again, a person may conclude that all men grasp at Pleasure, because all aim likewise at Life and Life is an act of Working, and every man works at and with those things which also he best likes; the musical man, for instance, works with his hearing at music; the studious man with his intellect at speculative questions, and so forth. And Pleasure perfects the acts of Working, and so Life after which men grasp. No wonder then that they aim also at Pleasure, because to each it perfects Life, which is itself choiceworthy. (We will take leave to omit the question whether we choose Life for Pleasure's sake or Pleasure for Life's sake; becuse these two plainly are closely connected and admit not of separation; since Pleasure comes not into being without Working, and again, every Working Pleasure perfects.)

And this is one reason why Pleasures are thought to differ in kind, because we suppose that things which differ in kind must be perfected by things so differing: it plainly being the case with the productions of Nature and Art; as animals, and trees, and pictures, and statues, and houses, and furniture; and so we suppose that in like manner acts of Working which are different in kind are perfected by things differing in kind. Now Intellectual Workings differ specifically from those of the Senses, and these last from one another; therefore so do the Pleasures which perfect them.

This may be shown also from the intimate connection subsisting between each Pleasure and the Working which it perfects: I mean, that the Pleasure proper to any Working increases that Working; for they who work with Pleasure sift all things more closely and carry them out to a greater degree of nicety; for instance, those men become geometricians who take Pleasure in geometry, and they apprehend particular points more completely: in like manner men who are fond of music, or architecture, or anything else, improve each on his own pursuit, because they feel Pleasure in them. Thus the Pleasures aid in increasing the Workings, and things which do so aid are proper and peculiar: but the things which are proper and peculiar to others specifically different are themselves also specifically different.

Yet even more clearly may this be shown from the fact that the Pleasures arising from one kind of Workings hinder other Workings; for instance, people who are fond of flute-music cannot keep their attention to conversation or discourse when they catch the sound of a flute; because they take more Pleasure in flute-playing than in the Working they are at the time engaged on; in other words, the Pleasure attendant on flute-playing destroys the Working of conversation or discourse.

Much the same kind of thing takes place in other cases, when a person is engaged in two different Workings at the same time: that is, the pleasanter of the two keeps pushing out the other, and, if the disparity in pleasantness be great, then more and more till a man even ceases altogether to work at the other.

This is the reason why, when we are very much pleased with anything whatever, we do nothing else, and it is only when we are but moderately pleased with one occupation that we vary it with another: people, for instance, who eat sweetmeats in the theatre do so most when the performance is indifferent.

Since then the proper and peculiar Pleasure gives accuracy to the Workings and makes them more enduring and better of their kind, while those Pleasures which are foreign to them mar them, it is plain there is a wide difference between them: in fact, Pleasures foreign to any Working have pretty much the same effect as the Pains proper to it, which, in fact, destroy the Workings; I mean, if one man dislikes writing, or another calculation, the one does not write, the other does not calculate; because, in each case, the Working is attended with some Pain: so then contrary effects are produced upon the Workings by the Pleasures and Pains proper to them, by which I mean those which arise upon the Working, in itself, independently of any other circumstances. As for the Pleasures foreign to a Working, we have said already that they produce a similar effect to the Pain proper to it; that is they destroy the Working, only not in like way.

Well then, as Workings differ from one another in goodness and badness, some being fit objects of choice, others of avoidance, and others in their nature indifferent, Pleasures are similarly related; since its own proper Pleasure attends on each Working: of course that proper to a good Working is good, that proper to a bad, bad: for even the desires for what is noble are praiseworthy, and for what is base blameworthy.

Furthermore, the Pleasures attendant on Workings are more closely connected with them even than the desires after them: for these last are separate both in time and nature, but the former are close to the Workings, and so indivisible from them as to raise a question whether the Working and the Pleasure are identical; but Pleasure does not seem to be an Intellectual Operation nor a Faculty of Perception, because that is absurd; but yet it gives some the impression of being the same from not being separated from these.

As then the Workings are different so are their Pleasures; now Sight differs from Touch in purity, and Hearing and Smelling from Taste; therefore, in like manner, do their Pleasures; and again, Intellectual Pleasures from these Sensual, and the different kinds both of Intellectual and Sensual from one another.

It is thought, moreover, that each animal has a Pleasure proper to itself, as it has a proper Work; that Pleasure of course which is attendant on the Working. And the soundness of this will appear upon particular inspection: for horse, dog, and man have different Pleasures; as Heraclitus says, an ass would sooner have hay than gold; in other words, provender is pleasanter to asses than gold. So then the Pleasures of animals specifically different are also specifically different, but those of the same, we may reasonably suppose, are without difference.

Yet in the case of human creatures they differ not a little: for the very same things please some and pain others: and what are painful and hateful to some are pleasant to and liked by others. The same is the case with sweet things: the same will not seem so to the man in a fever as to him who is in health: nor will the invalid and the person in robust health have the same notion of warmth. The same is the case with other things also.

Now in all such cases that is held to *be* which impresses the good man with the notion of being such and such; and if this is a second maxim (as it is usually held to be), and Virtue, that is, the Good man, in that he is such, is the measure of everything, then those must be real Pleasures which give him the impression of being so and those things pleasant in which he takes Pleasure. Nor is it at all astonishing that what are to him unpleasant should give another person the impression of being pleasant, for men are liable to many corruptions and marrings; and the things in question are not pleasant really, only to these particular persons, and to them only as being thus disposed.

Well, of course, you may say, it is obvious that we must not assert those which are confessedly disgraceful to be real Pleasures, except to depraved tastes: but of those which are thought to be good what kind, or which, must we say is *The Pleasure of Man?* is not the answer plain from considering the Workings, because the Pleasures follow upon these?

Whether then there be one or several Workings which belong to the perfect and blessed man, the Pleasures which perfect these Workings must be said to be specially and properly *The Pleasures of Man*; and all the rest in a secondary sense, and in various degrees according as the Workings are related to those highest and best ones.

Now that we have spoken about the Excellences of both kinds, and Friendship in its varieties, and Pleasures, it remains to sketch out Happiness, since we assume that to be the one End of all human things: and we shall save time and trouble by recapitulating what was stated before.

Well then, we said that it is not a State merely; because, if it were, it might belong to one who slept all his life through and merely vegetated, or to one who fell into very great calamities: and so, if these possibilities displease us and we would rather put it into the rank of some kind of Working (as was also said before), and Workings are of different kinds (some being necessary and choiceworthy with a view to other things, while others are so in themselves), it is plain we must rank Happiness among those choiceworthy for their own sakes and not among those which are so with a view to something further: because Happiness has no lack of anything but is self-sufficient.

By choiceworthy in themselves are meant those from which nothing is sought beyond the act of Working: and of this kind are thought to be the actions according to Virtue, because doing what is noble and excellent is one of those things which are choiceworthy for their own sake alone.

And again, such amusements as are pleasant; because people do not choose them with any further purpose: in fact they receive more harm than profit from them, neglecting their persons and their property. Still the common run of those who are judged happy take refuge in such pastimes, which is the reason why they who have varied talent in such are highly esteemed among despots; because they make themselves pleasant in those things which these aim at, and these accordingly want such men.

Now these things are thought to be appurtenances of Happiness because men in power spend their leisure herein: yet, it may be, we cannot argue from the example of such men: because there is neither Virtue nor Intellect necessarily involved in having power, and yet these are the only sources of good Workings: nor does it follow that because these men, never having tasted pure and generous Pleasure, take refuge in bodily ones, we are therefore to believe them to be more choiceworthy: for children too believe that those things are most excellent which are precious in their eyes.

We may well believe that as children and men have different ideas as to what is precious so too have the bad and the good: therefore, as we have many times said, those things are really precious and pleasant which seem so to the good man: and as to each individual that Working is most choiceworthy which is in accordance with his own state to the good man that is so which is in accordance with Virtue.

Happiness then stands not in amusement; in fact the very notion is absurd of the End being amusement, and of one's toiling and enduring hardness all one's life long with a view to amusement: for everything in the world, so to speak, we choose with some further End in view, except Happiness, for that is the End comprehending all others. Now to take pains and to labour with a view to amusement is plainly foolish and very childish: but to amuse one's self with a view to steady employment afterwards, as Anacharsis says, is thought to be right: for amusement is like rest, and men want rest because unable to labour continuously.

Rest, therefore, is not an End, because it is adopted with a view to Working afterwards.

Again, it is held that the Happy Life must be one in the way of Excellence, and this is accompanied by earnestness and stands not in amusement. Moreover those things which are done in earnest, we say, are better than things merely ludicrous and joined with amusement: and we say that the Working of the better part, or the better man, is more earnest; and the Working of the better is at once better and more capable of Happiness.

Then, again, as for bodily Pleasures, any ordinary person, or even a slave, might enjoy them, just as well as the best man living: but Happiness no one supposes a slave to share except so far as it is implied in life: because Happiness stands not in such pastimes but in the Workings in the way of Excellence, as has also been stated before.

Now if Happiness is a Working in the way of Excellence of course that Excellence must be the highest, that is to say, the Excellence of the best Principle. Whether then this best Principle is Intellect or some other which is thought naturally to rule and to lead and to conceive of noble and divine things, whether being in its own nature divine or the most divine of all our internal Principles, the Working of this in accordance with its own proper Excellence must be the perfect Happiness.

That it is Contemplative has been already stated: and this would seem to be consistent with what we said before and with truth: for, in the first place, this Working is of the highest kind, since the Intellect is the highest of our internal Principles and the subjects with which it is conversant the highest of all which fall within the range of our knowledge.

Next, it is also most Continuous: for we are better able to contemplate than to do anything else whatever, continuously.

Again, we think Pleasure must be in some way an ingredient in Happiness, and of all Workings in accordance with Excellence that in the way of Science is confessedly most pleasant: at least the pursuit of Science is thought to contain Pleasures admirable for purity and permanence; and it is reasonable to suppose that the employment is more pleasant to those who have mastered, than to those who are yet seeking for, it.

And the Self-Sufficiency which people speak of will attach chiefly to the Contemplative Working: of course the actual necessaries of life are needed alike by the man of science, and the just man, and all the other characters; but, supposing all sufficiently supplied with these, the just man needs people towards whom, and in concert with whom, to practise his justice; and in like manner the man of perfected self-mastery, and the brave man, and so on of the rest; whereas the man of science can contemplate and speculate even when quite alone, and the more entirely he deserves the appellation the more able is he to do so: it may be he can do better for having fellow-workers but still he is certainly most Self-Sufficient.

Again, this alone would seem to be rested in for its own sake, since nothing results from it beyond the fact of having contemplated; whereas from all things which are objects of moral action we do mean to get something beside the doing them, be the same more or less.

Also, Happiness is thought to stand in perfect rest; for we toil that we may rest, and war that we may be at peace. Now all the Practical Virtues require either society or war for their Working, and the actions regarding these are thought to exclude rest; those of war entirely, because no one chooses war, nor prepares for war, for war's sake: he would indeed be thought a bloodthirsty villain who should make enemies of his friends to secure the existence of fighting and bloodshed. The Working also of the statesman excludes the idea of rest, and, beside the actual work of government, seeks for power and dignities or at least Happiness for the man himself and his fellow-citizens: a Happiness distinct from the national Happiness which we evidently seek as being different and distinct.

If then of all the actions in accordance with the various virtues those of policy and war are pre-eminent in honour and greatness, and these are restless, and aim at some further End, and are not choiceworthy for their own sakes, but the Working of the Intellect, being apt for contemplation, is thought to excel in earnestness, and to aim at no End beyond itself, and to have Pleasure of its own which helps to increase the Working; and if the attributes of Self-Sufficiency, and capacity of rest, and unweariedness (as far as is compatible with the infirmity of human nature), and all other attributes of the highest Happiness, plainly belong to this Working, this must be perfect Happiness, if attaining a complete duration of life; which condition is added because none of the points of Happiness is incomplete.

But such a life will be higher than mere human nature, because a man will live thus, not in so far as he is man but in so far as there is in him a divine Principle: and in proportion as this Principle excels his composite nature so far does the Working thereof excel that in accordance with any other kind of Excellence: and therefore, if pure Intellect, as compared with human nature, is divine, so too will the life in accordance with it be divine compared with man's ordinary life.

Yet must we not give ear to those who bid one as man to mind only man's affairs, or as mortal only mortal things; but, so far as we can, make ourselves like immortals and do all with a view to living in accordance with the highest Principle in us; for small as it may be in bulk yet in power and preciousness it far more excels all the others [than they it in bulk].

In fact this Principle would seem to constitute each man's "Self," since it is supreme and above all others in goodness: it *would* be absurd then for a man not to choose his own life but that of some other.

And here will apply an observation made before, that whatever is proper to each is naturally best and pleasantest to him: such then is to Man the life in accordance with pure Intellect (since this Principle is most truly Man), and if so, then it is also the happiest.

And second in degree of Happiness will be that Life which is in accordance with the other kind of Excellence, for the Workings in accordance with this are proper to Man: I mean, we do actions of justice, courage, and the other virtues, towards one another, in contracts, services of different kinds, and in all kinds of actions and feelings too, by observing what is befitting for each: and all these plainly are proper to man. Further, the Excellence of the Moral character is thought to result in some points from physical circumstances, and to be, in many, very closely connected with the passions.

Again, Practical Wisdom and Excellence of the Moral character are very closely united; since the Principles of Practical Wisdom are in accordance with the Moral Virtues and these are right when they accord with Practical Wisdom.

These moreover, as bound up with the passions, must belong to the composite nature, and the Excellences or Virtues of the composite nature are proper to man: therefore so too will be the life and Happiness which is in accordance with them. But that of the Pure Intellect is separate and distinct: and let this suffice upon the subject, since great exactness is beyond our purpose.

It would seem, moreover, to require supply of external goods to a small degree, or certainly less than the Moral Happiness: for, as far as necessaries of life are concerned, we will suppose both characters to need them equally (though, in point of fact, the man who lives in society does take more pains about his person and all that kind of thing; there will really be some little difference), but when we come to consider their Workings there will be found a great difference.

I mean, the liberal man must have money to do his liberal actions with, and the just man to meet his engagements (for mere intentions are uncertain, and even those who are unjust make a pretence of wishing to do justly), and the brave man must have power, if he is to perform any of the actions which appertain to his particular Virtue, and the man of perfected self-mastery must have opportunity of temptation, else how shall he or any of the others display his real character?

(By the way, a question is sometimes raised, whether the moral choice or the actions have most to do with Virtue, since it consists in both: it is plain that the perfection of virtuous action requires both: but for the actions many things are required, and the greater and more numerous they are the more.) But as for the man engaged in Contemplative Speculation, not only are such things unnecessary for his Working, but, so to speak, they are even hindrances: as regards the Contemplation at least; because of course in so far as he is Man and lives in society he chooses to do what Virtue requires, and so he will need such things for maintaining his character as Man though not as a speculative philosopher.

And that the perfect Happiness must be a kind of Contemplative Working may appear also from the following consideration: our conception of the gods is that they are above all blessed and happy: now what kind of Moral actions are we to attribute to them: those of justice? nay, will they not be set in a ridiculous light if represented as forming contracts, and restoring deposits, and so on? well then, shall we picture them performing brave actions, withstanding objects of fear and meeting dangers, because it is noble to do so? or liberal ones? but to whom shall they be giving? and further, it is absurd to think they have money or anything of the kind. And as for actions of perfected self-mastery, what can theirs be? would it not be a degrading praise that they have no bad desires? In short, if one followed the subject into all details all the circumstances connected with Moral actions would appear trivial and unworthy of gods.

Still, every one believes that they live, and therefore that they Work because it is not supposed that they sleep their time away like Endymion: now if from a living being you take away Action, still more if Creation, what remains but Contemplation? So then the Working of the Gods, eminent in blessedness, will be one apt for Contemplative Speculation: and of all human Workings that will have the greatest capacity for Happiness which is nearest akin to this.

A corroboration of which position is the fact that the other animals do not partake of Happiness, being completely shut out from any such Working.

To the gods then all their life is blessed; and to men in so far as there is in it some copy of such Working, but of the other animals none is happy because it in no way shares in Contemplative Speculation.

Happiness then is co-extensive with this Contemplative Speculation, and in proportion as people have the act of Contemplation so far have they also the being happy, not incidentally, but in the way of Contemplative Speculation because it is in itself precious.

So Happiness must be a kind of Contemplative Speculation; but since it is Man we are speaking of he will need likewise External Prosperity, because his Nature is not by itself sufficient for Speculation, but there must be health of body, and nourishment, and tendance of all kinds.

However, it must not be thought, because without external goods and man cannot enjoy high Happiness, that therefore he will require many and great goods in order to be happy: for neither Self-Sufficiency, nor Action, stand in Excess, and it is quite possible to act nobly without being ruler of sea and land, since even with moderate means a man may act in accordance with Virtue.

And this may be clearly seen in that men in private stations are thought to act justly, not merely no less than men in power but even more: it will be quite enough that just so much should belong to a man as is necessary, for his life will be happy who works in accordance with Virtue.

Solon perhaps drew a fair picture of the Happy, when he said that they are men moderately supplied with external goods, and who have achieved the most noble deeds, as he thought, and who have lived with perfect self-mastery: for it is quite possible for men of moderate means to act as they ought.

Anaxagoras also seems to have conceived of the Happy man not as either rich or powerful, saying that he should not wonder if he were accounted a strange man in the judgment of the multitude: for they judge by outward circumstances of which alone they have any perception.

And thus the opinions of the Wise seem to be accordant with our account of the matter: of course such things carry some weight, but truth, in matters of moral action, is judged from facts and from actual life, for herein rests the decision. So what we should do is to examine the preceding statements by referring them to facts and to actual life, and when they harmonise with facts we may accept them, when they are at variance with them conceive of them as mere theories.

Now he that works in accordance with, and pays observance to, Pure Intellect, and tends this, seems likely to be both in the best frame of mind and dearest to the Gods: because if, as is thought, any care is bestowed on human things by the Gods then it must be reasonable to think that they take pleasure in what is best and most akin to themselves (and this must be the Pure Intellect); and that they requite with kindness those who love and honour this most, as paying observance to what is dear to them, and as acting rightly and nobly. And it is quite obvious that the man of Science chiefly combines all these: he is therefore dearest to the Gods, and it is probable that he is at the same time most Happy.

Thus then on this view also the man of Science will be most Happy.

Now then that we have said enough in our sketchy kind of way on these subjects; I mean, on the Virtues, and also on Friendship and Pleasure; are we to suppose that our original purpose is completed? Must we not rather acknowledge, what is commonly said, that in matters of moral action mere Speculation and Knowledge is not the real End but rather Practice: and if so, then neither in respect of Virtue is Knowledge enough; we must further strive to have and exert it, and take whatever other means there are of becoming good.

Now if talking and writing were of themselves sufficient to make men good, they would justly, as Theognis observes, have reaped numerous and great rewards, and the thing to do would be to provide them: but in point of fact, while they plainly have the power to guide and stimulate the generous among the young and to base upon true virtuous principle any noble and truly high-minded disposition, they as plainly are powerless to guide the mass of men to Virtue and goodness; because it is not their nature to be amenable to a sense of shame but only to fear; nor to abstain from what is low and mean because it is disgraceful to do it but because of the punishment attached to it: in fact, as they live at the beck and call of passion, they pursue their own proper pleasures and the means of securing them, and they avoid the contrary pains; but as for what is noble and truly pleasurable they have not an idea of it, inasmuch as they have never tasted of it.

Men such as these then what mere words can transform? No, indeed! it is either actually impossible, or a task of no mean difficulty, to alter by words what has been of old taken into men's very dispositions: and, it may be, it is a ground for contentment if with all the means and appliances for goodness in our hands we can attain to Virtue.

The formation of a virtuous character some ascribe to Nature, some to Custom, and some to Teaching. Now Nature's part, be it what it may, obviously does not rest with us; but belongs to those who in the truest sense are fortunate, by reason of certain divine agency.

Then, as for Words and Precept, they, it is to be feared, will not avail with all; but it may be necessary for the mind of the disciple to have been previously prepared for liking and disliking as he ought; just as the soil must, to nourish the seed sown. For he that lives in obedience to passion cannot hear any advice that would dissuade him, nor, if he heard, understand: now him that is thus how can one reform? in fact, generally, passion is not thought to yield to Reason but to brute force. So then there must be, to begin with, a kind of affinity to Virtue in the disposition; which must cleave to what is honourable and loath what is disgraceful. But to get right guidance towards Virtue from the earliest youth is not easy unless one is brought up under laws of such kind; because living with self-mastery and endurance is not pleasant to the mass of men, and specially not to the young. For this reason the food, and manner of living generally, ought to be the subject of legal regulation, because things when become habitual will not be disagreeable.

Yet perhaps it is not sufficient that men while young should get right food and tendance, but, inasmuch as they will have to practise and become accustomed to certain things even after they have attained to man's estate, we shall want laws on these points as well, and, in fine, respecting one's whole life, since the mass of men are amenable to compulsion rather than Reason, and to punishment rather than to a sense of honour.

And therefore some men hold that while lawgivers should employ the sense of honour to exhort and guide men to Virtue, under the notion that they will then obey who have been well trained in habits; they should impose chastisement and penalties on those who disobey and are of less promising nature; and the incurable expel entirely: because the good man and he who lives under a sense of honour will be obedient to reason; and the baser sort, who grasp at pleasure, will be kept in check, like beasts of burthen by pain. Therefore also they say that the pains should be such as are most contrary to the pleasures which are liked.

As has been said already, he who is to be good must have been brought up and habituated well, and then live accordingly under good institutions, and never do what is low and mean, either against or with his will. Now these objects can be attained only by men living in accordance with some guiding Intellect and right order, with power to back them.

As for the Paternal Rule, it possesses neither strength nor compulsory power, nor in fact does the Rule of any one man, unless he is a king or some one in like case: but the Law has power to compel, since it is a declaration emanating from Practical Wisdom and Intellect. And people feel enmity towards their fellow-men who oppose their impulses, however rightly they may do so: the Law, on the contrary, is not the object of hatred, though enforcing right rules.

The Lacedæmonian is nearly the only State in which the framer of the Constitution has made any provision, it would seem, respecting the food and manner of living of the people: in most States these points are entirely neglected, and each man lives just as he likes, ruling his wife and children Cyclops-Fashion.

Of course, the best thing would be that there should be a right Public System and that we should be able to carry it out: but, since as a public matter those points are neglected, the duty would seem to devolve upon each individual to contribute to the cause of Virtue with his own children and friends, or at least to make this his aim and purpose: and this, it would seem, from what has been said, he will be best able to do by making a Legislator of himself: since all public systems, it is plain, are formed by the instrumentality of laws and those are good which are formed by that of good laws: whether they are written or unwritten, whether they are applied to the training of one or many, will not, it seems, make any difference, just as it does not in music, gymnastics, or any other such accomplishments, which are gained by practice.

For just as in Communities laws and customs prevail, so too in families the express commands of the Head, and customs also: and even more in the latter, because of blood-relationship and the benefits conferred: for there you have, to begin with, people who have affection and are naturally obedient to the authority which controls them.

Then, furthermore, Private training has advantages over Public, as in the case of the healing art: for instance, as a general rule, a man who is in a fever should keep quiet, and starve; but in a particular case, perhaps, this may not hold good; or, to take a different illustration, the boxer will not use the same way of fighting with all antagonists.

It would seem then that the individual will be most exactly attended to under Private care, because so each will be more likely to obtain what is expedient for him. Of course, whether in the art of healing, or gymnastics, or any other, a man will treat individual cases the better for being acquainted with general rules; as, "that so and so is good for all, or for men in such and such cases:" because general maxims are not only said to be but are the object-matter of sciences: still this is no reason against the possibility of a man's taking excellent care of some *one* case, though he possesses no scientific knowledge but from experience is exactly acquainted with what happens in each point; just as some people are thought to doctor themselves best though they would be wholly unable to administer relief to others. Yet it may seem to be necessary nevertheless, for one who wishes to become a real artist and well acquainted with the theory of his profession, to have recourse to general principles and ascertain all their capacities: for we have already stated that these are the object-matter of sciences.

If then it appears that we may become good through the instrumentality of laws, of course whoso wishes to make men better by a system of care and training must try to make a Legislator of himself; for to treat skilfully just any one who may be put before you is not what any ordinary person can do, but, if any one, he who has knowledge; as in the healing art, and all others which involve careful practice and skill.

Will not then our next business be to inquire from what sources, or how one may acquire this faculty of Legislation; or shall we say, that, as in similar cases, Statesmen are the people to learn from, since this faculty was thought to be a part of the Social Science? Must we not admit that the Political Science plainly does not stand on a similar footing to that of other sciences and faculties? I mean, that while in all other cases those who impart the faculties and themselves exert them are identical (physicians and painters for instance) matters of Statesmanship the Sophists profess to teach, but not one of them practises it, that being left to those actually engaged in it: and these might really very well be thought to do it by some singular knack and by mere practice rather than by any intellectual process: for they neither write nor speak on these matters (though it might be more to their credit than composing speeches for the courts or the assembly), nor again have they made Statesmen of their own sons or their friends.

One can hardly suppose but that they would have done so if they could, seeing that they could have bequeathed no more precious legacy to their communities, nor would they have preferred, for themselves or their dearest friends, the possession of any faculty rather than this.

Practice, however, seems to contribute no little to its acquisition; merely breathing the atmosphere of politics would never have made Statesmen of them, and therefore we may conclude that they who would acquire a knowledge of Statesmanship must have in addition practice.

But of the Sophists they who profess to teach it are plainly a long way off from doing so: in fact, they have no knowledge at all of its nature and objects; if they had, they would never have put it on the same footing with Rhetoric or even on a lower: neither would they have conceived it to be "an easy matter to legislate by simply collecting such laws as are famous because of course one could select the best," as though the selection were not a matter of skill, and the judging aright a very great matter, as in Music: for they alone, who have practical knowledge of a thing, can judge the performances rightly or understand with what means and in what way they are accomplished, and what harmonises with what: the unlearned must be content with being able to discover whether the result is good or bad, as in painting.

Now laws may be called the performances or tangible results of Political Science; how then can a man acquire from these the faculty of Legislation, or choose the best? we do not see men made physicians by compilations: and yet in these treatises men endeavour to give not only the cases but also how they may be cured, and the proper treatment in each case, dividing the various bodily habits. Well, these are thought to be useful to professional men, but to the unprofessional useless. In like manner it may be that collections of laws and Constitutions would be exceedingly useful to such as are able to speculate on them, and judge what is well, and what ill, and what kind of things fit in with what others: but they who without this qualification should go through such matters cannot have right judgment, unless they have it by instinct, though they may become more intelligent in such matters.

Since then those who have preceded us have left uninvestigated the subject of Legislation, it will be better perhaps for us to investigate it ourselves, and, in fact, the whole subject of Polity, that thus what we may call Human Philosophy may be completed as far as in us lies.

First then, let us endeavour to get whatever fragments of good there may be in the statements of our predecessors; next, from the Politics we have collected, ascertain what kind of things preserve or destroy Communities, and what, particular Constitutions; and the cause why some are well and others ill managed, for after such inquiry, we shall be the better able to take a concentrated view as to what kind of Constitution is best, what kind of regulations are best for each, and what laws and customs.

To this let us now proceed.

NOTES

P. 2, l. 12. For this term, as here employed, our language contains no equivalent expression except an inconvenient paraphrase.

There are three senses which it bears in this treatise: the first (in which it is here employed) is its strict etymological signification, "The science of Society;" and this includes everything which can bear at all upon the well-being of Man in his social capacity, "Quicquid agunt homines nostri est farrago libelli." It is in this view that it is fairly denominated most commanding and inclusive.

The second sense (in which it occurs next, just below) is "Moral Philosophy." Aristotle explains the term in this sense in the Rhetoric (i. 2) ἡ περὶ τὰ ἤθη πραγματεία ἣν δίκαιόν ἐστι προσαγορεύειν πολιτικήν. He has principally in view in this treatise the moral training of the Individual, the branch of the Science of Society which we call Ethics Proper, bearing the same relation to the larger Science as the hewing and squaring of the stones to the building of the Temple, or the drill of the Recruit to the manœuvres of the field. Greek Philosophy viewed men principally as constituent parts of a πόλις, considering this function to be the real End of each, and this state as that in which the Individual attained his highest and most complete development.

The third sense is "The detail of Civil Government," which Aristotle expressly states (vi. 8) was the most common acceptation of the term.

P. 3, l. 6. Matters of which a man is to judge either belong to some definite art or science, or they do not. In the former case he is the best judge who has thorough acquaintance with that art or science, in the latter, the man whose powers have been developed and matured by education. A lame horse one would show to a farrier, not to the best and wisest man of one's acquaintance: to the latter one would apply in a difficult case of conduct.

Experience answers to the first, a state of self-control to the latter.

P. 3, l. 17. In the last chapter of the third book of this treatise it is said of the fool, that his desire of pleasure is not only insatiable, but indiscriminate in its objects, πανταχόθεν.

P. 4, l. 3. 'Αρχὴ is a word used in this treatise in various significations.

The primary one is "beginning or first cause," and this runs through all its various uses.

"Rule," and sometimes "Rulers," are denoted by this term; the initiative being a property of Rule.

"Principle" is a very usual signification of it, and in fact the most characteristic of the Ethics. The word Principle means "starting-point." Every action has two beginnings, that of Resolve (οὖ ἕνεκα), and that of Action (ὅθεν ἡ κίνησις). I desire praise of men: this then is the beginning of Resolve. Having considered how it is to be attained, I resolve upon some course, and this Resolve is the beginning of Action.

The beginnings of Resolve, 'Αρχαὶ or Motives, when formally stated, are the major premisses of what Aristotle calls the συλλογίσμοι τῶν πρακτῶν, i.e. the reasoning into which actions may be analysed.

Thus we say that the desire of human praise was the motive of the Pharisees, or the principle on which they acted.

Their practical syllogism then would stand thus:

> Whatever gains human praise is to be done;
> Public praying and almsgiving gain human praise:
> ∴ Public praying and almsgiving are to be done.

The major premisses may be stored up in the mind as rules of action, and this is what is commonly meant by having principles good or bad.

P. 4, l. 8. The difficulty of this passage consists in determining the signification of the terms γνώριμα ημῖν ἀnd γνώριμα απλως.

I have translated them without reference to their use elsewhere, as denoting respectively what *is* and what *may be* known. All truth is γνώριμα ἀπλῶς, but that alone ἡμῖν which we individually realise, therefore those principles alone are γνώριμα ἡμῖν which *we have received as true*. From this appears immediately the necessity of good training as preparatory to the study of Moral Philosophy: for good training in habits will either work principles into our nature, or make us capable of accepting them as soon as they are put before us; which no mere intellectual training can do. The child who has been used to obey his parents may never have heard the fifth Commandment: but it is in the very texture of his nature, and the first time he hears it he will recognise it as morally true and right: the principle is in his case a fact, the reason for which he is as little inclined to ask as any one would be able to prove its truth if he should ask.

But these terms are employed elsewhere (Analytica Post. I. cap. ii. sect. 10) to denote respectively particulars and universals. The latter are so denominated, because principles or laws must be supposed to have existed before the instances of their operation. Justice must have existed before just actions, Redness before red things: but since what we meet with are the concrete instances (from which we gather the principles and laws), the particulars are said to be γνωπιμώτερα ἡμῖν.

Adopting this signification gives greater unity to the whole passage, which will then stand thus. The question being whether we are to assume principles, or obtain them by an analysis of facts, Aristotle says, "We must begin of course with what is known: but then this term denotes either particulars or universals: perhaps we then must begin with particulars: and hence the necessity of a previous good training in habits, etc. (which of course is beginning with particular facts), for a fact is a starting-point, and if this be sufficiently clear, there will be no want of the reason for the fact in addition."

The objection to this method of translation is, that ἀρχαὶ occurs immediately afterwards in the sense of "principles."

Utere tuo judicio nihil enim impedio.

P. 4, l. 37. Or "prove themselves good," as in the Prior Analytics, ii. 25, ἄπαντα πιστεύομεν κ. τ. λ.: but the other rendering is supported by a passage in Book VIII. chap. ix. οἱ δ᾽ ὑπὸ τῶν ἐπιεικῶν καὶ εἰδότων ὀρεγόμενοι τιμῆς βεβαιῶσαι τὴν οἰκείαν δόξαν ἐφίενται περὶ αὐτῶν. χαίρουσι δὴ ὅτι εἰσὶν ἀγαθοί, πιστεύοντες τῇ τῶν λεγόντων κρίσει.

P. 5, l. 7. θέσις meant originally some paradoxical statement by any philosopher of name enough to venture on one, but had come to mean any dialectical question. Topics, I. chap. ix.

P. 5, l. 9. A lost work, supposed to have been so called, because containing miscellaneous questions.

P. 5, l. 11. It is only quite at the close of the treatise that Aristotle refers to this, and allows that θεωρία constitutes the highest happiness because it is the exercise of the highest faculty in man: the reason of thus deferring the statement being that till the lower, that is the moral, nature has been reduced to perfect order, θεωρία cannot have place; though, had it been held out from the first, men would have been for making the experiment at once, without the trouble of self-discipline.

P. 5, l. 17. Or, as some think, "many theories have been founded on them."

P. 6, l. 19. The list ran thus:—

τὸ πέρας	τὸ ἄρειρον	τὸ εὐθὺ	τὸ καμπύλον
τὸ περισσὸν	τὸ ἄρτιον	τὸ φῶς	τὸ σκότος
τὸ ἒν	τὸ πλῆθος	τὸ τετράγωνον	τὸ ἑτερόμηκες
τὸ δεξιὸν	τὸ ἀριστερὸν	τὸ ἠρεμοῦν	τὸ κινούμενον
τὸ ἄρρεν	τὸ θῆλυ	τὸ ἀγαθόν	τὸ κακόν

P. 6, l. 20. Plato's sister's son.

P. 7, l. 17. This is the capital defect in Aristotle's eyes, who being eminently practical, could not like a theory which not only did not necessarily lead to action, but had a tendency to discourage it by enabling unreal men to talk finely. If true, the theory is merely a way of stating facts, and leads to no action.

P. 8, l. 27. *i.e.* the identification of Happiness with the Chief Good.

P. 8, l. 38. *i.e.* without the capability of addition.

P. 8, l. 40. And then Happiness would at once be shown not to be the Chief Good. It is a contradiction in terms to speak of adding to the Chief Good. See Book X. chap. ii. δῆλον ὡς οὐδ᾽ ἄλλο οὐδὲν τἀγαθὸν ἂν εἴη ὃ μετά τινος τῶν καθ᾽ αὐτὸ ἀγαθῶν αἱρετώτερον γίνεται.

P. 9, l. 25. *i.e.* as working or as quiescent.

P. 10, l. 19. This principle is more fully stated, with illustrations, in the Topics, I. chap. ix.

P. 10, l. 23. Either that of the bodily senses, or that of the moral senses. "Fire burns," is an instance of the former; "Treason is odious," of the latter.

P. 11, l. 20. I have thought it worth while to vary the interpretation of this word, because though "habitus" may be equivalent to all the senses, of ἕξις, "habit" is not, at least according to our colloquial usage: we commonly denote by "habit" a state formed by habituation.

P. 11, l. 26. Another and perhaps more obvious method of rendering this passage is to apply καλῶν κἀγαθῶν to things, and let them depend grammatically on ἐπήβολοι. It is to be remembered, however, that καλός κἀγαθὸς bore a special and well-known meaning: also the comparison is in the text more complete, and the point of the passage seems more completely brought out.

P. 11, l. 40. "Goodness always implies the love of itself, an affection to goodness." (Bishop Butler, Sermon xiii.) Aristotle describes pleasure in the Tenth Book of this Treatise as the result of any faculty of perception meeting with the corresponding object, vicious pleasure being as truly pleasure as the most refined and exalted. If Goodness then implies the love of itself, the percipient will always have its object present, and pleasure continually result.

P. 12, l. 14. In spite of theory, we know as a matter of fact, that external circumstances are necessary to complete the idea of Happiness: not that Happiness is capable of addition, but that when we assert it to be identical with virtuous action we must understand that it is to have a fair field; in fact, the other side of βίος τέλειος.

P. 12, l. 33. It is remarkable how Aristotle here again shelves what he considers an unpractical question. If Happiness were really a direct gift from Heaven, independently of human conduct, all motive to self-discipline and moral improvement would vanish. He shows therefore that it is no depreciation of the value of Happiness to suppose it to come partly at least from ourselves, and he then goes on with other reasons why we should think with him.

P. 13, l. 2. This term is important: what has been maimed was once perfect: he does not contemplate as possible the case of a man being born incapable of virtue, and so of happiness.

P. 13, l. 13. But why give materials and instruments, if there is no work to do?

P. 14, l. 8. The supposed pair of ancestors.

P. 14, l. 13. Solon says, "Call no man happy till he is dead."
He must mean
either, The man when dead *is* happy (*a*),
  or,   The man when dead *may be said to have been* happy (*b*).
If the former, does he mean positive happiness (α)?
             or only freedom from unhappiness(β)?
We cannot allow (α),
Men's opinions disallow (β),
We revert now to the consideration of (*b*).

P. 14, l. 32. The difficulty was raised by the clashing of a notion commonly held, and a fact universally experienced. Most people conceive that Happiness should be abiding, every one knows that fortune is changeable. It is the notion which supports the definition, because we have therein based Happiness on the most abiding cause.

P. 15, l. 33. The term seems to be employed advisedly. The Choragus, of course, dressed his actors *for their parts;* not according to their fancies or his own.

Hooker has (E. P. v. lxxvi. 5) a passage which seems to be an admirable paraphrase on this.

"Again that the measure of our outward prosperity be taken by proportion with that which every man's estate in this present life requireth. External abilities are instruments of action. It contenteth wise artificers to have their instruments proportionable to their work, rather fit for use than huge and goodly to please the eye. Seeing then the actions of a servant do not need that which may be necessary for men of calling and place in the world, neither men of inferior condition many things which greater personages can hardly want; surely they are blessed in worldly respects who have wherewith to perform what their station and place asketh, though they have no more."

P. 15, l. 33. The meaning is this: personal fortunes, we have said, must be in certain weight and number to affect our own happiness; this will be true, of course, of those which are reflected on us from our friends: and these are the only ones to which the dead are supposed to be liable: add then the difference of sensibility which it is fair to presume, and there is a very small residuum of joy or sorrow.

P. 15, l. 38. Always bearing in mind that man "never continueth in one stay."

P. 16, l. 25. This is meant for an exhaustive division of goods, which are either so *in esse* or *in posse*.

If *in esse*, they are either above praise, or subjects of praise. Those *in posse*, here called faculties, are good only when rightly used. Thus Rhetoric is a faculty which may be used to promote justice or abused to support villainy. Money in like way.

P. 17, l. 3. Eudoxus, a philosopher holding the doctrine afterwards adopted by Epicurus respecting pleasure, but (as Aristotle testifies in the Tenth Book) of irreproachable character.

P. 17, l. 10. See the Rhetoric, Book I. chap. ix.

P. 18, l. 36. The unseen is at least as real as the seen.

P. 19, l. 1. The terms are borrowed from the Seventh Book, and are here used in their strict philosophical meaning. The ἐγκρατὴς is he who has bad or unruly appetites, but whose reason is strong enough to keep them under. The ἀκρατὴς is he whose appetites constantly prevail over his reason and previous good resolutions.

By the law of habits the former is constantly approximating to a state in which the appetites are wholly quelled. This state is called σωφροσύνη, and the man in it σώφρων. By the same law, the remonstrances of reason in the latter grow fainter and fainter till they are silenced forever. This state is called ἀκολασία, and the man in it ἀκόλαστος.

P. 19, l. 8. This is untranslatable. As the Greek phrase, ἔχειν λογόν τινος, really denotes substituting that person's λόγος for one's own, so the Irrational nature in a man of self-control or perfected self-mastery substitutes the orders of Reason for its own impulses. The other phrase means the actual possession of mathematical truths as part of the mental furniture, *i.e.* knowing them.

P. 19, l. 20. ἕξιν may be taken as opposed to ἐνέργειαν, and the meaning will be, to show a difference between Moral and Intellectual Excellences, that men are commended for merely having the latter, but only for exerting and using the former.

P. 20, l. 1. Which we call simply virtue.

P. 20, l. 3. For nature must of course supply the capacity.

P. 20, l. 15. Or "as a simple result of nature."

P. 21, l. 34. This is done in the Sixth Book.

P. 21, l. 41. It is, in truth, in the application of rules to particular details of practice that our moral Responsibility chiefly lies: no rule can be so framed, that evasion shall be impossible. See Bishop Butler's Sermon on the character of Balaam, and that on Self-Deceit.

P. 22, l. 40. The words ἀκόλαστος and δειλὸς are not used here in their strict significations to denote confirmed states of vice: the ἐγκρατὴς necessarily feels pain, because he must always be thwarting passions which are a real part of his nature; though this pain will grow less and less as he nears the point of σωφροσύνη or perfected Self-Mastery, which being attained the pain will then, and then only, cease entirely. So a certain degree of fear is necessary to the *formation* of true courage. All that is meant here is, that no habit of courage or self-mastery can be said to be matured, until pain altogether vanishes.

P. 23, l. 18. Virtue consists in the due regulation of *all* the parts of our nature: our passions are a real part of that nature, and as such have their proper office; it is an error then to aim at their extirpation. It is true that in a perfect moral state emotion will be rare, but then this will have been gained by regular process, being the legitimate result of the law that "passive impressions weaken as active habits are strengthened, by repetition." If musical instruments are making discord, I may silence or I may bring them into harmony: in either case I get rid of discord, but in the latter I have the positive enjoyment of music. The Stoics would have the passions rooted out, Aristotle would have them cultivated: to use an apt figure (whose I know not), They would pluck the blossom off at once, he would leave it to fall in due course when the fruit was formed. Of them we might truly say, *Solitudinem faciunt, pacem appellant.* See on this point Bishop Butler's fifth Sermon, and sect. ii. of the chapter on Moral Discipline in the first part of his Analogy.

P. 24, l. 38. I have adopted this word from our old writers, because our word *act* is so commonly interchanged with *action.* Πρᾶξις (action) properly denotes the whole process from the conception to the performance. Πρᾶγμα (fact) only the result. The latter may be right when the former is wrong: if, for example, a murderer was killed by his accomplices. Again, the πρᾶξις may be *good* though the πρᾶγμα be wrong, as if a man under erroneous impressions does what would have been right if his impressions had been true (subject of course to the question how far he is guiltless of his original error), but in this case we could not call the πρᾶξις *right*. No repetition of πράγματα goes to form a habit. See Bishop Butler on the Theory of Habits in the chapter on Moral Discipline, quoted above, sect. ii. "And in like manner as habits belonging to the body," etc.

P. 25, l. 10. Being about to give a strict logical definition of Virtue, Aristotle ascertains first what is its genus τί ἐστιν.

P. 25, l. 26. That is, not for *merely having* them, because we did not make ourselves.

See Bishop Butler's account of our nature as containing "particular propensions," in sect. iv. of the chapter on Moral Discipline, and in the Preface to the Sermons.

P. 26, l. 17. This refers to the division of quantity (πόσον) in the Categories. Those Quantities are called by Aristotle Continuous, whose parts have position relatively to one another, as a line, surface, or solid; those discrete, whose parts have no such relation, as numbers themselves, or any string of words grammatically unconnected.

P. 26, l. 28. Numbers are in arithmetical proportion (more usually called progression), when they increase or decrease by a common difference: thus, 2, 6, 10 are so, because $2 + 4 = 6; 6 + 4 = 10$; or *vice versa*, $10 - 4 = 6; 6 - 4 = 2$.

P. 27, l. 28. The two are necessary, because since the reason itself may be perverted, a man must have recourse to an external standard: we may suppose his λόγος originally to have been a sufficient guide, but when he has injured his moral perceptions in any degree, he must go out of himself for direction.

P. 28, l. 25. This is one of the many expressions which seem to imply that this treatise is rather a collection of notes of a *vivâ voce* lecture than a set formal treatise. "The table" of virtues and vices probably was sketched out and exhibited to the audience.

P. 28, l. 38. Afterwards defined as

"All things whose value is measured by money."

P. 29, l. 15. We have no term exactly equivalent: it may be illustrated by Horace's use of the term *hiatus*,

"Quid dignum tanto feret hic promissor hiatu?" A. P. 138. Opening the mouth wide gives a promise of something great to come; if nothing great does come, this is a case of χαυνότης, or fruitless and unmeaning *hiatus*; the transference to the present subject is easy.

P. 29, l. 28. In like manner *we* talk of laudable ambition, implying of course there may be that which is not laudable.

P. 30, l. 33. An expression of Bishop Butler's, which corresponds exactly to the definition of νέμεσις in the Rhetoric.

P. 31, l. 28. That is, in the same genus: to be contraries, things must be generically connected. τὰ πλεῖστον ἀλλήλων διεστηκότα τῶν ἐν τῷ αὐτῷ γένει ἐναντία ὁρίζονται. Categories, iv. 15.

P. 32, l. 30. "Δεύτερος πλοῦς is a proverb," says the Scholiast on the Phædo, "used of those who do anything safely and cautiously, inasmuch as they who have miscarried in their first voyage, set about their preparations for the second cautiously;" and he then alludes to this passage.

P. 32, l. 38. That is, you must allow for the *recoil*.

"Naturam expellas furca tamen usque recurret."

P. 33, l. 3. This illustration sets in so clear a light the doctrines entertained respectively by Aristotle, Eudoxus, and the Stoics regarding pleasure, that it is worth while to go into it fully.

The reference is to Iliad iii. 154–160. The old counsellors, as Helen comes upon the city wall, acknowledge her surpassing beauty, and have no difficulty in understanding how both nations should have incurred such suffering for her sake: still, fair as she is, home she must go, that she bring not ruin on themselves and their posterity.

This exactly represents Aristotle's relation to Pleasure: he does not, with Eudoxus and his followers, exalt it into the Summum Bonum (as Paris would risk all for Helen), nor does he with the Stoics call it wholly evil, as Hector might have said that the woes Helen had caused had "banished all the beauty from her cheek;" but, with the aged counsellors, admits its charms, but aware of their dangerousness resolves to deny himself; he "feels her sweetness, yet defies her thrall."

P. 33, l. 18. Αἴσθησις is here used as an analogous noun, to denote the faculty which, in respect of moral matters, discharges the same function that bodily sense does in respect of physical objects. It is worth while to notice how in our colloquial language we carry out the same analogy. We say of a transaction, that it "looks ugly," "sounds oddly," is a "nasty job," "stinks in our nostrils," is a "hard dealing."

P. 35, l. 40. A man is not responsible for being θήρατος, because "particular propensions, from their very nature, must be felt, the objects of them being present; though they cannot be gratified at all, or not with the allowance of the moral principle." But he is responsible for being εὐθήρατος, because, though thus formed, he "might have improved and raised himself to an higher and more secure state of virtue by the contrary behaviour, by steadily following the moral principle, supposed to be one part of his nature, and thus withstanding that unavoidable danger of defection which necessarily arose from propension, the other part of it. For by thus preserving his integrity for some time, his danger would lessen; since propensions, by being inured to submit, would do it more easily and of course: and his security against this lessening danger would increase; since the moral principle would gain additional strength by exercise, both which things are implied in the notion of virtuous habits." (From the chapter on Moral Discipline in the Analogy, sect. iv.) The purpose of this disquisition is to refute the Necessitarians; it is resumed in the third chapter of this Book.

P. 36, l. 23. Virtue is not only the duty, but (by the laws of the Moral Government of the World) also the interest of Man, or to express it in Bishop Butler's manner, Conscience and Reasonable Self-love are the two principles in our nature which of right have supremacy over the rest, and these two lead in point of fact to the same course of action. (Sermon II.)

P. 36, l. 23. Any ignorance of particular facts affects the rightness not of the πρᾶξις, but of the πρᾶγμα; but ignorance of, i.e. incapacity to discern, Principles, shows the Moral Constitution to have been depraved, i.e. shows Conscience to be perverted, or the sight of Self-love to be impaired.

P. 37, l. 21. ἕνεκα primarily denotes the relation of cause and effect: all circumstances which in any way contribute to a certain result are ἕνεκα that result.

From the power which we have or acquire of deducing future results from present causes we are enabled to act towards, with a view to produce, these results: thus ἕνεκα comes to mean not causation merely, but *designed* causation: and so οὗ ἕνεκα is used for Motive, or final cause.

It is the primary meaning which is here intended; it would be a contradiction in terms to speak of a man's being ignorant of his own Motive of action.

When the man "drew a bow at a venture and smote the King of Israel between the joints of the harness" (I Kings xxii. 23), he did it ἕνεκα τοῦ ἀπόκτειναι the King of Israel, in the primary sense of ἕνεκα: that is to say, the King's death was *in fact the result*, but could not have been the motive, of the shot, because the King was disguised and the shot was at a venture.

P. 37, l. 26. Bishop Butler would agree to this: he says of settled deliberate anger, "It seems *in us* plainly connected with a sense of virtue and vice, of moral good and evil." See the whole Sermon on Resentment.

P. 37, l. 27. Aristotle has, I venture to think, rather quibbled here, by using ἐπιθυμία and its verb, equivocally: as there is no following his argument without condescending to the same device, I have used our word lust in its ancient signification. Ps. xxiv. 12, "What man is he that lusteth to live?"

P. 37, l. 31. The meaning is, that the *onus probandi* is thrown upon the person who maintains the distinction; Aristotle has a *primâ facie* case. The whole passage is one of difficulty. Cardwell's text gives the passage from δοκεῖ δὲ as a separate argument. Bekker's seems to intend αἱ δὲ πράξεις as a separate argument: but if so, the argument would be a mere *petitio principii*. I have adopted Cardwell's reading in part, but retain the comma at ἄμφω, and have translated the last four words as applying to the whole discussion, whereas Cardwell's reading seems to restrict them to the last argument.

P. 38, l. 36. *i.e.* on objects of Moral Choice; opinion of this kind is not the same as Moral Choice, because actions alone form habits and constitute character: opinions are in general *signs* of character, but when they begin to be acted on they cease to be opinions, and merge in Moral Choice.

> "Treason doth never prosper: what's the reason?
> When it doth prosper, none dare call it Treason."

P. 40, l. 37. The introduction of the words διὰ τίνος seems a mere useless repetition, as in the second chapter ἐν τίνι added to περὶ τί.

These I take for some among the many indications that the treatise is a collection of notes for lectures, and not a finished or systematic one.

P. 41, l. 8. Suppose that three alternatives lay before a man, each of the three is of course an object of Deliberation; when he has made his choice, the alternative chosen does not cease to be in its nature an object of Deliberation, but superadds the character of being chosen and so distinguished. Three men are admitted candidates for an office: the one chosen is the successful candidate; so of the three βουλευτὰ, the one chosen is the βουλευτὸν προαιρετὸν.

P. 41, l. 13. Compare Bishop Butler's "System of Human Nature," in the Preface to the Sermons.

P. 41, l. 22. These words, ἐκ τοῦ βουλεύσασθαι—βούλευσιν, contain the account of the whole mental machinery of any action. The first step is a Wish, implied in the first here mentioned, viz. Deliberation, for it has been already laid down that Deliberation has for its object-matter means to Ends supposed to be set before the mind: the next step is Deliberation, the next Decision, the last the definite extending of the mental hand towards the object thus selected; the two last constitute προαίρεσις in its full meaning. The word ὄρεξις means literally "a grasping at or after:" now as this physically may be either vague or definite, so too may the mental act: consequently the term as transferred to the mind has two uses, and denotes either the first wish, βούλησις, or the last definite movement, Will in its strict and proper sense. These two uses are recognised in the Rhetoric (i. 10), where ὄρεξις is divided into ἄλογος and λογιστική.

The illustration then afforded by the polities alluded to is this: as the Kings first decided and then announced their decision for acceptance and execution by their subjects, so Reason, having decided on the course to be taken, communicates its decision to the Will, which then proceeds to move τὰ ὀργανικὰ μέρη. To instance in an action of the mixed kind mentioned in the first chapter: safe arrival at land is naturally desired; two means are suggested, either a certain loss of goods, or trying to save both lives and goods: the question being debated, the former is chosen; this decision is communicated to the Will, which causes the owner's hands to throw overboard his goods: the act is denominated voluntary, because the Will is consenting; but in so denominating it, we leave out of sight how that consent was obtained. In a purely compulsory case the agent never gets beyond the stage of Wish, for no means are in his power and deliberation therefore is useless; consequently there is neither Decision nor Will, in other words, no Choice.

P. 41, l. 39. Compare the statement in the Rhetoric, i. 10, ἔστι δ᾽ ἡ μὲν βούλησις ἀγαθοῦ ὄρεξις (οὐδεὶς γὰρ βούλεται ἀλλ' ἢ ὅταν οἰηθῇ εἶναι ἀγαθόν).

P. 43, l. 33. A stone once set in motion cannot be recalled, because it is then placed under the operation of natural laws which cannot be controlled or altered: so too in Moral declension, there is a point at which gravitation operates irretrievably, "there is a certain bound to imprudence and misbehaviour, which being transgressed, there remains no place for repentance in the natural course of things." Bishop Butler's Analogy, First Part, chap. ii.

P. 44, l. 35. Habits being formed by acting in a certain way under certain circumstances, we can only choose how we will act, not what circumstances we will have to act under.

P. 45, l. 30. "*Moral* Courage" is our phrase.

P. 46, l. 38. The meaning of this passage can scarcely be conveyed except by a paraphrase.

"The object of each separate act of working is that which accords with the habit they go to form; Courage is the habit which separate acts of bravery go to form, therefore the object of these is that which accords with Courage, *i.e.* Courage itself. But Courage is honourable (which implies that the end and object of it is honour, since things are denominated according to their end and object), therefore the object of each separate act of bravery is honour."

P. 47, l. 35. For true Courage is required, 1. Exact appreciation of danger. 2. A Proper motive for resisting fear. Each of the Spurious kinds will be found to fail in one or other, or both.

P. 48, l. 22. This may merely mean, "who give strict orders" not to flinch, which would imply the necessity of compulsion. The word is capable of the sense given above, which seems more forcible.

P. 48, l. 28. See Book VI chap. xiii. near the end. Σωκράτης μὲν οὖν λόγους τὰς ἀρετὰς ᾤετο εἶναι (ἐπιστήμας γὰρ εἶναι πάσας).

P. 48, l. 33. Such as the noise, the rapid movements, and apparent confusion which to an inexperienced eye and ear would be alarming. So Livy says of the Gauls, v. 27, Nata in *vanos* tumultus gens.

P. 49, l. 13. In Coronea in Bœotia, on the occasion of the citadel being betrayed to some Phocians. "The regulars" were Bœotian troops, the πολιτικὰ Coroneans.

P. 49, l. 15. By the difference of tense it seems Aristotle has mixed up two things, beginning to speak of the particular instance, and then carried into the general statement again. This it is scarce worth while to imitate.

P. 52, l. 14. The meaning of the phrase κατὰ συμβεβηκὸς, as here

used, is given in the Seventh Book, chap. x. εἰ γάρ τις τοδὶ διὰ τοδὶ
αἱρεῖται ἢ διώκει, καθ' αὑτὸ μὲν τοῦτο διώκει καὶ αἱρεῖται, κατὰ
συμβεβηκὸς δὲ τὸ πρότερον.

P. 73, l. 17. Perhaps "things which reflect credit on them" as on page
72.

P. 75, l. 32. Book VII.

P. 76, l. 9. Each term is important: to make up the character of
Justice, men must have the capacity, do the acts, and do them from
moral choice.

P. 76, l. 27. But not always. Φιλεῖν, for instance, has two senses, "to
love" and "to kiss," μισεῖν but one. Topics, I. chap. xiii. 5.

P. 76, l. 31. *Things* are ὁμώνυμα which have only their name in
common, being in themselves different. The ὁμωνυμία is *close* therefore when the difference though real is but slight. There is no English
expression for ὁμωνυμία, "equivocal" being applied to a term and not
to its various significates.

P. 77, l. 15. See Book I chap. i. τοιαύτην δέ τινα πλάνην ἔχει καὶ
τἀγαθά, κ.τ.λ.

P. 78, l. 23. A man habitually drunk in private is viewed by our law
as confining his vice to himself, and the law therefore does not attempt
to touch him: a religious hermit may be viewed as one who confines
his virtue to his own person.

P. 79, l. 13. See the account of Sejanus and Livia. Tac. Annal. iv. 3.

P. 79, l. 36. Cardwell's text, which here gives ταράνομον, yields a
much easier and more natural sense. All Injustice violates law, but only
the particular kinds violate equality; and therefore

the unlawful : the unequal :: universal Injustice : the particular *i.e.*
as whole to part.

There is a reading which also alters the words within the parenthesis,
but this hardly affects the gist of the passage.

P. 80, l. 16. There are two reasons why the characters are not necessarily coincident. He is a good citizen, who does his best to carry out
the πολιτεία under which he lives, but this may be faulty, so therefore
pro tanto is he.

Again, it is sufficient, so far as the Community is concerned, that he
does the facts of a good man: but for the perfection of his own individual character, he must do them virtuously. A man may move rightly in
his social orbit, without revolving rightly on his own axis.

The question is debated in the Politics, iii. 2. Compare also the distinction between the brave man, and good soldier (supra, Book III.
chap. xii.), and also Bishop Butler's first Sermon.

P. 81, l. 2. Terms used for persons.

P. 81, l. 17. By μοναδικὸς ἀριθμὸς is meant numbers themselves, 4, 20, 50, etc., by ὅλως ἀριθμὸς these numbers exemplified, 4 horses, 20 sheep, etc.

P. 81, l. 31. The profits of a mercantile transaction (say £1000) are to be divided between A and B, in the ratio of 2 to 3 (which is the real point to be settled); then,

A : B :: 400 : 600.

A : 400 :: B : 600 (permutando, and assuming a value for A and B, so as to make them commensurable with the respective sums).

A+400 : B+600 : : A : B. This represents the actual distribution: its fairness depending entirely on that of the first proportion.

P. 82, l. 16. *i.e.* Corrective Justice is wrought out by subtraction from the wrong doer and addition to the party injured.

P. 82, l. 40. Her Majesty's "Justices."

P. 83, l. 29. I have omitted the next three lines, as they seem to be out of place here, and to occur much more naturally afterwards: it not being likely that they were originally twice written, one is perhaps at liberty to give Aristotle the benefit of the doubt, and conclude that he put them where they made the best sense.

P. 83, l. 35. This I believe to be the meaning of the passage, but do not pretend to be able to get it out of the words.

P. 84, l. 9. This is apparently contrary to what was said before, but not really so. Aristotle does not mean that the man in authority struck wrongfully, but he takes the extreme case of simple Reciprocation: and in the second case, the man who strikes one in authority commits two offences, one against the person (and so far they are equal), and another against the office.

P. 84, l. 21. χάρις denotes, 1st, a kindly feeling issuing in a gratuitous act of kindness; 2ndly, the effect of this act of kindness on a generous mind; 3rdly, this effect issuing in a requital of the kindness.

P. 85, l. 37. The Shoemaker would get a house while the Builder only had (say) one pair of shoes, or at all events not so many as he ought to have. Thus the man producing the least valuable ware would get the most valuable, and *vice versa*.

Adopting, as I have done, the reading which omits οὐ at δει ἄγειν, we have simply a repetition of the caution, that before Reciprocation is attempted, there must be the same ratio between the wares as between the persons, *i.e.* the ratio of equality.

If we admit οὐ, the meaning may be, that you must not bring into the proportion the difference mentioned above (ἑτέρων καὶ οὐκ ἴσων), since for the purposes of commerce all men are equal.

Say that the Builder is to the Shoemaker as 10 : 1. Then there must be the same ratio between the wares: consequently the highest artist will carry off the most valuable wares, thus combining in himself both ὑπερόχαι. The following are the three cases, given 100 pr. shoes = 1 house.

Builder	:	Shoemaker	::	1 pr. shoes	:	1 house—*wrong*.
———		———.		100 pr. shoes	:	1 house—*right*.
———		———.		10 (100 pr. shoes)	:	1 house—*wrong*.

P. 87, l. 14. Every unjust act embodies τὸ ἀδικὸν, which is a violation of τὸ ἴσον, and so implies a greater and a less share, the former being said to fall to the doer, the latter to the sufferer, of injury.

P. 87, l. 33. In a pure democracy men are absolutely, *i.e.* numerically, equal, in other forms only proportionately equal. Thus the meanest British subject is proportionately equal to the Sovereign: that is to say, is as fully secured in his rights as the Sovereign in hers.

P. 89, l. 3. Or, according to Cardwell's reading (κινητόν οὐ μέντοι πᾶν): "but amongst ourselves there is Just, which is naturally variable, but certainly all Just is not such." The sense of the passage is not affected by the reading. In Bekker's text we must take κινητὸν to mean the same as κινούμενον, *i.e.* "we admit there is no Just which has not been sometimes disallowed, still," etc. With Cardwell's, κινητὸν will mean "which not only *does* but naturally *may* vary."

P. 89, l. 25. Murder is unjust by the law of nature, Smuggling by enactment. Therefore any act which can be referred to either of these heads is an unjust act, or, as Bishop Butler phrases it, an act *materially* unjust. Thus much may be decided without reference to the agent. See the note on page 00, l. 16.

P. 91, l. 17. "As distinct from pain or loss." Bishop Butler's Sermon on Resentment. See also, Rhet. ii. 2 Def. of ὀργή.

P. 91, l. 21. This method of reading the passage is taken from Zell as quoted in Cardwell's Notes, and seems to yield the best sense. The Paraphrast gives it as follows:

"But the aggressor is not ignorant that he began, and so he feels himself to be wrong [and will not acknowledge that he is the aggressor], but the other does not."

P. 92, l. 12. As when a man is "*justified* at the Grass Market," *i.e.* hung.

P. 94, l. 25. Where the stock of good is limited, if any individual takes more than his share some one else must have less than his share: where it is infinite, or where there is no good at all, this cannot happen.

P. 96, l. 31. The reference is to chap. vii. where it was said that the law views the parties in a case of particular injustice as originally equal, but now unequal, the wrong doer the gainer and the sufferer the loser by the wrong, but in the case above supposed there is but *one* party.

P. 97, l. 24. So in the Politics, i. 2.

Ἡ μὲν γὰρ ψυχὴ τοῦ σώματος ἄρχει δεσποτικὴν ἀρχὴν, ὁ δὲ νοῦς τῆς ὀρεξέως πολιτικὴν καὶ δεσποτικήν.

Compare also Bishop Butler's account of human nature as a system—of the different authority of certain principles, and specially the supremacy of Conscience.

P. 98, l. 7. I understand the illustration to be taken from the process of lowering a weight into its place; a block of marble, or stone, for instance, in a building.

P. 99, l. 2. Called for convenience sake Necessary and Contingent matter.

P. 99, l. 6. One man learns Mathematics more easily than another, in common language, *he has a turn for* Mathematics, *i.e.* something in his mental conformation answers to that science. The Phrenologist shows the bump denoting this aptitude.

P. 99, l. 13. And therefore the question resolves itself into this, "What is the work of the Speculative, and what of the Practical, faculty of Reason." See the description of ἀρετὴ, II. 5.

P. 99, l. 24. πρᾶξις is here used in its strict and proper meaning.

P. 99, l. 25. That is to say, the Will waits upon deliberation in which Reason is the judge: when the decision is pronounced, the Will must act accordingly.

The question at issue always is, *Is this Good?* because the Will is only moved by an impression of Good: the Decision then will be always *Aye or No*, and the mental hand is put forth to grasp in the former case, and retracted in the later.

So far is what must take place in *every* Moral Action, right or wrong, the Machinery of the mind being supposed uninjured: but to constitute a good Moral Choice, *i.e.* a good Action, the Reason must have said Aye when it ought.

The cases of faulty action will be, either when the Machinery is perfect but wrongly directed, as in the case of a deliberate crime; or when the direction given by the Reason is right but the Will does not move in accordance with that direction; in other words, when the Machinery is out of order; as in the case of the ἀκρατὴς—video meliora proboque, Deteriora sequor.

P. 99, l. 34. See the note on Ἀρχὴ on page 4, l. 3.

P. 100, l. 22. The mind attains truth, either for the sake of truth itself (ἁπλῶς), or for the sake of something further (ἕνεκά τινος). If the first, then either syllogistically (ἐπιστήμη), non-syllogistically (νοῦς), or by union of the two methods (σοφία). If the second, either with a view to *act* (φρόνησις), or with a view to *make* (τέχνη).

Otherwise. The mind contemplates Matter Necessary or Contingent. If necessary, Principles (νοῦς), Deductions (ἐπιστήμη), or Mixed (σοφία). If Contingent, Action (φρόνησις), Production (τέχνη). (Giphanius quoted in Cardwell's notes.)

P. 100, l. 32. The cobbler is at his last; why? to make shoes, which are to clothe the feet of some one: and the price to be paid, *i.e.* the produce of his industry, is to enable him to support his wife and children; thus his production is subordinate to Moral Action.

P. 100, l. 34. It may be fairly presumed that Aristotle would not thus have varied his phrase without some real difference of meaning. That difference is founded, I think, on the two senses of ὄρεξις before alluded to (note, p. 41, l. 22). The first impulse of the mind towards Action may be given either by a vague desire or by the suggestion of Reason. The vague desire passing through the deliberate stage would issue in Moral Choice: Reason must enlist the Will before any Action can take place.

Reason ought to be the originator in all cases, as Bishop Butler observes that Conscience should be: if this were so, every act of Moral Choice would be ὀρεκτικὸς νοῦς.

But one obvious function of the feelings and passions in our composite nature is to instigate Action, when Reason and Conscience by themselves do not: so that as a matter of fact our Moral Choice is, in general, fairly described as ὄρεξις διανοητική. See Bishop Butler's Sermon II. and the First upon Compassion.

P. 100, l. 35. It is the opening statement of the Post. Analytics.

P. 100, l. 38. Aristotle in his logical analysis of Induction, Prior. Analytics II. 25, defines it to be "the proving the inherence of the major term in the middle (*i.e.* proving the truth of the major premiss in fig. I.) through the minor term." He presupposes a Syllogism in the first Figure with an universal affirmative conclusion, which reasons, of course, from an universal, which universal is to be taken as proved by Induction. His doctrine turns upon a canon which he there quotes. "If of one and the same term two others be predicated, one of which is co-

extensive with that one and the same, the other may be predicated of
that which is thus coextensive." The fact of this coextensiveness must
be ascertained by νοῦς, in other words, by the Inductive Faculty. We
will take Aldrich's instance.

All Magnets attract iron ⎫ Presupposed Syllogism reasoning from
A B C are Magnets   ⎬ a universal.
A B C attract iron.   ⎭

A B C attract iron   (Matter of observation and experiment)

All Magnets are A B C   (Assumed by νοῦς, *i.e.* the Inductive
                             faculty)

All Magnets attract iron   (Major premiss of the last Syllogism
                             proved by taking the minor term of
                             that for the middle term of this.)

Or, according to the canon quoted above:
                A B C are Magnets.
                A B C attract iron.

But νοῦς tells me that the term Magnets is coextensive with the term
A B C, therefore of all Magnets I may predicate that they attract iron.

Induction is said by Aristotle to be διὰ πάντων, but he says in the
same place that for this reason we must *conceive* (νοεῖν) the term containing the particular Instances (as A B C above), as composed of all
the Individuals.

If Induction implied actual examination of all particular instances it
would cease to be Reasoning at all and sink into repeated acts of
Simple Apprehension: it is really the bridging over of a chasm, not the
steps cut in the rock on either side to enable us to walk down into and
again out of it. It is a branch of probable Reasoning, and its validity depends *entirely* upon the quality of the particular mind which performs
it. Rapid Induction has always been a distinguishing mark of Genius:
the certainty produced by it is Subjective and not Objective. It may be
useful to exhibit it Syllogistically, but the Syllogism which exhibits it is
either nugatory, or contains a premiss *literally* false. It will be found
useful to compare on the subject of Induction *as the term is used by
Aristotle*, Analytica Prior. II. 25, 26. Analytica Post I. 1, 3, and I. Topics
VI. I. and X.

P. 101, l. 3. The reference is made to the Post Analyt. I. II. and it is
impossible to understand the account of ἐπιστήμη without a perusal
of the chapter; the additions to the definition referred to relate to the

nature of the premisses from which ἐπιστήμη draws its conclusions: they are to be "true, first principles, incapable of any syllogistic proof, better known than the conclusion, prior to it, and causes of it." (See the appendix to this Book.)

P. 101, l. 17. This is the test of correct logical division, that the *membra dividentia* shall be opposed, i.e. not included the one by the other.

P. 101, l. 17. The meaning of the ἐπεὶ appears to be this: the appeal is made in the first instance to popular language, just as it was in the case of ἐπιστήμη, and will be in those of φρόνησις and σοφία. We commonly call Architecture an Art, and it is so and so, therefore the name Art and this so and so are somehow connected: to prove that connection to be "coextensiveness," we predicate one of the other and then simply convert the proposition; which is the proper test of any logical definition, or of any specific property. See the Topics, I. vi.

P. 101, l. 38. See the parable of the unjust Steward, in which the popular sense of φρόνησις is strongly brought out; ἐπῄνεσεν ὁ κύριος τὸν οἰκόνομον τῆς ἀδικίας ὅτι φρονίμως ἐποίησεν ὅτι οἱ υἱοὶ τοῦ αἰῶνος τούτου φρονιμώτεροι, κ. τ. λ. — Luke xvi. 8.

P. 102, l. 1. Compare the ἁπλῶς and καθ᾽ ἕκαστα πεπαιδευμένος of Book I. chap. 1.

P. 102, l. 28. The two aspects under which Virtue may be considered as claiming the allegiance of moral agents are, that of being right, and that of being truly expedient; because Conscience and Reasonable Self-Love are the two Principles of our moral constitution naturally supreme: and "Conscience and Self-Love, *if we understand our true happiness*, always lead us the same way." Bishop Butler, end of Sermon III.

And again:

"If by *a sense of interest* is meant a practical regard to what is upon the whole our Happiness: this is not only coincident with the principle of Virtue or Moral Rectitude, but is a part of the idea itself. And it is evident this Reasonable Self-Love wants to be improved as really as any principle in our nature. . . . So little cause is there for Moralists to disclaim this principle." From the note on sect. iv. of the chapter on Moral Discipline, Analogy, part I, chap. v.

P. 102, l. 34. See the note on Ἀρχή on page 4, l. 3.

The student will find it worth while to compare this passage with the following. — Chap. xiii. of this book beginning ἡ δ᾽ ἕξις τῷ ὄμματι τούτῳ κ. τ. λ. — vii. 4. ἔτι καὶ ὧδε φυσικῶς. κ. τ. λ. vii. 9. — ἡ γὰρ ἀρετὴ καὶ ἡ μοχθηρία. κ. τ. λ. — iii. 7 *ad finem*. εἰ δέ τις λέγοι. κ. τ. λ.

P. 103, l. 1. This is not quite fair. Used in its strict sense, Art does not admit of degrees of excellence any more than Practical Wisdom. In popular language we use the term "wiser man," as readily as "better artist:" really denoting in each case different degrees of approximation to Practical Wisdom and Art respectively; διὰ τὸ γίνεσθαι τοὺς ἐπαίνους δι' ἀναφορᾶς. I. 12.

P. 103, l. 3. He would be a *better Chymist* who should poison intentionally, than he on whose mind the prevailing impression was that "Epsom Salts mean Oxalic Acid; and Syrup of Senna Laudanum."

P. 103, l. 31. The term Wisdom is used in our English Translation of the Old Testament in the sense first given to Σοφία here. "Then wrought Bezaleel and Aholiab, and every *wise-hearted man, in whom the Lord put wisdom and understanding* to know how to work all manner of work for the service of the Sanctuary." Exodus xxxvi. 1.

P. 104, l. 1. ἐπιστήμη and Νοῦς, (in the strict sense, for it is used in many different senses in this book) are different parts of the whole function σοφία; ἐπιστήμη takes in conclusions, drawn by strict reasoning from Principles of a certain kind which Νοῦς supplies. It is conceivable that a man might go on gaining these principles by Intuition and never reasoning from them, and so Νοῦς might exist independent of ἐπιστήμη, but not this without that. Put the two together, the head to the trunk, and you form the living being Σοφία. There are three branches of σοφία according to Greek Philosophy, Θεολογικὴ, Μαθηματικὴ, Φυσικὴ. Science is perhaps the nearest English term, but we have none really equivalent.

P. 104, l. 3. πολιτικὴ is here used in its most extensive sense, φρόνησίς would be its chief Instrument.

P. 104, l. 22. The faculty concerned with which is Φυσικὴ Σοφία.

P. 105, l. 12. In every branch of Moral Action in which Practical Wisdom is employed there will be general principles, and the application of them; but in some branches there are distinct names appropriated to the operations of Practical Wisdom, in others there are not.

Thus Practical Wisdom, when employed on the general principles of Civil Government, is called Legislation; as administering its particular functions it is called simply Government. In Domestic Management, there are of course general Rules, and also the particular application of them; but here the faculty is called only by one name. So too when Self-Interest is the object of Practical Wisdom.

P. 105, l. 23. χειροτέχναι, "our mere Operatives in Public business." (Chalmers.)

P. 105, l. 28. Practical Wisdom may be employed either respecting

Self, (which is φρόνησις proper)
or not-Self, i.e. either one's family = οἰκονομική,
or one's community = πολιτική,

but here the supreme and subordinate are distinguished; the former is νομοθετική, the latter πολιτική proper, whose functions are deliberation and the administration of justice.

P. 106, l. 3. But where can this be done, if there be no community? see Horace's account of the way in which his father made him reap instruction from the examples in the society around him. I. Sat. iv. 105, etc. See also Bishop Butler, Analogy, part I. chap. v. sect. iii.

The whole question of the Selfish Morality is treated in Bishop Butler's first three and the eleventh Sermons, in which he shows the coincidence in *fact* of of enlightened Self-Love and Benevolence *i.e.* love of others. Compare also what is said in the first Book of this treatise, chap. v., about αὐταρκεία.

P. 106, l. 5. More truly "implied," namely, that Practical Wisdom results from experience.

P. 106, l. 10. This observation seems to be introduced, simply because suggested by the last, and not because at all relevant to the matter in hand.

P. 106, l. 12. An instance of Principles gained αἰσθήσει. (Book I. chap. viii.)

P. 106, l. 22. Particulars are called ἔσχατα because they are last arrived at in the deliberative process; but a little further on we have the term applied to first principles, because they stand at one extremity, and facts at the other, of the line of action.

P. 106, l. 31. I prefer the reading ἡ φρόνησις, which gives this sense; "Well, as I have said, Practical Wisdom is this kind of sense, and the other we mentioned is different in kind." In a passage so utterly unimportant, and thrown in almost colloquially, it is not worth while to take much trouble about such a point.

P. 107, l. 2. The definition of it in the Organon (Post. Analyt. I. xxiv.), "a happy conjecture of the middle term without time to consider of it."

The quæstio states the phænomena, and the middle term the causation the rapid ascertaining of which constitutes ἀγχίνοια.

All that receives light from the sun is bright on the side next to the sun.

The moon receives light from the sun,

∴ The moon is bright on the side next the sun.

The ἀγχινοία consists in rapidly and correctly accounting for the observed fact, that the moon is bright on the side next to the sun.

P. 107, l. 10. Opinion is a complete, deliberation an incomplete, mental act.

P. 107, l. 28. The End does not sanctify the Means.

P. 107, l. 37. The meaning is, there is one End including all others; and in this sense φρόνησις is concerned with means, not Ends: but there are also many subordinate Ends which are in fact Means to the Great End of all. Good counsel has reference not merely to the grand End, but to the subordinate Ends which φρόνησις selects as being right means to the Grand End of all.

P. 108, l. 1. The relative οὗ might be referred to τὸ σύμφερον, but that εὐβουλία has been already divided into two kinds, and this construction would restrict the name to one of them, namely that πρός τι τέλος as opposed to that πρὸς τὸ τέλος ἁπλῶς.

P. 108, l. 26. We have no term which at all approximates to the meaning of this word, much less will our language admit of the play upon it which connects it with συγγνώμη.

P. 108, l. 35. Meaning, of course, all those which relate to Moral Action. φρόνησις is equivalent to εὐβουλία, σύνεσις, γνώμη, and νοῦς (in the new sense here given to it).

The faculty which guides us truly in all matters of Moral Action is φρόνησις, *i.e.* Reason directed by Goodness or Goodness informed by Reason. But just as every faculty of body and soul is not actually in operation at the same time, though the Man is acting, so proper names are given to the various Functions of Practical Wisdom.

Is the φρόνιμος forming plans to attain some particular End? he is then εὔβουλος—is he passing under review the suggestions of others? he is συνετὸς—is he judging of the acts of others? he admits γνώμη to temper the strictness of justness—is he applying general Rules to particular cases? he is exercising νοῦς πρακτικὸς or αἴσθησις—which in each and all he is φρόνιμος.

P. 108, l. 40. See note, on p. 106.

P. 109, l. 9. There are cases where we must simply accept or reject without proof: either when Principles are propounded which are prior to all reasoning, or when particular facts are brought before us which are simply matters of αἴσθησις. Aristotle here brings both these cases within the province of νοῦς, *i.e.* he calls by this name the Faculty which attains Truth in each.

P. 109, l. 14. *i.e.* of the συλλογισμοὶ τῶν πρακτῶν.

P. 109, l. 15. See the note on Ἀρχὴ on p. 4, l. 3. As a matter of fact and mental experience the Major Premiss of the Practical Syllogism is wrought into the mind by repeatedly acting upon the Minor Premiss (*i.e.* by ἐθισμός).

> All that is pleasant is to be done,
> This is pleasant,
> ∴ This is to be done.

By habitually acting on the Minor Premiss, *i.e.* on the suggestions of ἐπιθυμία, a man comes really to hold the Major Premiss. Aristotle says of the man destitute of all self-control that he is firmly persuaded that it is his proper line to pursue the gratification of his bodily appetites, διὰ τὸ τοιοῦτος εἶναι οἷος διώκειν αὐτάς. And his analysis of ἀκρασία (the state of progress towards this utter abandonment to passion) shows that each case of previous good resolution succumbing to temptation is attributable to ἐπιθυμία suggesting its own Minor Premiss in place of the right one. Book VII. 8 and 5.

P. 109, l. 26. The *consequentia* is this:

There are cases both of principles and facts which cannot admit of reasoning, and must be authoritatively determined by νοῦς. What makes νοῦς to be a true guide? only practice, *i.e.* Experience, and *therefore*, etc.

P. 109, l. 41. This is a note to explain ὑγίεινα and εὐεκτικὰ; he gives these three uses of the term ὑγίεινα in the Topics, I. xiii. 10,

$$\text{ὑγίεινον λέγεται} \begin{cases} \text{τὸ μὲν ὑγίειας ποιητικὸν,} \\ \text{τὸ δὲ φυλακτικὸν,} \\ \text{τὸ δὲ σημαντικὸν.} \end{cases}$$

Of course the same will apply to εὐεκτικὸν.

P. 110, l. 21. $\left.\begin{array}{l}\text{Healthiness is the formal} \\ \text{Medicine is the efficient}\end{array}\right\}$ cause of health.

See Book X. chap. iv. ὥσπερ οὐδ᾽ ἡ ὑγίεια καὶ ὁ ἰατρὸς ὁμοίως αἴτιά ἐστι τοῦ ὑγιαίνειν.

P. 110, l. 26. φρόνησις is here used in a partial sense to signify the Intellectual, as distinct from the Moral, element of Practical Wisdom.

P. 110, l. 28. This is another case of an observation being thrown in *obiter*, not relevant to, but suggested by, the matter in hand.

P. 110, l. 31. See Book II. chap. iii, and V. xiii.

P. 111, l. 6. The article is supplied at πανούργους, because the abstract word has just been used expressly in a bad sense. "Up to anything" is the nearest equivalent to πανούργους, but too nearly approaches to a colloquial vulgarism.

P. 111, l. 13. See the note on Ἀρχὴ on page 4, l. 3.

P. 111, l. 14. And for the Minor, of course.

"This particular action is———."

We may paraphrase τὸ τέλος by τί δεῖ πράττειν—τί γὰρ δεῖ πράττειν ἢ μὴ, τὸ τέλος αὐτῆς ἐστιν᾽ i.e. τῆς φρονησέως.—(Chap. xi. of this Book.)

P. 111, l. 18. "Look asquint on the face of truth." Sir T. Browne, Religio Medici.

P. 111, l. 24. The term σωφρονικοὶ must be understood as governing the signification of the other two terms, there being no single Greek term to denote in either case mere dispositions towards these Virtues.

P. 111, l. 27. Compare the passage at the commencement of Book X. νῦν δὲ φαίνονται . . . κατοκώχιμον ἐκ τῆς ἀρετῆς.

P. 111, l. 41. It must be remembered that φρόνησις is used throughout this chapter in two senses, its proper and complete sense of Practical Wisdom, and its incomplete one of merely the Intellectual Element of it.

P. 115, l. 1. The account of Virtue and Vice hitherto given represents rather what men *may be* than what they *are*. In this book we take a practical view of Virtue and Vice, in their ordinary, every day development.

P. 115, l. 14. This illustrates the expression, "*Deceits* of the Flesh."

P. 118, l. 14. Another reading omits the μὴ: the meaning of the whole passage would be exactly the same: it would then run, "if he had been convinced of the rightness of what he does, *i.e.* if he were now acting on conviction, he might stop in his course on a change of conviction."

P. 119, l. 27. Major and minor Premisses of the συλλογισμοὶ πῶν πρακτῶν.

P. 119, l. 32. Some necessarily implying knowledge of the particular, others not.

P. 120, l. 10. As a modern parallel, take old Trumbull in Scott's "Red Gauntlet."

P. 120, l. 35. That is, as I understand it, either the major or the minor premiss: it is true, that "all that is sweet is pleasant;" it is true also, that "this is sweet:" what is contrary to Right Reason is the bringing in this minor to the major, *i.e.* the universal maxim, forbidding to taste. Thus;

a man goes to a convivial meeting with the maxim in his mind "All excess is to be avoided;" at a certain time his αἴσθησις tells him "This glass is excess." As a matter of mere reasoning, he cannot help receiving the conclusion "This glass is to be avoided:" and supposing him to be morally sound he would accordingly abstain. But ἐπιθυμία, being a simple tendency towards indulgence, suggests, in place of the minor premiss "This is excess," its own premiss "This is sweet;" this again suggests the self-indulgent maxim or principle ('Ἀρχὴ), "All that is sweet is to be tasted," and so, by strict logical sequence, proves "This glass is to be tasted."

The solution then of the phænomenon of ἀκρασία is this: that ἐπιθυμία, by its direct action on the animal nature, swamps the suggestions of Right Reason.

On the high ground of Universals, ἐπιστήμη i.e. ὀρθὸς λόγος easily defeats ἐπιθυμία. The ἀκρατὴς, an hour before he is in temptation, would never deliberately prefer the maxim "All that is sweet is to be tasted" to "All excess is to be avoided." The ἀκόλαστος would.

Horace has a good comment upon this (II. Sat. 2).

> Quæ virtus et quanta, boni, sit vivere parvo
>
> · · · · · ·
>
> Discite, *non inter lances mensasque nitentes*
> Verùm hìc *impransi* mecum disquirite.

Compare also Proverbs xxiii. 31. "Look not thou upon the wine when it is red," etc.

P. 121, l. 6. ὅρον. Aristotle's own account of this word (Prior Analyt. ii. 1) is εἰς ὃν διαλύεται ἡ πρότασις; but both in the account of νοῦς and here it seems that the proposition itself is really indicated by it.

P. 122, l. 9. The Greek would give "avoids excessive pain," but this is not true, for the excess of pain would be ground for excuse: the warrant for translating as in the text, is the passage occurring just below διώκει τὰς ὑπερβολὰς καὶ φεύγει μετρίας λύπας.

P. 122, l. 33. Compare Bishop Butler on Particular Propensions, Analogy, Part I. chap. v. sect. iv.

P. 123, l. 16. That is, they are to the right states as Vice to Virtue.

P. 124, l. 39. Consult in connection with this Chapter the Chapter on ὀργὴ in the Rhetoric, II. 2, and Bishop Butler's Sermon on Resentment.

P. 125, l. 29. The reasoning here being somewhat obscure from the concisement of expression, the following exposition of it is subjoined.

Actions of Lust are wrong actions done with pleasure,
Wrong actions done with pleasure are more justly objects of wrath,[1]
Such as are more justly objects of wrath are more unjust,
∴Actions of Lust are more unjust.

P. 127, l. 8. τῶν δὴ λεχθέντων. Considerable difference of opinion exists as to the proper meaning of these words. The emendation which substitutes ἀκρατὴς for ἀκόλαστος removes all difficulty, as the clause would then naturally refer to τῶν μὴ προαιρουμένων: but Zell adheres to the reading in the text of Bekker, because the authority of MSS. and old editions is all on this side.

I understand μᾶλλον as meant to modify the word μαλακίας, which properly denotes that phase of ἀκρασία (not ἀκολασία) which is caused by pain.

The ἀκόλαστος *deliberately* pursues pleasure and declines pain: if there is to be a distinct name for the latter phase, it comes under μαλακία more nearly than any other term, though perhaps not quite properly.

Or the words may be understood as referring to the class of wrong acts caused by avoidance of pain, whether deliberate or otherwise, and then of course the names of μαλακία and ἀκολασία may be fitly given respectively.

P. 128, l. 20. "If we went into a hospital where all were sick or dying, we should think those least ill who were insensible to pain; a physician who knew the whole, would behold them with despair. And there is a mortification of the soul as well as of the body, in which the first symptoms of returning hope are pain and anguish." Sewell, Sermons to Young Men (Sermon xii.).

P. 128, l. 31. Before the time of trial comes the man deliberately makes his Moral Choice to act rightly; but, at the moment of acting, the powerful strain of desire makes him contravene this choice: his Will does not act in accordance with the affirmation or negation of his Reason. His actions are therefore of the mixed kind. See Book III. chap. i., and note on page 000.

P. 129, l. 31. Let a man be punctual *on principle* to any one engagement in the day, and he must, as a matter of course, keep all his others

---

[1] ὕβρις is introduced as the single instance from which this premiss is proved inductively. See the account of it in the Chapter of the Rhetoric referred to in the preceding note.

in their due places relatively to this one; and so will often wear an appearance of being needlessly punctilious in trifles.

P. 130, l. 25. Because he is destitute of these minor springs of action, which are intended to supply the defects of the higher principle.

See Bishop Butler's first Sermon on Compassion, and the conclusion of note on p. 97.

P. 135, l. 30. Abandoning Bekker's punctuation and reading μὴ ἀγαθόν; yields a better sense.

"Why will he want it on the supposition that it is not good? He can live even with Pain: because," etc.

P. 136, l. 6. φεύγει may be taken perhaps as equivalent to φεύγουσι and so balance χαίρουσι. But compare Chapter viii. (Bekker).

P. 139, l. 1. "Owe no man anything, but to *love* one another: for he that loveth another *hath fulfilled the Law.*" Romans xiii. 8.

P. 139, l. 12. κεραμεῖς. The Proverb in full is a line from Hesiod,

καὶ κεραμεὺς κεραμεῖ κοτέει καὶ τέκτονι τέκτων.

P. 140, l. 14. In this sense, therefore, is it sung of Mrs. Gilpin, that she

"two stone bottles found,
To hold the liquor that she *loved*,
And keep it safe and sound."

P. 142, l. 15. Cardwell's reading, ταύτῃ γὰρ ὅμοιοι, καὶ τὰ λοιπά, is here adopted, as yielding a better sense than Bekker's.

P. 146, l. 14. The Great man will have a right to look for more Friendship than he bestows; but the Good man *can* feel Friendship only for, and in proportion to, the goodness of the other.

P. 148, l. 3. See note on page 52, l. 14.

P. 153, l. 28. See I. Topics, Chap. v. on the various senses of ταὐτον.

P. 154, l. 23. "For the mutual society, help, and comfort that the one ought to have of the other, both in prosperity and adversity."

P. 156, l. 13. Which one would be assuming he was, if one declined to recognise the obligation to requite the favour or kindness.

P. 165, l. 12. "Neither the Son of man, that He should *repent.*" Numbers xxiii. 19.

"In a few instances the Second Intention, or Philosophical employment of a Term, is more extensive than the First Intention, or popular use." Whately, Logic, iii. 10.

P. 166, l. 9. "I have sometimes considered in what troublesome case is that Chamberlain in an Inn who being but one is to give attendance to many guests. For suppose them all in one chamber; yet, if one shall command him to come to the window, and the other to the table, and another to the bed, and another to the chimney, and another to come upstairs, and another to go downstairs, and all in the same instant, how would he be distracted to please them all? And yet such is the sad condition of my soul by nature; not only a servant but a slave unto sin. Pride calls me to the window, gluttony to the table, wantonness to the bed, laziness to the chimney, ambition commands me to go upstairs, and covetousness to come down. Vices, I see, are as well contrary to themselves as to Virtue." (Fuller's Good Thoughts in Bad Times. Mix't Contemplations, viii.)

P. 179, l. 12. See note, p. 00.

P. 179, l. 20. See Book II. chap. ix.

P. 180, l. 26. See Book I. chap. v. ad finem.

P. 181, l. 14. The notion alluded to is that of the ἰδέα; that there is no real substantial good except the αὐτὸ ἄγαθον, and therefore whatever is so called is so named in right of its participation in that.

P. 181, l. 20. See note on page 103, l. 1.

P. 181, l. 33. Movement is, according to Aristotle, of six kinds:

From not being to being	Generation
From being to not being	Destruction
From being to being more	Increase
From being to being less	Diminution
From being here to being there	Change of Place
From being in this way to being in that . .	Alteration

} Categories, chap. xi

P. 181, l. 40. A may go to sleep quicker than B, but cannot *do more sleep* in a given time.

P. 182, l. 7. Compare Book III. chap. vi. ὥσπερ καὶ ἐπὶ τῶν σωμάτων, κ. τ. λ.

P. 183, l. 33. Which is of course a γένεσις.

P. 183, l. 35. That is, subordinate Movements are complete before the whole Movement is.

P. 184, l. 23. Pleasure is so instantaneous a sensation, that it cannot be conceived divisible or incomplete: the longest continued Pleasure is only a succession of single sparks, so rapid as to give the appearance of a stream, of light.

P. 187, l. 2. A man is as effectually hindered from taking a walk by the ἀλλοτρία ἡδονὴ of reading a novel, as by the οἰκεία λύπη of gout in the feet.

P. 189, l. 40. I have thus rendered σπουδὴ (οὐκ ἀγνοῶν τὸ ἁμαρτανόμενον); but, though the English term does not represent the depth of the Greek one, it is some approximation to the truth to connect an earnest serious purpose with Happiness.

P. 190, l. 30. Bishop Butler, *contrà* (Sermon XV.).

"Knowledge is not our proper Happiness. Whoever will in the least attend to the thing will see that it is the gaining, not the having, of it, which is the entertainment of the mind." The two statements may however be reconciled. Aristotle may be well understood only to mean, that the pursuit of knowledge will be the pleasanter, the freer it is from the minor hindrances which attend on *learning*.

P. 191, l. 6. The clause immediately following indicates that Aristotle felt this statement to be at first sight startling, Happiness having been all the way through connected with ἐνέργεια, but the statement illustrates and confirms what was said in note on page 5, l. 11.

P. 191, l. 17. That is to say, he aims at producing not merely a happy aggregate, but an aggregate of happy individuals. Compare what is said of Legislators in the last chapter of Book I. and the first of Book II.

P. 192, l. 19. See note, page 110, l. 26.

DOVER·THRIFT·EDITIONS

All books complete and unabridged. All 5³⁄₁₆" x 8¹⁄₄," paperbound.

A selection of the more than 200 titles in the series.

POETRY

101 GREAT AMERICAN POEMS, The American Poetry & Literacy Project (ed.). (Available in U.S. only.) 40158-8

ENGLISH ROMANTIC POETRY: An Anthology, Stanley Appelbaum (ed.). 256pp. 29282-7

DOVER BEACH AND OTHER POEMS, Matthew Arnold. 112pp. 28037-3

SELECTED POEMS FROM "FLOWERS OF EVIL," Charles Baudelaire. 64pp. 28450-6

BHAGAVADGITA, Bhagavadgita. 112pp. 27782-8

THE BOOK OF PSALMS, King James Bible. 128pp. 27541-8

IMAGIST POETRY: AN ANTHOLOGY, Bob Blaisdell (ed.). 176pp. (Available in U.S. only.) 40875-2

BLAKE'S SELECTED POEMS, William Blake. 96pp. 28517-0

SONGS OF INNOCENCE AND SONGS OF EXPERIENCE, William Blake. 64pp. 27051-3

THE CLASSIC TRADITION OF HAIKU: An Anthology, Faubion Bowers (ed.). 96pp. 29274-6

BEST POEMS OF THE BRONTË SISTERS (ed. by Candace Ward), Emily, Anne, and Charlotte Brontë. 64pp. 29529-X

SONNETS FROM THE PORTUGUESE AND OTHER POEMS, Elizabeth Barrett Browning. 64pp. 27052-1

MY LAST DUCHESS AND OTHER POEMS, Robert Browning. 128pp. 27783-6

POEMS AND SONGS, Robert Burns. 96pp. 26863-2

SELECTED POEMS, George Gordon, Lord Byron. 112pp. 27784-4

SELECTED CANTERBURY TALES, Geoffrey Chaucer. 144pp. 28241-4

THE RIME OF THE ANCIENT MARINER AND OTHER POEMS, Samuel Taylor Coleridge. 80pp. 27266-4

WAR IS KIND AND OTHER POEMS, Stephen Crane. 64pp. 40424-2

THE CAVALIER POETS: An Anthology, Thomas Crofts (ed.). 80pp. 28766-1

SELECTED POEMS, Emily Dickinson. 64pp. 26466-1

SELECTED POEMS, John Donne. 96pp. 27788-7

SELECTED POEMS, Paul Laurence Dunbar. 80pp. 29980-5

"THE WASTE LAND" AND OTHER POEMS, T. S. Eliot. 64pp. (Available in U.S. only.) 40061-1

THE CONCORD HYMN AND OTHER POEMS, Ralph Waldo Emerson. 64pp. 29059-X

THE RUBÁIYÁT OF OMAR KHAYYÁM: FIRST AND FIFTH EDITIONS, Edward FitzGerald. 64pp. 26467-X

A BOY'S WILL AND NORTH OF BOSTON, Robert Frost. 112pp. (Available in U.S. only.) 26866-9

THE ROAD NOT TAKEN AND OTHER POEMS, Robert Frost. 64pp. (Available in U.S. only.) 27550-7

HARDY'S SELECTED POEMS, Thomas Hardy. 80pp. 28753-X

"GOD'S GRANDEUR" AND OTHER POEMS, Gerard Manley Hopkins. 80pp. 28729-7

A SHROPSHIRE LAD, A. E. Housman. 64pp. 26468-8

LYRIC POEMS, John Keats. 80pp. 26871-3

DOVER·THRIFT·EDITIONS

FICTION

DOVER·THRIFT·EDITIONS

FICTION

THE NECKLACE AND OTHER SHORT STORIES, Guy de Maupassant. 128pp. 27064-5
BARTLEBY AND BENITO CERENO, Herman Melville. 112pp. 26473-4
THE OIL JAR AND OTHER STORIES, Luigi Pirandello. 96pp. 28459-X
THE GOLD-BUG AND OTHER TALES, Edgar Allan Poe. 128pp. 26875-6
TALES OF TERROR AND DETECTION, Edgar Allan Poe. 96pp. 28744-0
THE QUEEN OF SPADES AND OTHER STORIES, Alexander Pushkin. 128pp. 28054-3
THE STORY OF AN AFRICAN FARM, Olive Schreiner. 256pp. 40165-0
FRANKENSTEIN, Mary Shelley. 176pp. 28211-2
THREE LIVES, Gertrude Stein. 176pp. (Available in U.S. only.) 28059-4
THE STRANGE CASE OF DR. JEKYLL AND MR. HYDE, Robert Louis Stevenson. 64pp.
  26688-5
TREASURE ISLAND, Robert Louis Stevenson. 160pp. 27559-0
GULLIVER'S TRAVELS, Jonathan Swift. 240pp. 29273-8
THE KREUTZER SONATA AND OTHER SHORT STORIES, Leo Tolstoy. 144pp. 27805-0
THE WARDEN, Anthony Trollope. 176pp. 40076-X
FIRST LOVE AND DIARY OF A SUPERFLUOUS MAN, Ivan Turgenev. 96pp. 28775-0
FATHERS AND SONS, Ivan Turgenev. 176pp. 40073-5
ADVENTURES OF HUCKLEBERRY FINN, Mark Twain. 224pp. 28061-6
THE ADVENTURES OF TOM SAWYER, Mark Twain. 192pp. 40077-8
THE MYSTERIOUS STRANGER AND OTHER STORIES, Mark Twain. 128pp. 27069-6
HUMOROUS STORIES AND SKETCHES, Mark Twain. 80pp. 29279-7
AROUND THE WORLD IN EIGHTY DAYS, Jules Verne. 160pp. 41111-7
CANDIDE, Voltaire (François-Marie Arouet). 112pp. 26689-3
GREAT SHORT STORIES BY AMERICAN WOMEN, Candace Ward (ed.). 192pp. 28776-9
"THE COUNTRY OF THE BLIND" AND OTHER SCIENCE-FICTION STORIES, H. G. Wells. 160pp.
  (Available in U.S. only.) 29569-9
THE ISLAND OF DR. MOREAU, H. G. Wells. 112pp. (Available in U.S. only.) 29027-1
THE INVISIBLE MAN, H. G. Wells. 112pp. (Available in U.S. only.) 27071-8
THE TIME MACHINE, H. G. Wells. 80pp. (Available in U.S. only.) 28472-7
THE WAR OF THE WORLDS, H. G. Wells. 160pp. (Available in U.S. only.) 29506-0
ETHAN FROME, Edith Wharton. 96pp. 26690-7
SHORT STORIES, Edith Wharton. 128pp. 28235-X
THE AGE OF INNOCENCE, Edith Wharton. 288pp. 29803-5
THE PICTURE OF DORIAN GRAY, Oscar Wilde. 192pp. 27807-7
JACOB'S ROOM, Virginia Woolf. 144pp. (Available in U.S. only.) 40109-X
MONDAY OR TUESDAY: Eight Stories, Virginia Woolf. 64pp. (Available in U.S. only.) 29453-6

NONFICTION

POETICS, Aristotle. 64pp. 29577-X
POLITICS, Aristotle. 368pp. 41424-8
NICOMACHEAN ETHICS, Aristotle. 256pp. 40096-4
MEDITATIONS, Marcus Aurelius. 128pp. 29823-X
THE LAND OF LITTLE RAIN, Mary Austin. 96pp. 29037-9
THE DEVIL'S DICTIONARY, Ambrose Bierce. 144pp. 27542-6
THE ANALECTS, Confucius. 128pp. 28484-0
CONFESSIONS OF AN ENGLISH OPIUM EATER, Thomas De Quincey. 80pp. 28742-4
NARRATIVE OF THE LIFE OF FREDERICK DOUGLASS, Frederick Douglass. 96pp. 28499-9

DOVER·THRIFT·EDITIONS

NONFICTION

THE SOULS OF BLACK FOLK, W. E. B. Du Bois. 176pp. 28041-1

SELF-RELIANCE AND OTHER ESSAYS, Ralph Waldo Emerson. 128pp. 27790-9

THE LIFE OF OLAUDAH EQUIANO, OR GUSTAVUS VASSA, THE AFRICAN, Olaudah Equiano. 192pp. 40661-X

THE AUTOBIOGRAPHY OF BENJAMIN FRANKLIN, Benjamin Franklin. 144pp. 29073-5

TOTEM AND TABOO, Sigmund Freud. 176pp. (Available in U.S. only.) 40434-X

LOVE: A Book of Quotations, Herb Galewitz (ed.). 64pp. 40004-2

PRAGMATISM, William James. 128pp. 28270-8

THE STORY OF MY LIFE, Helen Keller. 80pp. 29249-5

TAO TE CHING, Lao Tze. 112pp. 29792-6

GREAT SPEECHES, Abraham Lincoln. 112pp. 26872-1

THE PRINCE, Niccolò Machiavelli. 80pp. 27274-5

THE SUBJECTION OF WOMEN, John Stuart Mill. 112pp. 29601-6

SELECTED ESSAYS, Michel de Montaigne. 96pp. 29109-X

UTOPIA, Sir Thomas More. 96pp. 29583-4

BEYOND GOOD AND EVIL: Prelude to a Philosophy of the Future, Friedrich Nietzsche. 176pp. 29868-X

THE BIRTH OF TRAGEDY, Friedrich Nietzsche. 96pp. 28515-4

COMMON SENSE, Thomas Paine. 64pp. 29602-4

SYMPOSIUM AND PHAEDRUS, Plato. 96pp. 27798-4

THE TRIAL AND DEATH OF SOCRATES: Four Dialogues, Plato. 128pp. 27066-1

A MODEST PROPOSAL AND OTHER SATIRICAL WORKS, Jonathan Swift. 64pp. 28759-9

CIVIL DISOBEDIENCE AND OTHER ESSAYS, Henry David Thoreau. 96pp. 27563-9

SELECTIONS FROM THE JOURNALS (Edited by Walter Harding), Henry David Thoreau. 96pp. 28760-2

WALDEN; OR, LIFE IN THE WOODS, Henry David Thoreau. 224pp. 28495-6

NARRATIVE OF SOJOURNER TRUTH, Sojourner Truth. 80pp. 29899-X

THE THEORY OF THE LEISURE CLASS, Thorstein Veblen. 256pp. 28062-4

DE PROFUNDIS, Oscar Wilde. 64pp. 29308-4

OSCAR WILDE'S WIT AND WISDOM: A Book of Quotations, Oscar Wilde. 64pp. 40146-4

UP FROM SLAVERY, Booker T. Washington. 160pp. 28738-6

A VINDICATION OF THE RIGHTS OF WOMAN, Mary Wollstonecraft. 224pp. 29036-0

PLAYS

PROMETHEUS BOUND, Aeschylus. 64pp. 28762-9

THE ORESTEIA TRILOGY: Agamemnon, The Libation-Bearers and The Furies, Aeschylus. 160pp. 29242-8

LYSISTRATA, Aristophanes. 64pp. 28225-2

WHAT EVERY WOMAN KNOWS, James Barrie. 80pp. (Available in U.S. only.) 29578-8

THE CHERRY ORCHARD, Anton Chekhov. 64pp. 26682-6

THE SEA GULL, Anton Chekhov. 64pp. 40656-3

THE THREE SISTERS, Anton Chekhov. 64pp. 27544-2

UNCLE VANYA, Anton Chekhov. 64pp. 40159-6

THE WAY OF THE WORLD, William Congreve. 80pp. 27787-9

BACCHAE, Euripides. 64pp. 29580-X

MEDEA, Euripides. 64pp. 27548-5

THE MIKADO, William Schwenck Gilbert. 64pp. 27268-0